A HISTORY
of the AMISH
REVISED AND UPDATED

A HISTORY
of the AMISH

REVISED AND UPDATED

STEVEN M. NOLT

Good Books

Intercourse, PA 17534
800/762-7171
www.goodbks.com

Photography Credits

Covers: front and back, Doyle Yoder.

Jerry Irwin/Good Books, 4, 237, 243, 333; Jan Gleysteen, 7, 11, 16, 23, 25, 28, 31, 37, 42, 54, 69, 99, 103, 116; *Mirror of the Martyrs* (copyright 2003, Good Books, Intercourse, PA 17534), 13; The People's Place, 33, 73, 83; Pearl L. Sensenig/Mennonite Disaster Service, 47; Mennonite Historical Library, Goshen, IN, 52 (both), 60, 74, 101, 106, 147; John A. Parmer, 81; Doyle Yoder, 90, 112, 292, 323; J. Lemar Mast, 119; Mennonite Church USA Archives, Goshen, IN, 127 (Edward J. Yoder Collection), 164, 165 (John E. Sharp Collection), 199 (Historical Committee Collection), 221 (both, Michael Richard Collection), 229 (C. Henry Smith Collection), 240 (S.D. Guengerich Collection), 295 (Mennonite World Conference Collection); John Stahly, 130; Thomas J. Meyers, 141; Steven M. Nolt, 143; Heritage Historical Library, 151; Steven R. Estes, 179, 190, 264; Louetta M. Miller, 181; Illinois State Historical Library, 184; Harold Thut, 194; James R. Burkett, 206; Della Bender Miller, 211; Nelson P. Springer, 219; *Pennsylvania Mennonite Heritage,* 222 (both), 225; Horst Gerlach, 226; *The Amish in America: Settlements that Failed, 1840-1960* (Pathway Publishers, Aylmer, ON), 232; Ivan H. and Alice Martin Stoltzfus, 248; Lancaster (PA) Mennonite Historical Society, 258; Mennonite Library and Archives, North Newton, KS, 267; Kenneth Pellman, 272; Dottie Kauffmann, 274; Melvin S. and Mary Ellen Stoltzfoos Stoltzfus, 277; Richard Reinhold, 286; Ed Sachs, 301; BERRY'S WORLD reprinted by permission of NEA, Inc., 303; Wide World Photos, 305, 319; *Globe and Mail* (Toronto), 320; Christian Aid Ministries, 330.

Design by Dawn J. Ranck

A HISTORY OF THE AMISH
Copyright © 1992, 2003 by Good Books, Intercourse, Pennsylvania 17534
International Standard Book Number: 1-56148-393-1
Library of Congress Catalog Card Number: 92-29684

Library of Congress Cataloging-in-Publication Data

Nolt, Steven M.
    A history of the Amish / Steven M. Nolt.
      p. cm.
    Includes bibliographical references and index.
    ISBN 1-56148-393-1
    1. Amish—History. I. Title
BX8129-A6N65   1992
289.7'3—dc20
                                      92-29684
                                         CIP

Table of Contents

In memory of Abner F. Beiler (1917-2002)
who encouraged me to write the first edition of this book.

Acknowledgments

If the themes of community and mutual aid have been important in Amish history, they also play central roles in the process of writing a book. I received generous assistance and advice from numerous people while preparing the original and revised versions of this volume. Special notice must go to the staffs of the Lancaster (Pa.) Mennonite Historical Society; Archives of the Mennonite Church USA, Goshen, Ind.; and Mennonite Historical Library of Goshen (Ind.) College, as well as to the director of the Heritage Historical Library, Aylmer, Ont., who aided this project in many ways. Several Amish people in Indiana, Ohio, Ontario, and Pennsylvania read portions of the manuscript and offered suggestions and corrections. Others who supplied helpful information and critiques include Steven R. Estes, Donald B. Kraybill, Thomas J. Meyers, Joe Springer, Jan Gleysteen, J. Craig Haas, and Perry Klopfenstein. Steve Scott deserves special thanks for the time and assistance he has given me over the years. I continue to marvel at the support Merle Good and Phyllis Pellman Good showed for a novice author's first book and appreciate their interest in my producing a thoroughly revised edition.

For some reason it is customary to thank family members last, even though their contributions—often in indirect, but no less essential, ways—are the most important of all. To Rachel (who has lived with Amish historical work for almost a dozen years now), Lydia, and Esther, thanks for all your love.

Steven M. Nolt
Goshen, Indiana, 2003

1.
A Reformation Heritage

> *"We have been united to stand fast in the Lord."*
> — Anabaptist leaders, 1527

The Amish story

For many Americans the dawning of the twentieth century offered optimism and opportunity. A pervasive spirit of expectancy buoyed hopes that a better, brighter future was breaking into the present. The advances of science and the wonders of technology that had amazed attendees of the 1892 World's Columbia Exposition in Chicago disappointed few in the decade that followed. On the international stage, the United States was becoming an imperial power, while at home its efforts seemingly turned more toward social and urban reform and renewal. Western civilization offered itself as the world's salvation for the arriving hundred years, and with the moral and emotional catastrophe of world wars and a Great Depression still beyond the horizon, even America's churches were confident that 1900 marked the beginning of a new "Christian Century."

In McVeytown, Mifflin County, Pennsylvania, 64-year-old Amishman Jonathan K. Hartzler was not so sure. Hartzler was a rather progressive-thinking man himself, but as he considered the situation of his own people at the beginning of the

Amish families going home from church, Conewango Valley, New York. While the Old Order Amish are hardly isolated from modern society, they remain decidedly out-of-step with twenty-first century North American culture.

new century, his progressivism failed to chase nagging questions from his mind. Would his people survive the next hundred years? Why, he wondered, were some Amish congregations near his home declining almost to the point of extinction? And why, he also asked, were some members of his church prone "to look upon the dark side" of their own people and uncritically gaze "upon the bright side of churches in other denominations"? Such "unfavorable comparisons" were driving some Amish to predict the doom of their own group.[1]

Mustering his own optimism, Hartzler decided "to get at the truth" and "seek for the causes of the decline, and by the help of God, remove them." Carefully, he gathered detailed information on Amish church membership and migration, bracing himself for the results. Happily, he found that the Amish churches in his home state—far from declining—had actually grown by nearly three-quarters in the last half of the 1800s. Now Hartzler, too, believed he could be optimistic about the future.

As he reflected on the drama of God's activity in the world, Hartzler began to see in Amish history more than a human story. "Persecution drove our forefathers from their homes," he remembered. But despite the difficulties of those days, "they became one of God's means to carry the gospel from the old world to the new." As later generations of Pennsylvania Amish moved westward, they, too, "probably far more than they were aware" were "led by the hand of God," he concluded.

Yes, Hartzler could see his people playing a part in a God-ordained manifest destiny, much as many American politicians saw their own nation. Yet Hartzler's bright vision was also tinted with typical Amish humility—a distraction that rarely bothered the leaders in Washington. God's "goodness has been so great," the old man realized, while his Amish church had been "so wayward and so unworthy." But therein lay Hartzler's faith: God would be as faithful in the twentieth century as he had been "in Bible times. His compassions fail not; they are new every morning."[2]

More than a century later the Amish not only persist, but also remain a growing, vibrant group in North America. With their rejection of automobile ownership, public utility electricity, and the fads and fashions of Madison Avenue, they annually attract countless tourists and academics who see in Old Order people everything from images of nostalgic conservatism to icons of postmodern environmentalism. Yet the Amish are really none of these things. They are not timeless figures frozen in the past, nor the poster-children of political activists. Taken on their own terms, the Old Order Amish are a living, dynamic church—a committed Christian community whose members have taken seriously the task of discipleship and group witness. From their background in the Protestant Reformation, to their 1693 beginnings in the Swiss and south Rhine Valley, and from their immigration to North America, to their efforts to be a people in the midst of many modern pressures, the Amish have persevered through a remarkable past.

Migrating, dividing, struggling, and sticking together, the Amish people have lived a story that is rich and deep. Still connected to the faith that encouraged Jonathan K. Hartzler, today's Amish have persisted and changed and continued their story. Like Hartzler's turn-of-the-century progressive musings on westward expansion, the Amish story at times seems to be a very North American tale. But it is also a different story from that of its host societies, as the Amish faith has led its communities on strikingly divergent paths in contemporary Canada and the United States.

Understanding the Amish story requires the breadth of vision of Jonathan K. Hartzler. Hartzler looked both to his people's faith and to their European origins in order to make sense of their life in 1900. That Hartzler remembered the persecution of his forebears in Europe is no surprise. The Amish are one of several spiritual heirs of the Protestant Reformation's Anabaptist movement,[3] and the source of Hartzler's faith had roots deep in turbulent sixteenth-century Europe.

A turbulent sixteenth century

In the early 1500s a number of political and economic woes troubled Western Europe. For more than 50 years a population explosion had outstripped the Continent's ability to feed itself. Inflation of prices and rents drove land-owning peasants into poverty, while in the towns and cities a growing group of powerful and wealthy merchants and craftspeople challenged the rule of hereditary nobles. University scholars grew sharply critical of state corruption.

The menacing power of the Ottoman Turks to the east threatened feelings of national security. Kings struggled not only to wrest power and authority from local nobles, but also against rival monarchs across Europe. Anxiety only grew as the printing press shrank the European world. No longer were events in Paris and Vienna so distant; the printed page relayed messages of doom, destruction, and social unrest from city to

The Grossmünster (Great Church) in Zurich, Switzerland, where Reformer Huldrych Zwingli presided. The Anabaptist movement in Zurich began in 1525.

city in a matter of days. Free from direct state control, the new press circulated ideas and arguments in a way that often increased anxiety and discontent.

Amid the turbulence of early sixteenth-century Western European life, the church still stitched the social fabric together. For more than a thousand years Western Europe had been united in "One Holy Catholic and Apostolic Church." During the fourth century, with the support of the Roman emperors, Christianity had evolved from a persecuted movement to the only officially sanctioned religion in the Roman Empire. Under a now presumably Christian empire, bishops and priests received special privileges, and eventually the bishop of Rome was accorded particular prestige. The church and the imperial state were linked in building a common, unified, and Christian civilization. Dissent against the One Church also became a crime against state and society.

In time, the western half of the Roman Empire crumbled, but the church remained to pick up the pieces. Throughout the Middle Ages the Pope, as bishop of Rome, led Christians in building a holy civilization in Western Europe. The church offered God's salvation to all who sought divine grace through participation in the sacraments (especially the Holy Communion), which the church regulated carefully.

But the church did more than oversee the way to heaven. The church mediated national conflicts, crowned rulers, patronized the fine arts, supported higher education, and encouraged trade and exploration. The church had led Western Europe for a millennium, but now, in the early sixteenth century, society was splintering and the church itself was breaking up—a fact that frightened many people as much as any political or economic bad news.

To be sure, some popes had been pawns of French kings and German emperors, and church councils and activist priests frequently had counseled reform. But after 1517 the trouble in the church was different. The Roman Catholic Church was actually losing its moral and political authority in some parts of Europe. In that year the Wittenburg monk and lecturer Martin Luther had proposed a whole series of changes, not only of church structure—as many reformers had done before—but also in the interpretation of key church doctrines.[4]

Luther and the Protestant Reformation

Luther proposed revolutionary challenges to some of Rome's basic teachings. Luther insisted that "salvation by grace through faith alone" meant that God's saving grace comes directly to each Christian on the basis of his or her individual faith, and that it is not mediated through the church's sacraments. Such thinking undercut the church's importance and authority. By the time he officially broke with Rome in 1521,

Luther was also championing church decision-making based solely on Bible study instead of tradition and canon law, and the use of the German language instead of Latin to make worship more understandable to the lay people.

Printers promoted Luther's ideas widely across German-speaking Europe and beyond. A number of German princes also supported him, both for political and religious reasons. Church leaders in other places began introducing some of Luther's teachings into their own parishes. An important fellow-reformer was Huldrych Zwingli, priest at the Great Church in the Swiss city of Zurich. Like Luther, Zwingli preached salvation by grace through faith alone, rejected the doctrine of purgatory and advocated the marriage of clergy. Zwingli also taught the symbolic, rather than physical, presence of Jesus' body and blood in the bread and wine of communion.

As early as 1518, Zwingli's teaching attracted reform-minded young men and women in the Zurich area. By 1522 small groups of these students and craftspeople began meeting in private homes for Bible study and prayer.[5] They were excited by the ideas of the Reformation, but also troubled because they feared Zwingli's reforms were losing momentum and might even be reversed. Zwingli, like Luther, often relied on the government to implement religious change. Luther and Zwingli seemingly could not imagine a society without a strong leader; when they removed the pope from their social scheme, they replaced Rome's power and authority with that of a local prince or magistrate.

Radicals in Zurich

This state-church strategy troubled the reform-minded Zurich youth who feared the Zurich City Council was now controlling the church. When Zwingli's reforms strengthened the Council's power (such as his rejection of Rome's authority over Zurich), the city fathers readily agreed. But when the changes involved the Council's own sacrifice (such as relaxing the unjust tithes that the city extorted from the surrounding rural villages), the Council stalled.

Moreover, because the church routinely baptized all infants, it by definition included all citizens among its members. In practical terms this meant that the church adjusted its moral expectations and standards downward, seeking a lowest common denominator to support its inclusive character. Virtually everyone was a member of the church regardless of their level of commitment or interest. The church could not demand the high ethics of Christ's Sermon on the Mount from those who were nominally Christian simply because they were citizens. Instead it settled for expedient personal and social ethics, and Jesus' teachings often were disregarded in the face of political realities.

This government-guided church reform bothered the young Zurich dissenters. If the Word of God was to form the church, they contended, then no human government should stand in the way. In 1524, when Zwingli concluded that aspects of the Catholic mass were unbiblical and should be discarded, the City Council balked. Zwingli conceded to the Council, irking the radicals.

Gradually the dissenters realized that the recovery of the church as they understood it from the New Testament could occur only on radically different grounds from both those being used by Rome and the Reformers. These radicals, it turned out, were working with a different concept of the church itself. For them the church was a community of Christians voluntarily committed to imitating Christ and to each other. Baptism—the sign of church membership and commitment—was only for adults or those old enough to choose the path of discipleship. The state could have no part in controlling or directing the activities and doctrines of the church. The church must be free of government control.

Salvation came by grace through faith, these radicals believed, but it was more than a future ticket to heaven. It transformed one's present life with God and with other people.

Since Christ taught peaceful nonviolence and nonresistance to worldly enemies, radical Christian obedience prohibited participation in either the military or the judicial arms of the state. The New Testament church demonstrated sharing of personal goods and practicing mutual aid among Christians, and the dissenters took those teachings seriously as well.

Anabaptism is born

Before long the ideas of the voluntary, "free church" radicals clashed with the Zurich Council, which demanded a unified church and state on its own terms. Some dissenters refused to have their infant children baptized because the children were not yet old enough to understand the implications of Christ's

Anabaptists met secretly for worship in this Swiss cave near Wappenswil.

teachings. The city demanded that the radicals stop meeting, have their children baptized, and expel the non-Zurichers from among them. Snubbing the Council, the dissenters met on January 21, 1525 and baptized one another, signaling their own conscious decision to follow Christ and form a church apart from the state. Since they all had been baptized as infants many years before, this new adult baptism was literally a second baptism (in Latin, *anabaptismus*). For their part, these Anabaptists, as they were now called, claimed that their infant baptisms had been meaningless.

Such disobedience to the state church was intolerable in Zurich. Both Zwingli and the Council sensed that Anabaptist ideas challenged the unity of the church and the state and was socially subversive. In rejecting infant baptism, the Anabaptists separated the political tie between church membership and citizenship. By challenging the unity of the church, the Anabaptists shredded the social fabric. In rejecting the state's authority in matters of religion, the Anabaptists threatened anarchy, and, by refusing military service, the Anabaptists made the city vulnerable to foreign attack.

Anabaptists were imprisoned and exiled, fined and threatened. Meanwhile their ideas, already present in the rural countryside around Zurich, spawned a number of fellowships beyond the city walls. Even the threat of the death penalty failed to halt the movement. Within several years, Anabaptist groups emerged elsewhere in Switzerland and in southern Germany, the Austrian Tyrol, and Moravia. Itinerant preachers, dissident booksellers, and traveling merchants spread the message, calling people to receive God's grace and form a faithful church free of state interference and embodying Jesus' life and teaching.[6]

The plight of persecution

During the next century, the Anabaptists faced ferocious persecution. Anabaptists were jailed, tortured, burned, beheaded, or sold as galley slaves forced to row themselves to death on the Mediterranean. Some of the Swiss city-states employed "Anabaptist hunters" who tracked down suspected citizens and were paid by the head. When Anabaptist groups sprang up in northern Germany and the Netherlands, authorities there also reacted harshly. Perhaps some four thousand Anabaptists were killed in the decades after 1525.[7]

As a result, Anabaptist meetings might take place at night, in the woods, or among small groups. Leaders traveled secretly and had to hide precious and illegal tracts and devotional materials. Members lived in fear, and some recanted their beliefs, returned to the state churches, and even betrayed one-time associates. The century of persecution left lasting marks on the Anabaptist movement.[8] The re-baptizers developed a deep distrust of larger society and a fairly negative view of government,

During the sixteenth century, several thousand Anabaptists were executed, including Maria and Ursula van Beckum in 1544. Etching by Jan Luyken.

which they encountered most often in the form of judicial brutality. Generations later and half a world away in North America, Anabaptist descendants still recounted the stories of those who suffered.

In addition to fostering a tendency to withdraw, the fierce opposition further encouraged values of simplicity and piety that the Anabaptists already saw in the Bible. The line dividing the suffering church and the cruel world became all too clear. The world was arrogant, wealthy, proud, and violent. The Anabaptists saw themselves as meek, simple, humble, and nonresistant. While some of these characteristics may have been typical of rural Swiss and south German people generally, the experience of persecution accentuated them among the Anabaptists.

In part, Anabaptist church life reflected these desperate times as well, with its fairly flexible nature. Local congregations were self-standing, each with its own ordained leadership who preached and provided pastoral care, as well as looking after the material needs of members and collecting and distributing money for the poor. Swiss Anabaptists allowed lay members to lead worship and teach if no ordained leader was available, though performing the rites of baptism, communion, ordination, and marriage was reserved for senior ministers called "elders" (later, in North America, they came to be called "bishops"). However, the most important roles for Anabaptist leaders—elders or junior ministers—were modeling daily Christian discipleship and guiding church discipline.

Anabaptist agreement

If the rather decentralized nature of the Anabaptist movement provided something of a survival strategy, it also posed its own problems. Within two years of Anabaptism's beginnings, some of its leaders sensed a need to outline what held their diverse collection of local fellowships together. Gathering in the village of Schleitheim on the Swiss-German border, Swiss and south

German Anabaptists who called themselves simply "Brethren" or "Swiss Brethren" began by declaring their definition of the church. "We have been united to stand fast in the Lord," they announced, "as obedient children of God, sons and daughters, who have been and shall be separated from the world in all that we do and leave undone, and . . . completely at peace."[9]

The Swiss Brethren then went on to agree on seven foundational elements of church life and Christian conduct. They started with adult baptism and church discipline. Discipline was a key issue for the Swiss Brethren and would remain so for their spiritual descendants. The matter was also in part immediate because the Swiss Brethren were being subjected to discipline themselves in the form of state imprisonment and torture for abandoning officially sanctioned churches. In contrast, the discipline advocated by the Anabaptists was nonviolent. The Anabaptists excommunicated and barred from fellowship those who fell into unrepentant sin.

While milder than its executioner-enforced state church equivalent, church discipline for the Swiss Brethren was nevertheless critically important. Since they affirmed both the voluntary nature of the church and the high ethical standards of personal discipleship, the Brethren also had to grapple with what to do when people decided to stop following Jesus. Creating a committed church required the discernment of definite boundaries. But if the New Testament was clear that Christians should avoid "the world," it was less clear what such avoidance involved. For the time being, the Swiss Brethren avoided the question itself, but most seemed to feel that barring the unrepentant from the communion table kept church integrity pure enough.

Trouble in the north

The Anabaptists in northern Europe soon had to wrestle with church discipline in a situation that was less theoretical than that of their south German and Swiss brothers and sisters.

Anabaptist ideas emerged in northern Germany in 1530 and spread immediately in the Netherlands, where the movement grew rapidly. This northern Anabaptism had some different emphases from those in Switzerland and the south Rhine Valley. Notably in the north there was great enthusiasm for the

Anabaptist leader Menno Simons.

imminent Second Coming of Christ, with bold predictions about impending events before that Great Day. Some Anabaptists were uncomfortable with the fanaticism associated with these predictions and preferred a "quiet and peaceable life" of obedience to Jesus' teachings. Others, however, set out with force to usher in the new Messianic Age. Ironically, these Anabaptists took up the sword in order to create an Anabaptist church-state. Capturing the city of Münster in 1534, these Anabaptists turned the tables on the state churches and began to persecute and punish anyone who refused to be baptized as an adult!

Within a year, an army jointly raised by Catholics and Protestants crushed the Münster takeover. But the aftershocks of the struggle shook the nonviolent northern Anabaptists who had rejected the actions at Münster from the start. Fearful state authorities connected the actions at Münster with all the Anabaptist groups, even those that denounced any form of violent coercion. Following Münster, persecution of the Anabaptists became severe in the Netherlands and northern Germany since officials had clear evidence that Anabaptism could spark militant revolution.

With its members scattered, discouraged, and scared, nonviolent Dutch Anabaptism struggled to redefine itself. Into this disorganized movement came a former Dutch Catholic priest named Menno Simons.[10] Menno had been a secret Anabaptist sympathizer for some years, but in 1536 he denounced the violence and mayhem of Münster and openly joined the peaceful wing of the movement. For the next quarter century, Dutch Anabaptist leaders worked to nurture the peaceful fellowships across northern Europe. So influential was Menno's role in particular that by 1545 some officials were linking Anabaptists with his name and labeling some "Mennonites."

Menno needed to distance himself and his fellow believers from the debacle of Münster. No longer was it possible simply to refuse spiritual fellowship with the fanatical Anabaptists of the Münster stripe; peaceful Anabaptists could not even risk associating with them. The unrepentant, excommunicated Anabaptists who espoused violence had to be avoided in social and personal relationships, Menno and others taught.[11]

Other questions challenged Dutch Anabaptists, as well. Some European theologians and church reformers began to promote the notion that the church was simply "spiritual" and "other-worldly," which opened for question the significance of Christian relationships and the importance of ethics in this life. In corrective reaction to such teaching, Menno and the "Mennonite" Anabaptists placed even more emphasis on purging sin from the ranks of the church and on the separation of believers from the apostate. Christians needed to avoid, or "shun," the unrepentant.[12]

In the course of a few years, some northern Anabaptists became increasingly extreme in their practice of shunning excommunicated members (the practice was known as *Meidung* in German). Some would have nothing at all to do with former church members. Others even called for the suspending of the marriage relationship when the church excommunicated one of the partners. Apparently Menno tried to play a mediating role between those who called for strict and for milder application of excommunication, but in the end Menno sided with those who called for social avoidance.[13]

Disagreements around shunning repeatedly stifled church unity among the Anabaptists. In 1554, when the Dutch and northern European Mennonites finally formulated a specific statement on avoidance and excommunication, the Swiss and south German Mennonites* rejected it as too harsh. Three years later, a well-attended conference of Swiss and southern

---

* The Swiss and south German Anabaptists did not use the term *Mennonite* to describe themselves. Most often they went by the name *Swiss Brethren*. In the interest of simplifying terminology, however, this chapter and several that follow will use the term Mennonite to identify these Swiss and south German Anabaptists.

leaders sent a delegation north to visit Menno and to suggest that the Dutch practice of shunning was going too far.

Eventually, however, the Swiss and south German Mennonites agreed to recognize social avoidance in some way. Perhaps they made this concession to their Dutch brothers and sisters for the sake of church unity. Or perhaps the Swiss and south Germans actually were persuaded that the New Testament called on Christians to limit social contacts with wayward believers as a means of urging restoration. Either way, in 1568 and again in 1591, the south German Mennonites adopted church confessions that called for socially avoiding those members who left the church unrepentant.[14] To what extent the south Germans actually practiced what they preached is unclear. Meanwhile, in the north, decades of harshly administered church discipline were beginning to tear the Dutch Mennonites apart.

Decisions at Dordrecht

In 1632, however, the long struggle over shunning in the north seemed to be resolved. In an historic meeting held in the Dutch city of Dordrecht, Dutch and northern Mennonite leaders drew up a church unity agreement known as the *Dordrecht Confession.*[15] The confession became a long-lasting and highly influential Mennonite confession of faith. It outlined doctrine from creation to Christ's second coming. The next-to-last of its 18 articles dealt with avoidance. The article endorsed the wisdom of ending business and social relationships with those who broke their baptismal vows. Faithful Christians could not conscientiously support the life and lifestyle of those who gave up the way of discipleship, it argued.

But Dordrecht also called for "Christian moderation" in the use of avoidance. The church was still to feed, clothe, and otherwise help excommunicated members who were in need, "according to the love and teaching of Christ and the apostles." The church could not view the shunned as "enemies," it cau-

Martyrs Mirror:
Anabaptist History Among the Amish

In the late sixteenth century the Dutch government took a tolerant stance toward Anabaptists. Socially accepted, Mennonites gradually moved into mainstream culture and eventually became economically prosperous. By the mid-1600s they had achieved a "golden age" and filled the ranks of wealthy merchants, physicians, artists, and artisans.

Dutch Mennonite minister Thieleman Jansz. van Braght feared his people were acculturating. Would they forget the New Testament teaching on simplicity, humility, and the suffering church as they became more socially secure in this life? Braght believed that one way to call the church to faithfulness was to remind it of its martyr past. He began collecting stories of Anabaptist martyrs from court records and other books. In 1660 he published them in a 1,478-page tome entitled *The Bloody Theater,* or *Martyrs Mirror.*

The book included explanation of Mennonite beliefs (including shunning), as well as hundreds of gripping martyr tales. About 100 of the stories were made more graphic in the book's second edition of 1685 when Dutch artist Jan Luyken provided 104 copper engraved illustrations.

Many Mennonites believed the book implicitly taught non-resistance to violence since the stories recounted those who chose suffering over fighting when faced with persecution. In 1748, confronted with the threat of frontier warfare, Pennsylvania Mennonites had the book translated into German.

In 1780 Amish elder Hans Nafziger of Essingen, Germany made arrangements to reprint the Pennsylvania edition in Europe for his Amish congregations in the Palatinate and Alsace. Nafziger worked on the project with Peter Weber, a neighboring Mennonite minister. In war-torn Europe these stories would do their people good, they believed. Meanwhile the Amish in North America were also reading the German *Martyrs Mirror*, and several decades later in 1849 Mifflin County, Pennsylvania Amishman Shem Zook issued a new German language edition of the book. Amish-owned Pathway Publishers still keeps a German edition of the martyr book in print.

Today the *Martyrs Mirror* is found in Amish homes, and references to it are common in Amish circles. The book also has supported the idea that the world is not to be fully trusted. The themes of separation, suffering, and faithfulness ring from its pages. No doubt the piety and experiences of martyrs in the sixteenth-century shape Amish life and thought in the twenty-first.

See Thieleman J. van Braght, *The Bloody Theater; or Martyrs Mirror of the Defenseless Christians* (Scottdale, Pa.: Herald Press, 1998). See also John S. Oyer and Robert S. Kreider, *Mirror of the Martyrs*, sec. ed. (Intercourse, Pa.: Good Books, 2003).

tioned, but rather should ask the erring to amend their lives and "be reconciled to God" and the church.

The Dordrecht Confession seemed to strike a balance by presenting a moderate form of shunning which aimed to keep clear boundaries of Christian ethics, while urging those who had left the church to return. Accepted by many congregations in the north, the document circulated among the Mennonites in south Germany and Switzerland as well, as did many of Menno's writings that advocated social avoidance. A generation later, in 1660, Alsatian Mennonite ministers and deacons representing congregations recently emigrated from Switzerland officially adopted as their own the Dordrecht statement with its article on shunning.[16] Yet at least one of those signers did not approve of the article on social avoidance.[17] Even though other Swiss Anabaptists also rejected shunning, they too offered the Dordrecht Confession when the government in Bern demanded an outline of their doctrine.[18]

After more than one hundred years of debate and argument among the Anabaptist-Mennonites, the controversy over social avoidance seemed to die down after 1660. By then many Mennonites seemed officially to sanction the shunning of unrepentant former church members. Had the Mennonites finally achieved "unity in the Lord," or was the issue still unresolved?

Survival strategies

While the south German and Swiss Mennonites were trying to resolve their internal disagreements over discipline, they also confronted continued persecution and opposition from the state and the state church. After 1614 Swiss authorities avoided creating religious martyrs. Instead of public executions, civic leaders used imprisonment, fines, and exile to discourage Anabaptist growth. Beginning in 1635, Swiss city councils, especially the one that governed the area around Bern, tried systematically to rid their lands of Swiss Brethren.

In 1648, Europe hailed the end of the terribly destructive Thirty Years War. Fought over political ambitions and alliances that were often complicated by Protestant and Catholic rivalries, the war had taken the lives of more than half the inhabitants of some areas. The enormity of death and pillage was staggering. Also devastating was the fact that farmland which had lain untilled in the midst of war was reverting to forest, thereby threatening survivors with famine.

Within the dire conditions left by the conflict, princes hurried to find settlers to cultivate their war-ravaged acres. The situation was so desperate that many even considered taking on outcast Anabaptist tenants. By at least 1653 persecuted Swiss Brethren began to move down the Rhine River into the wasted lands on its west bank, known as the Palatinate. Eleven years later one of the Palatinate's dukes issued a special offer of toleration to the Swiss Brethren (he called them "Mennists," cor-

A prison cell at Trachselwald Castle, Switzerland, in which Anabaptists were imprisoned.

rectly associating them with their fellow Mennonites in the North). The Mennonites would receive religious freedom for themselves, the duke promised, but they could not proselytize, meet in large groups, or construct church buildings. Despite these restrictions and heavier taxes, some Mennonites saw the offer as better than the harassment and threat of deportation they faced in Switzerland.[19]

Simultaneously, several French nobles invited Swiss Brethren to move into lands just north of Switzerland on the west bank of the Rhine. Known as Alsace, the region was home to German-speaking Alsatians, but governed by religiously tolerant French aristocrats. Small numbers of Anabaptists had lived in both the Palatinate and Alsace for several generations, but the large migrations after 1670 changed Mennonite church life there.[20] The new immigrants came in large numbers and maintained their social and churchly ties to Switzerland.

Ausbund:
Anabaptist Hymnal of the Amish

In 1535 a group of Anabaptists traveling from Moravia to southwestern Germany were captured on the Bavarian border. Placed in the Passau castle prison, some spent nearly five years there before authorities freed them. Others died in the dungeon. During the imprisonment, to occupy themselves and encourage one another, the prisoners wrote 53 hymns. Many of the lyrics spoke of sorrow, loneliness, and the imminence of death, but the hymns were also hopeful since their authors believed that suffering was to be expected in this life and was nothing compared with the glory of heaven.

By at least 1564, the hymns were printed in book form. The book proved popular, and soon other favorite hymns, including many lengthy martyr ballads with dozens of stanzas, joined the Passau collection. Only 19 years after its first known edition, the prison hymnbook was reissued with 130 songs. This printing was the first to receive the *Ausbund* title.

The hymns stress Anabaptist themes such as believer's baptism, nonviolence, and the suffering of Christ's followers. Many of the tunes associated with the hymn texts were popular secular ones now put with religious lyrics. The *Ausbund* was the Anabaptists' most common worship book other than the Bible. German-speaking European Mennonites and Amish continued to use the Ausbund some 300 years after its first words were sung in the Passau prison.

In North America Mennonites used the book regularly until about 1800. The Amish continued to sing from the book into the nineteenth century, and today nearly all Old Order Amish congregations use it or adaptations of it. Today's *Ausbund* contains 140 hymns, a brief doctrinal statement, and a short selection of Swiss Anabaptist martyr biographies. No printed music is included in the volume; all tunes have been passed on oral-ly over time. While some of the tunes have been forgotten and many greatly embellished, the Amish have preserved a valuable piece of Reformation-era hymnody. Contemporary Amish church life has been enriched and influenced by the singing of *Ausbund* hymns. The stories of martyrdom and persecution strengthen the Amish sense of humility and dependence on God and remind them of their heritage.

See *Ausbund: das ist, Etliche schöne Christliche Lieder* (Lancaster, Pa.: Verlag von den Amischen Gemeinden in Lancaster County, Pa., 1997). For more information, see Paul M. Yoder, et al., *Four Hundred Years with the Ausbund* (Scottdale, Pa.: Herald Press, 1964) or the Amish-authored volume Benuel S. Blank, *The Amazing Story of the Ausbund* (Narvon, Pa.: the author, 2001). About half the *Ausbund* song texts are translated into English in *Songs of the Ausbund, v. 1: History and Translations of Ausbund Hymns* (Millersburg, Ohio: Ohio Amish Library, 1998).

The castle at Passau on the Danube. Anabaptists imprisoned here wrote hymns that became the nucleus of the Ausbund *hymnal.*

Mennonite congregations in Switzerland, the Palatinate, and Alsace were now more closely connected than before.

Anabaptist survival into the mid-1600s had not been easy, and opposition had surfaced from many quarters. Still these often scattered and marginalized members of society had sought to be a church composed of committed disciples of Christ who had experienced God's salvation and were living witnesses to an alternative way of life. At times, this vision itself had been a stumbling block, as the Anabaptists disagreed on how the church should relate to those who were not disciples. The tension of being *in* the world, but not *of* it, had sometimes been too great. But most Anabaptists had not given up living in that tension, choosing rather, they said, "to persevere along the path we have entered upon, unto the glory of God and of Christ His Son."[21]

2.
Amish Beginnings, 1693-1711

"There you have it."

— Peter Zimmerman announcing the
beginning of the Amish church

Curious times

In 1690 the Swiss and south Rhine Mennonite world was still one of uncertainty, opposition, and persecution, reminiscent of the early days of Anabaptism. But it was also a world in which Mennonites experienced the goodwill, respect, and even admiration of neighbors.[1] This curious mix of confrontation and cooperation formed a context for heated Mennonite debate about the church and its relationship to society—debate that eventually resulted in division.

State opposition to the Swiss Brethren-Mennonites, especially in the Canton of Bern had continued throughout the 1600s. Waves of harassment, peaking in 1670 and the early 1690s, included repeated rounds of official mandates, fines, and threats of banishment or imprisonment. These attempts to expel completely the Mennonites from Switzerland were behind the emigration of hundreds of Swiss Mennonites to Alsace and the Palatinate during those years.

Those who remained behind in the Swiss heartland often survived through a combination of strategies that could include

The Emme River Valley in Switzerland, home of many Swiss Brethren (Mennonites), including Hans Reist.

occasional attendance at state churches or public denials of Anabaptist affiliation.[2] In other cases, living through trying times was eased by the support of sympathetic, non-Anabaptist neighbors. If the late seventeenth century witnessed renewed persecution, it also saw the emergence of a sort of grassroots admiration of Swiss Mennonites. Common people, sick of civic corruption and state church religiosity, saw the separatist Anabaptists as model Christians. An official investigation in 1692 unearthed opinions like that of a women who, when asked if she were a Mennonite, replied, "No, to tell the truth I am not worthy to be an Anabaptist . . . they are such a holy people." The depth of this popularity, in fact, was embarrassing to civil magistrates and resulted in targeted efforts to pressure local state church members and village leaders to comply with anti-Anabaptist legislation. Early in 1693 a Swiss Reformed pastor named Georg Thormann authored a book against the Anabaptists, driven to do so by the fact that too many common people saw the Mennonites "as saints, as the salt of the earth, as the true and chosen people and the proper core of all Christians."[3]

The combination of rekindled persecution and newfound public favor meant that the issue of the church's relationship to the world was not just theoretical. During times of state harassment, friendly neighbors could mean the difference between imprisonment and freedom. They interceded on behalf of Mennonite acquaintances, hid them, or made important social and political contacts for them. But this environment placed the Mennonites in a peculiar position. Having long seen themselves as a people separate from and in opposition to "the world," what did it mean that at least some in that world seemed to like them? What were they to make of these worldly state church admirers? The designations they gave their neighbors—Half-Anabaptists (*Halbtäufer*) or True-Hearted (*treuherzige*) People—suggested some of the Mennonite ambivalence towards them. At the same time, plagued by discrimination and social stigma, many Mennonites eagerly turned to the True-Hearted for help.

Not surprisingly, the alliance was especially strong in Switzerland where official opposition was harshest and Mennonites families had built up generations of networks of connections with the True-Hearted. Connections with the True-Hearted were less important in the Palatinate and Alsace where persecution was less acute and where Mennonite immigrants and refugees had arrived more recently and lacked a long history of neighborly contacts.[4] In any case, Mennonites were unsure how to regard their sympathetic friends. In an era when all churches—Catholic, Lutheran, and Reformed—branded most of those outside of their own groups as heretical, the Mennonites were not alone in viewing ecumenical relations as problematic.

For the Anabaptists, though, the difficulty was all the more perplexing because they advocated adult baptism and separation from sinful, worldly social structures as a mark of true Christian discipleship. Were the True-Hearted saved? They had not been voluntarily baptized as adult believers. If they were saved, then the practice of adult baptism was potentially meaningless. The True-Hearted also refused to leave their respectable and socially secure state church memberships and continued through their tithes and offerings to support the very apparatus which persecuted the Mennonites. Were not the True-Hearted inconsistent and hypocritical? But could the Mennonites condemn the True-Hearted, especially when they exhibited such Christ-like ethics as "giving a cup of cold water" to their persecuted neighbors? Indeed, some True-Hearted people had put their very reputations and property on the line when they befriended the outcast Mennonites. How could the Mennonites criticize them? How could some Mennonites survive without them?

An old Anabaptist perspective on the problematic relationship was that Mennonites simply could not know whether or not the True-Hearted were saved; only God knew. Mennonites should pray for the True-Hearted and be grateful for their friendship, but there was no need to cut off relations with them or condemn them. This view was most common in Switzerland.

Another equally traditional line of reasoning circulated especially in Alsace and the Palatinate. This tradition drew on the strict Anabaptist distinction between the church and the world. For those who held this worldview, there was little or no middle ground—the True-Hearted were not saved, and the Mennonites should not pretend that they were nor rely on their help in times of trouble. God alone would see the persecuted through. Mennonites who held to this more dualistic view also made much of the Anabaptist practice of shunning those who recanted their professions of faith and joined the state church. Accepting the aid of True-Hearted family members who had returned to the state church violated the principle of social avoidance. Drawing on significant streams of earlier Mennonite thought, those who advocated this perspective had biblical and historic Anabaptist support for their call for separation and avoidance. Since Anabaptists believed that salvation and church membership had practical social implications, it followed that breaking those ties also carried consequences that were equally concrete and relational.

Jakob Ammann

Perhaps especially because of the unsettling nature of late seventeenth-century life, voices calling for spiritual renewal and a reassessment of Anabaptist identity began surfacing in

The Alsatian village of Markirch (today Sainte-Marie-aux-Mines). Jakob Ammann lived in this area from about 1695 to 1712.

south Rhine and Swiss Mennonites communities. One of those urging reform in church life was a Swiss elder named Jakob Ammann. A recent convert to Anabaptism, Ammann had moved north, perhaps as early as the 1680s, to minister in Alsatian congregations largely composed of Swiss migrants and refugees. The exact reason for Ammann's move to Alsace is not clear, but from the time he began agitating for changes in church life he had notable connections and support in the region. Most of the controversial events surrounding him, however, took place in Switzerland. Ammann's first call for reform was his proposal for more frequent communion services.[5]

In striving for literal obedience to the Bible, Swiss Mennonites had observed communion once a year because the first Lord's Supper instituted by Jesus had been a part of an annual Passover meal. By at least 1693, Ammann suggested that church life would be strengthened if congregations communed twice a year. Since the Mennonites had stressed preparing for the Lord's Supper by closely examining their lives and relationships with God and other people, having communion more often might encourage members to give greater attention to their Christian lives.

Also, the Anabaptists had always excluded from the communion table those living in open sin. A more frequent observance would also force congregations to deal more often with situations of wrongdoing and discipline. Since Ammann represented those who believed that Mennonites were becoming spiritually lax, he welcomed more attention to church order.

Ammann's congregations instituted a more frequent communion, but, when people in some other congregations asked their own leaders to make the same change, those elders and ministers, notably a Swiss elder named Hans Reist, balked at the idea of introducing a new practice. Perhaps threatened by the challenge of Ammann's strong personality or his popular appeal, Reist and several other elders rejected more frequent communion. They admitted that Ammann and those who agreed with him could do as they wished, but Reist and his associates made it clear that they considered the innovation unnecessary.

To avoid or not to avoid

Ammann believed Reist represented a weakening of Mennonite church life and resolve, a weakening Ammann abhorred. Reist was a friend of the True-Hearted and held out the possibility that they were saved without publicly confessing God's grace and receiving baptism. Nor did Reist practice social avoidance with those who left the church or who refused to confess their sins; he was comfortable merely with excluding them from the once-a-year communion table. So when some in Reist's congregation continued to clamor for more frequent communion and Reist called fellow ministers Niklaus

The confrontation between Jakob Ammann and Hans Reist as carved by Aaron Zook (1921-2003), a member of the Beachy Amish church.

Hans Reist

Hans Reist (often called Hüsli Hans) was a Swiss Brethren elder in the Emme River Valley east of Berne, Switzerland. Little is known about his life aside from bits of information preserved in letters chronicling his disagreements with Jakob Ammann. He was married to Barbara Ryser.

Reist knew persecution firsthand. In 1670 authorities expelled Hans and Barbara, penniless, from their village of Rotenbaum because the couple were Anabaptists. The Bern government confiscated the Reist house and sold most of their grain, animals, and furniture—including a loom. The state settled Reist's outstanding debts with the proceeds, and then kept about half the profits from the liquidation of the family's modest wealth.

Like many expelled Anabaptists, Reist broke exile in a few years and returned home. State records mention him again in 1686. In 1701 officials arrested Reist, and he promised to attend state church services and take the holy sacraments. Reist may have had no more intention of keeping that pledge than he had had of remaining in exile 30 years before, or he may have been willing to engage in acts of public piety that he considered meaningless in exchange for some measure of toleration. Reist was a leader who knew how to survive tough times and understood his own ability to compromise. Apparently he sympathized with the failings of others and allowed his church and the True-Hearted a fair degree of spiritual latitude.

A small collection of Reist's writings remain in the form of a 16-page booklet containing a prayer and a hymn. In line with Ammann's charge that Reist taught salvation for the True-Hearted, Reist's prayer petitions God "on behalf of all those peoples who do so much good unto us with food and drink and house and shelter, and who produce and show unto us great love and loyalty. Lord God, be their rich reward here and in the life eternal."

Reist's prayer suggests the pain he must have experienced in the schism with Ammann. "Draw us together," the elder prayed, "in Thy great love, and let no dissention or scattering come among us any more, but rather let us see, O Lord of Harvest, how great the harvest but how few Thy faithful workers are." Reist's hymn was a 46-stanza ballad recounting the biblical story of Abraham and Isaac.

For more information see Samuel Geiser's entry "Reist, Hans" in *The Mennonite Encyclopedia, vol. 4* (1959); Isaac Zürcher, "Hans Reist House and the 'Vale of Anabaptists,'" *Mennonite Quarterly Review* 66 (July 1992), 426-27; and Robert Friedmann, *Mennonite Piety Through the Centuries: Its Genius and Literature* (Goshen, Ind.: Mennonite Historical Society, 1949), 184-85. Mark Furner, "Lay Casuistry and the Survival of Later Anabaptists in Bern," *Mennonite Quarterly Review* 75 (October 2001), 455-56 (esp. n.105), 466. Reist's prayer appears in John D. Roth, ed., with Joe Springer, *Letters of the Amish Division: A Sourcebook* (Goshen, Ind.: Mennonite Historical Society, 1993), 147-52.

Moser and Peter Giger for counsel, Ammann decided to open the debate further. Ammann asked Moser and Giger to find out what Reist really believed about shunning.

Reist answered with the words of Jesus, replying that, "What goes into the mouth does not defile the person but what comes out of the mouth, that defiles a man" (Matthew 15:11).[6] The message to Ammann was clear: Reist believed that avoiding sin was only a spiritual possibility, not a matter with social or physical implications. Reist had no interest in practicing literal shunning of errant members as an attempt to win them back to the church.

Now Ammann believed that renewal in the church was all the more urgent if even seasoned leaders like Hans Reist failed to uphold a thoroughgoing separation from the world. In 1693 Ammann and three other like-minded ministers traveled through Swiss Mennonite communities, teaching the significance of social avoidance and questioning elders and ministers on their practice.

The party soon found that Reist's friend, Niklaus Moser, agreed with them that shunning was important; he also rejected the notion that the True-Hearted were saved. In the next town, Reist's other advising minister, Peter Giger, seemingly also confessed the importance of shunning. Buoyed by their newfound sympathy, Ammann's group traveled down into the Swiss Emme River Valley, with its notable Mennonite population, and summoned Hans Reist himself. The exchange between Reist and Ammann was heated. Reist rejected Ammann's call for shunning on the grounds that Jesus ate with known sinners and yet had kept himself pure. Christians in the late seventeenth century could do the same, Reist claimed.

But, Ammann countercharged, Reist was not keeping the church pure. A woman who had lied, and then repeatedly lied about her lying, was still considered a member of Reist's congregation even though her untruth had been revealed. For whatever reasons of favoritism, Reist had not practiced even the spiritual discipline he espoused. Here was proof for Ammann that Reist was drifting from the Anabaptist teachings of church purity and Christian ethics.

Ministers in a neighboring town suggested that Ammann call a general meeting of Swiss church leaders and settle the matter publicly. Niklaus Moser's barn served as the meeting place. Many elders and ministers did not show up—among them, Hans Reist. Sensing a growing tension between Ammann and Reist, Moser and Giger backed away from their earlier acceptance of shunning. At the meeting, they told Ammann that they would like to decide the issue only with the counsel of all of the ministers and thorough Bible study. After some discussion, those present decided to invite all leaders and lay members to another gathering in two weeks. Hopefully everyone would reach consensus then.

The next 14 days were filled with personal meetings and private correspondence. Through emissaries, Ammann tried to contact Reist, who still refused to say that the True-Hearted were not saved. Reist also circulated a letter criticizing Ammann and warning fellow ministers "not to give too much regard to the teachings and discipline of the younger [ministers]."[7] Ammann also reported that Reist claimed "more authority" than Ammann, even though both held the same church office. While the simmering dispute was much more than a simple personality clash, Reist's condescending attitude hurt efforts at reconciliation and seemed to invite confrontation.

The Niklaus Moser farm at Fridersmatt, in the Emme River Valley, was the site of numerous secret Swiss Anabaptist meetings. In 1693 it also served as a meeting place for one of the debates between Jakob Ammann and his supporters and those who sided with Hans Reist.

Jakob Ammann

In recent years historians have learned more about Jakob Ammann. The son of Michael and Anna (Rupp) Ammann, Jakob was born in 1644 near Erlenbach in the Swiss Canton of Bern. He was married to Verena Stüdler. As late as 1671 Jakob was a member in good standing of the Reformed Church, but by 1680, Swiss officials were reporting his conversion to Anabaptism. Records reveal official suspicion that his father had also become an Anabaptist.

Ammann probably lived in Steffisburg, Switzerland, prior to his public dispute with Hans Reist, and likely moved to Alsace in the 1680s, and to the Markirch Valley itself only in 1695. There, non-Anabaptist observers quickly recognized his leadership and influence. In 1696 a magistrate called Ammann the "leader of the new Anabaptist sect" and noted that he was "commonly called 'the Patriarch.'" Ammann successfully negotiated his people's exemptions from militia duty and from serving as municipal tax collectors, and in 1701 he won approval for an Amish family to raise a set of orphans without state interference.

In 1712 local authorities expelled Anabaptists from Alsace, and Ammann's whereabouts thereafter are unknown. In 1730 Ammann's daughter asked to resettle in the Canton of Bern. She told authorities that her father had been a Swiss Anabaptist minister, but that he was no longer living and had died outside the canton. As part of her repatriation she was told to join the Reformed Church; however, the evidence suggests she probably never did.

Like his father, Jakob Ammann was a tailor by trade, and French researcher Robert Baecher has written that it is "fitting that a tailor, one sensitive to the style of dress around him, would extend this concern to the strict and regulated attire that eventually became a hallmark of the Amish community."

Today few Amish know much about Ammann; when asked about their church's origins, most typically stress the biblical or Reformation roots of their faith. "The birthplace of Jacob Aymen [sic] we have not yet ascertained," wrote two Pennsylvania Amishmen in 1830, "nor yet the exact place of his residence—having never considered him a man of note, we do not deem the place of his nativity a matter of consequence." Nevertheless, today more than 180,000 people call themselves *Amish*.

For biographical material on Ammann, see Robert Baecher, "The 'Patriarche' of Sainte-Marie-aux-Mines," *Mennonite Quarterly Review* 74 (January 2000), 145-58; John Hüppi, "Identifying Jacob Ammann," *Mennonite Quarterly Review* 74 (April 2000), 329-39; and Mark Furner, "On the Trail of Jacob Ammann," *Mennonite Quarterly Review* 74 (April 2000), 326-28.

Days of division

When the day for the second general conference arrived, Hans Reist and several other ministers sympathetic to him did not appear. In the long moments of that tense situation, Ammann assured everyone that he did not want to cause a schism in the church, but he reminded them that matters could not be settled until Reist arrived. One of the women waiting for the discussion to get started left the meeting to find Reist and tell him that the group was waiting.

But Reist had no intention of meeting with Ammann or debating the issues under consideration. He sent word back to those at the Moser barn that he and other church leaders were involved in harvesting and were too busy to be bothered.

Hearing this, Ammann "almost became enraged and immediately placed Hans Reist, along with six other ministers, under the ban as a heretic."[8] The startling course of events left onlookers "horrified," and several people begged Ammann to be patient and let his temper cool.[9] Instead, Ammann turned and questioned five other men as to their views on shunning.

When their answers were conditional, Ammann expelled them from the church as well. Shocked at the apparent splitting of the church before their very eyes, the gathered Mennonites waited for someone to speak a word of peace—some word to undo all the harsh words that had just torn the church apart.

Instead, as if to validate all that had just happened, Ammann's associate, Peter Zimmerman, said, "There you have it," and the meeting broke up quickly and in confusion, with neither side offering the customary handshake.[10]

In the hours following that encounter, a number of leaders tried to resolve the crisis. Two of the ministers whom Ammann had excommunicated offered to hold a discussion to try and work out the groups' differences. After some hesitation, Ammann and his supporters agreed to attend the forum, which included Peter Giger and his congregation. The sides consented to one guideline: "that when someone is speaking, the other should listen."[11]

Ammann addressed the group first. When Giger next took his turn to present the views of the Reist group, Ammann got up to walk out. Angry that Ammann would not offer the same hearing that he had just received, Giger grabbed Ammann's shirtsleeve and said, "Let me also finish my speech." But Ammann "shook his arm loose" and left the room, dramatically bringing the meeting to a premature end.[12]

Although the division had not yet spread to Anabaptist communities beyond Switzerland, it was clear that there were now two distinct groups: the larger Mennonite community represented by Hans Reist, and the reforming "Ammann-ish" faction led by Jakob Ammann.[13] If before this encounter Swiss church leaders had underestimated Ammann's resolution or the seriousness with which he regarded reforming church life, they could do so no longer. Ammann intended to establish a disciplined church, even if it meant leaving behind most of his fellow Anabaptists.

The schism spreads

The story of what had transpired in Switzerland during 1693 soon spread to the other south Rhine Mennonite communities, and eventually to the Dutch and North German Mennonites. Thereafter letters flew back and forth, with all parties advising, scolding, questioning, and challenging both the Reist/Mennonite and Amish groups. Some Palatinate ministers wrote to the Amish and counseled them to be reconciled with the Reist people. They also wrote to the Alsatian congregations and warned them not to listen to Jakob Ammann.

Alsatian church leaders, however, claimed that Reist was the one to ignore. They were confused as to why Reist thought that social avoidance was a new teaching. The Alsatian congregations contended that Swiss Mennonites had accepted the biblical teaching of shunning some 30 years earlier. Why had Reist not practiced it, they wondered? Most Alsatians agreed that Ammann was the true reformer in the controversy—restoring classical Anabaptist doctrines that the Swiss had let slide. Earlier, Ammann had excommunicated several members of the Alsatian Mennonite congregation at Markirch who would not stop attending the services of the state church. The expelled had evidently tried to win some social acceptance by going to their local parish church. Ammann and other Alsatian leaders would allow no such compromise of faith for personal gain and social status.

Returning to his home in Alsace, Ammann responded to the past months' events with a long letter. He reminded those who called him a troublemaker that he had merely followed the three-part practice of church discipline outlined by Jesus in Matthew 18. Ammann privately confronted those who were erring and asked them to mend their ways. When they refused admonition, he visited them with several witnesses and only finally, as a last resort, was he forced to excommunicate those who would not reform. But Ammann also had words for those who as yet were not involved in the Reist-Ammann division.

The mill at Ohnenheim in Alsace. In 1660, Alsatian Mennonites met here and adopted the Dordrecht Confession as their statement of faith. Later, during the Ammann-Reist controversy, Palatinate Mennonites called a unity conference at the mill. That March 1964 gathering failed to bring peace, and the two groups remained divided.

Ammann sent a "letter of warning" to the Mennonite churches in the south Rhine and Swiss regions in which he demanded that men and women, ministers and lay members declare by February 20, 1694, whether they supported Reist or him. Although Ammann said he was open to someone showing him his error with scripture, he served notice that the Amish would shun "according to God's Word" those who did not decide by March 7.[14]

In response to events that seemed increasingly out of control, the Palatinate Mennonites called a conference of reconciliation at a mill in Alsace. The Palatinates proposed a compromise. They suggested that Reist had, in fact, been negligent in exercising church discipline and in teaching that the True-Hearted might be saved, but the Palatinates rejected Ammann's teaching on shunning the excommunicated. Grudgingly, the Swiss Mennonites—including Reist himself—agreed to the compromise.

The Amish, however, would not accept the proposed solution. The social avoidance of those who left the church, even to the point of not eating common meals together, was one of Ammann's major reforms; it was also the historic understanding of many Anabaptists. The only Amish response to the meeting at the mill was Ammann's banning and shunning of most of the Palatinate ministers, along with a large group of other people whom he had apparently not met.

The church at risk

The Swiss and south Rhine Mennonite communities had remained surprisingly united for more than a century and a half. During several months spanning 1693-1694, their fellowships were torn apart and mired in deep pain and resentment. Were the issues trite items of no lasting concern? Was the whole schism the result of personality conflicts blown out of proportion? While personality differences more than likely contributed to the disagreement, the issues involved were significant. The stakes were high. From the perspective of both sides, the church itself was at risk.

For Ammann, the danger the church faced was compromise. The Anabaptist reformers of 150 years earlier had given their lives for a church that would be a visible alternative to sinful society. Now some Mennonites were resorting to outward compromise, agreeing to attend state church catechism or even have their infants baptized to avoid exile. Relations with the True-Hearted were especially problematic, Ammann charged, because the half-commitment of such folks only mirrored the lack of full-fledged conviction on the part of many Anabaptists themselves. He also believed that Mennonites were willing to sacrifice humility and simplicity in their efforts to fit in with those around them. In contrast, Ammann required male members to wear untrimmed beards and forbade "haughty clothing."[15] Fashionable styles represented frivolous spending, and the use of buttons to fasten coats suggested the ornamental style of military uniforms; neither stood the test of the biblical injunction to avoid even the appearance of evil.

Moreover, if the Anabaptists had really believed that salvation was given by grace through faith, then the True-Hearted, who had not publicly accepted such grace and submitted to its accompanying symbol of water baptism, could not be saved. The same was true for what Ammann saw as the clear New Testament teaching of social avoidance: there was no middle ground.[16] In those regions where persecution was relatively light and compromise was a greater threat—Alsace, parts of the Palatinate, and the mountains south and west of Bern—Ammann received most of his support. He championed strict doctrinal interpretations and an activist approach that appealed to Mennonites who desired a strong group identity in an atmosphere of relative tolerance.[17]

For Reist and the old Mennonite communities in the Emme River Valley and parts of the Palatinate, the threat was anything but lost identity. Their identity as outcasts and the targets of state persecution was all too clear. For the Reist group, the threat to the church was a cold legalism. They already faced enough external threats. Shunning or stricter dress standards that would divide them from within were the last thing they needed. Nor were they keen to receive lectures on faithfulness from those who lived in relative safety outside of Bern.[18]

Additionally Reist could claim—probably quite accurately— that the Swiss Anabaptists had never practiced social avoidance, even if they had agreed to it in principle during unity discussions with their northern European Mennonite cousins years before. Ammann's insistence on implementing it now only stirred up trouble. Physical avoidance was simply not taught in the New Testament, as Reist read it. And as for the True-Hearted, Reist thought that it was presumptuous for humans to declare whether or not a person was saved, baptism notwithstanding. Yet despite their emphasis on openness and opposition to avoidance, it was the Mennonites who seemed to practice shunning when opportunities for reconciliation arrived.

The Amish ask for forgiveness and the Mennonites refuse

A few years after the Mennonite and Amish division, several Amish leaders felt they had acted too quickly in excommunicating so many people. They especially wondered if their actions were justified because they had not counseled with their own congregations before expelling the Reist group. Several Amish leaders—including Ammann himself—then excommunicated themselves from the church, symbolically demonstrating their repentance and desire to rejoin the larger Mennonite fellowship. The response of the Mennonites was disappointing at best. Some of the Reist group reveled in the Amish admittance that they had been too quick. Other Mennonites wrote letters equating Jakob Ammann with symbolic biblical figures of evil and doom.

Again the question of social avoidance surfaced and ended the unity talks. One Amish minister, Ulli Ammann (Jakob's younger brother), later wrote that the Amish had hoped to come to some agreement. "But this was all for naught. Our efforts could find no place among them," Uli Ammann lamented. "Instead, when they [the Mennonites] said something about the matter, they began with our faults and did not want to acknowledge that they themselves were guilty of making mistakes or had been a cause of our mistakes. So contention and division continued among the people . . . ."[19] In 1711 an Alsatian Mennonite fellowship considered reconciliation with Ulli Ammann and another Amish minister, but with unclear results. In any case, the division between the two groups persisted.[20]

In 1699 and 1700 Mennonite leaders rebuffed repeated Amish attempts to seek peace, even after some Amish again excommunicated themselves in self-humiliation. Mennonites reasoned that the Amish earlier had acted unjustly and now continued to claim that shunning was biblical. Additionally, the Amish observed a literal footwashing service as a part of their communion service, following the example of Jesus who had washed his disciples' feet during the first Lord's Supper (John 13). Most Swiss Mennonites thought that literal footwashing was an unnecessary ritual, even though it, like avoidance, was a part of the old Mennonite Dordrecht Confession.

Diverging paths
Throughout the turbulent years of Swiss and south Rhine Mennonite division, the War of Palatinate Succession ravaged both Alsace and the Palatinate. Meanwhile, the Bern government in Switzerland redoubled its efforts to drive Mennonites from its lands. Amid so much hardship along the Rhine and persecution in the Alps, the small group of Anabaptists split.

Four days before Christmas 1697, the north German Mennonite patriarch, 85-year-old minister and shipowner

Today Amish and Mennonites participate together in several cooperative ventures. Here Old Order Amish men help rebuild a structure near Salisbury, Pennsylvania, soon after tornadoes destroyed it in June 1998. The Salisbury cleanup and reconstruction was coordinated by Mennonite Disaster Service, a volunteer relief response effort supported by both Mennonites and Amish.

Gerrit Roosen of Hamburg, wondered about the connections between the larger events of European politics and Mennonite church life. Roosen worried over the war and its effects on his people, and over the new political division created by France's control of Alsace and the city of Strasbourg. He was also deeply saddened by the Mennonite-Amish division, well known as it was to northern Mennonites. Although the Dutch and north German Mennonites of Roosen's region had originally advocated shunning, they had recently practiced it less and less often. Roosen, in fact, rejected Ammann's conservative clothing and appearance regulations. In all of the Apostle Paul's letters, the old minister wrote, there was "not a single word in which he gave a law to any believers regarding what style of

Church Discipline and Matthew 18

An important Anabaptist belief was that Christians followed Jesus in life and death, regardless of practical consequences, and were reliant on God's enabling grace. Having made a commitment to God and the church to take up the way of discipleship, a believer would occasionally "fall away" by living in unrepentant sin or succumbing to false doctrine. It was the responsibility of the rest of the church, and especially the leaders, to plead with erring ones to change their ways. Eventually, if members refused to acknowledge wrongdoing, the church would excommunicate them. Such a dramatic step not only signaled the seriousness of the situation, but also might jolt the errant into repentance, a change of life, and reunion with the church.

For many Anabaptists a key Scripture addressing church discipline was Jesus' words to his disciples in Matthew 18:15-18.

Moreover if thy brother shall trespass against thee, go and tell him his fault between thee and him alone; if he shall hear thee, thou hast gained thy brother. But if he will not hear thee, then take with thee one or two more, that in the mouth of two or three witnesses every word may be established. And if he shall neglect to hear them, tell it unto the church: but if he neglect to hear the church, let him be unto thee as an heathen man and a publican. Verily I say unto you, Whatsoever ye shall bind on earth shall be bound in heaven: and whatsoever ye shall loose on earth shall be loosed in heaven.

These verses suggest a three-step sequence (private warning, warning with witnesses, and public warning) that must precede a member's expulsion from the church. The process ensured that church leaders did not excommunicate arbitrarily. More importantly, the three stages gave the errant one several opportunities to repent and find forgiveness.

How exactly these verses were applied in the life of the congregation was one of the significant points of disagreement between the Ammann and Reist groups. Both appealed to Scripture and Anabaptist-Mennonite history. Ammann argued that Reist had not followed Jesus' teaching closely enough when Reist had not excommunicated a member who told a series of lies, in spite of the fact that the congregation knew the situation and the member refused to repent.

The Reist group, on the other hand, thought it was Ammann who had not taken Matthew 18 seriously enough. They reminded Ammann that he had excommunicated fellow believers without offering them opportunities to repent when he expelled numerous Palatine Anabaptists whom he had never met, much less addressed privately or with witnesses.

The second major argument involving church discipline centered on what excommunication entailed. Ammann believed that the Bible clearly pointed to the social avoidance of the excommunicated. Reist, in contrast, felt that merely excluding the expelled one from the communion service was enough. Ammann could have found support in Scriptures such as Romans 16:17; 1 Corinthians 5:9-11; 2 Thessalonians 3:6, 14-15; 2 Timothy 3:2-5; and Titus 3:10. Reist alluded to passages like Matthew 9:10-13 and 15:11.

Personality issues aside, the Ammann-Reist controversy involved disagreements over significant Anabaptist issues of belief and practice: the nature of the church, its relationship to larger society, and the application of the important text in Matthew 18.

clothes they should have." Avoid undue luxury, of course, he added, but otherwise "I think it appropriate to follow the customs of the land and that of the people one is with and of one's surroundings."[21]

Roosen's ideas represented a growing consensus among European Mennonites. In the north, an emphasis on inner piety over outward appearance meant that simple lifestyle patterns and physical-social separation from the world were not so important as long as a person's heart was right. In the south, the Mennonites' very struggle to survive had brought the need to rely on the True-Hearted and often to define identity in ethnic, rather than disciplinary, terms. Ammann's position represented a different approach. The church as a visible and social reality needed boundaries equally physical and social. The separation from the world was not merely a matter of inner feeling, nor even the result of being a persecuted minority group. Church renewal came by way of commitment and community. In their own ways, both the Amish and the Mennonites were trying to safeguard the church.

Yet despite their renewed commitment to separation from the world, the Amish shared some things in common with other Western Europeans. After 1700, for example, the Amish were intrigued by the prospect of immigration to the "New World." North America beckoned the Amish as persuasively as it called their neighbors. Distinct though they were, Jakob Ammann's people were soon as caught up in colonization as their worldly state church neighbors. The lure of the Atlantic shunned no one.

3.
Migration and Persistence: The Amish in Europe, 1693-1801

> *"You are still one with us . . . in keeping to doctrine and congregational practice according to the old customs."*
> — admonition of elder Hans Nafziger
> to an immigrant minister, 1788

Searching for stability

The first century of Amish life was marked both by a continued outsider status, and by the emergence in many places of notably amiable relations between the Amish and influential non-Amish neighbors. In their own ways, these two developments encouraged the church's geographic spread. In 1693 the Amish were a tiny group concentrated in Alsace, with smaller numbers in the Palatinate and Switzerland. Pressure in all these areas, invitations to lease farms in other parts of western Germany and Eastern Europe, and the lure of North America all resulted in migration, so that by 1801, the Amish were worshiping from western Pennsylvania to Russian Volhynia.

Despite the church's dispersal to far-flung settlements, its identity remained intact. In the late 1700s elder Hans Nafziger of Essingen, Germany, visited fellow Amish in the Netherlands, ordained leaders in Alsace, and corresponded with minister

Popular images of eighteenth-century Swiss Anabaptists.

Christian Schowalter in Lancaster County, Pennsylvania. Such activity, along with Nazfiger's arranging to publish a German translation of the Dutch Anabaptist history book *Martyrs Mirror,* all pointed to ways that past experiences and contemporary relationships formed a persistent peoplehood. These were a separate people, called out of the world as a witness to the world. Nevertheless, they were still a part of that world even as they strove to be apart from it.

The tension between being a part of the community and being excluded outsiders was apparent even in the earliest years of the Amish church. After the 1693 division, a significant number of Swiss Anabaptists who sided with Ammann moved north to the valley of Markirch (in French Sainte-Marie-aux-Mines) in Alsace, which was then ruled by the religiously tolerant Lords of Ribeaupierre. While Anabaptists had been living in the Alsatian lowlands for some time, the influx of as many as 60 new families—including Ammann's household—into the Sainte-Marie-aux-Mines valley created a sizable new Amish community there.

Writing in 1702, a local Catholic priest noted that "in Sainte-Marie-aux-Mines [the] Anabaptists . . . are divided in three different sects and have no communication with each other as far as their religion is concerned." The largest was Ammann's notably plain group in which men "have a long beard and the men and women wear clothing made only of linen." A few Swiss refugees apparently aligned with Hans Reist "have shorter beards and everyone dresses in coarse cloth," while the third group—those Anabaptists who had been living in tolerant Alsatian villages for decades—"are about like the Catholics [in appearance]." None of the three groups had a "church building but meet in one of their homes (each one in his sect) which are often scattered in the mountains."

Clearly the Amish were distinguishable even from other Anabaptists, especially those whose long-standing presence in tolerant Alsace had resulted in their adaptation to local customs and appearance. Yet even as distinct outsiders, the Amish were able to find a welcome in Sainte-Marie-aux-Mines. Evidently, in fact, members of the French Reformed (Huguenot) Sainte-Marie-aux-Mines congregation had housed the Amish refugees when they first arrived after 1694. As the Amish established themselves in the area, they rented or even purchased some of the largest farms in the valley. Others took over area mills and lumber operations. Meanwhile, civil authorities appear to have sided with them when neighbors complained that the Amish should have to serve in certain civic roles. The Amish received a waiver in exchange for a fee.

This economic and even partial civic acceptance, however, existed in tension with the reality of being religious outsiders. During the early 1700s, Amish leaders were repeatedly involved in conflicts over conversion as individuals from state church backgrounds joined or sought to join the Anabaptists. Some disputes were quite public, such as Ammann's vocal arguments in the middle of the street with a Catholic priest upset over the possibility of proselytism. In the end, these religious tensions outweighed the ability of the Amish to find an economic and neighborly niche in the valley. In 1712 the French government overruled locally tolerant lords and ordered the expulsion of all Anabaptists from Alsace. Although the order never completely rooted out the Amish presence, it effectively dispersed important early Amish communities.[1]

If the expulsion orders pushed the Amish out, the possibility of settlement pulled them to nearby areas outside direct royal jurisdictions, such as Salm, Montbéliard, Hesse-Darmstadt, and the duchies of Lorraine and Zweibrücken. In some cases, refugees moved to territory open to Anabaptists for the first time, while in others, they went to places where fellow church members had long lived. As early as 1704, for example, Amish families had been living in Montbéliard, but the expulsions from Markirch swelled these numbers considerably. Eventually, most Amish were forced out of the very

The Schaaken Estate, near Korbach in Waldeck. Vinzenz and Anna (Zimmerman) Schwarzentruber were leaseholders here beginning in 1759.

areas in which Anabaptism had first sprouted. Only three small Amish congregations survived in Switzerland, all close to the Alsatian border.[2]

In most places, Amish and other religious minority refugees did not own land outright, but leased estates from landed nobility seeking tenants. The relationship between landlords and renters benefited both parties; leaseholders received toleration, while owners found a pool of especially loyal tenants who were dependant upon them for protection.[3] Landed nobles typically rented estates for periods of six to nine years, handing over responsibility for the estate farm, granting freedom of worship on estate land, and allowing leaseholders use of the nearby forests for raising livestock. Leaseholders could supplement their income by taking up trade in weaving or operating the estate distillery. In Waldeck some renters began making cheese.[4]

Often more than one household leased a single estate, and in the case of Amish renters, they sought to pass the lease to fellow church members. For example, in 1713 Christian Rupp leased an estate near Frieburg, which he renewed until his death in 1746, whereupon Michael Müller became the tenant. By that time, Müller had to pay nearly twice as much in annual rent and took a co-leaseholder. In 1772 the estate—still under the management of Müller and Zimmerman families—included 10 horses and foals, 32 oxen, 16 cows, 20 calves, 26 sheep, and 23 pigs. In 1800 the farm had a workforce of 23 who farmed 231 acres of tillable land, 128 acres of meadow, 119 acres of pastureland, and less than five acres of garden. All of this had to feed 35 people and generate enough cash to cover the annual lease payment.[5]

Identifiable Amish communities developed as leaseholders clustered in particular areas. The French-speaking territory of Montbéliard, for example, developed into a thriving Amish community, especially after 1750 under the leadership of elder Hans Rich.[6] As the eighteenth century wore on, the needs of growing families and the interests of territorial landlords both resulted in the formation of more communities. About 1775, Prince Carl Christian of Nassau-Weilburg invited four families—Nafziger, Unzicker, Schanz, and Schwarztraub households—to take up estates near Frankfurt, which they did. And by 1780, Amish were invited to Austrian-controlled land in Baden-Durlach.[7]

Harassment and hospitality

The welcome some found on the estates of wealthy landowners was part of the paradox of Amish life in these years: havens of toleration made necessary and possible by continued waves of persecution and harassment. Into the eighteenth century, Swiss authorities in Bern posted commissions for citizens who turned over Anabaptists to the state.[8] Certainly the Amish were not alone in suffering intolerance. In 1699 the government of Bern expelled the pastor of the city's largest state church because he had held unauthorized Bible study meetings.[9] In many places, both Catholics and Protestants—if they were minority members of their home territories—felt unwelcome. Nor were the Amish the only ones to benefit from the land-leasing agreements offered by nobles. Swiss Reformed households were also leaving Alpine valleys to become tenants on German and French farms to the north.

Yet if these lease agreements afforded the Amish some relief from religious persecution, they also could produce new tensions. As Swiss outsiders, the Amish—along with other Swiss leaseholders—were "free" people, not bound by traditional local rules that regulated the economic lives of surrounding peasants. Moreover, peasant farmers typically were banned from allowing their cattle, sheep, or pigs to use the estate forests, which were open only to the leaseholders. Opposition to the Amish, then, might stem from nonreligious resentments or might become entwined with religion only as frustrated peasants enlisted the help of sympathetic priests or pastors to protest the presence of Anabaptists. Such protests rarely resulted in nobles turning down leases, but they added to a context in which the Amish status as ethnic and religious outsiders remained, even though the nobles gave them a friendly welcome.

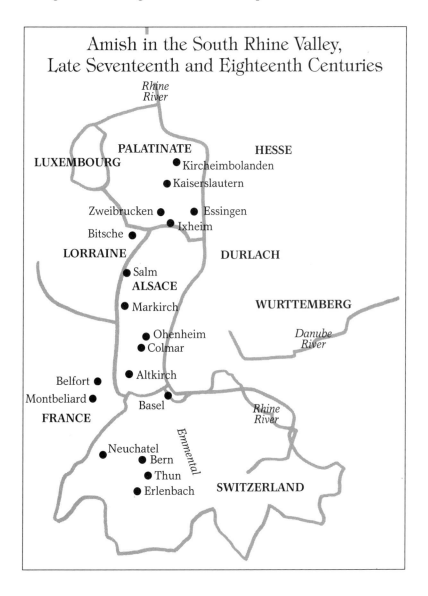

Amish in the South Rhine Valley, Late Seventeenth and Eighteenth Centuries

Despite such tensions and Amish commitments to separation from worldly society, there were notable examples of assistance and friendship across religious lines. If the Amish were separate, they were not necessarily withdrawn. Not only were landlords dependent upon them, but the Amish themselves at times relied on the goodwill of their non-Amish neighbors—even in cases where the issues clearly were matters of Amish concern. In 1729 Hans Hochstättler, a leaseholder near Frieburg, appealed to a nearby Reformed Church pastor to perform the marriage of Hochstättler's daughter Barbara and an Alsatian Anabaptists named Hans von Gunten. Barbara's pregnancy out of wedlock had resulted in her excommunication from the Amish church and the refusal of Amish elders to perform the wedding. The Reformed clergyman initially refused, citing the fact that services of the state church were unavailable to dissenters. Yet apparently the pastor liked Hochstättler, and so he wrote to his own superior asking permission to marry the couple as a gesture of goodwill. Clearly he did not approve of Amish religious customs, referring to Amish discipline as "their strange way of thinking," but he respected Hochstättler enough to put his own professional reputation on the line and to marry the couple "in a private ceremony and without pomp."[10]

Another somewhat surprising feature of Amish family life in this era was the number of mixed marriages between Amish and non-Amish partners. Because the Amish insisted on marriage only between church members, it seems these families were the result of one partner converting and joining the Amish later in life, while the other remained a state church adherent.[11] These sorts of ties—in addition to the economic links of leaseholding—connected Amish and non-Amish families and communities in peculiar ways.

If all of this seems a bit remarkable in light of Jakob Ammann's insistence on separation and avoiding dependence on the True-Hearted, perhaps it can be understood in a larger context. Amman was keenly interested in avoiding religious compromise to curry state favor. The Amish of the 1700s were still committed to those principles. If their daily conduct won them friends and some respect, that was another matter. Even if the development of neighborly connections resulted in some goodwill, the Amish were still spiritual outsiders subject to social sanction. In 1744, for example, when Nicholas Stoltzfus, a Lutheran hired hand on an Amish farm, asked to marry an Amish woman, state authorities permitted the nuptials only if the couple agreed to leave the area after the wedding.[12]

Such sanctions, though, often were rooted as much in the tensions accompanying economic competition, as in theological debate. In Baden-Durlach in the 1760s, for example, the Hochberg weaver's guild protested the presence of non-guild Amish weavers like Christian Gautsche and succeeded in keeping Gautsche from hiring a journeyman. After 1780 when Anabaptists moved into Austrian-ruled areas of Baden, economic resentments surfaced even more frequently. Locals denounced the Amish as foreigners and complained that nobles who rented estates to outsiders were unconcerned with the economic plight of local folks. One notable case of conflict involved a Catholic would-be renter who railed against a Catholic nunnery for preferring to lease its acres to Anabaptists heretics on the grounds that they were skilled farmers, instead of to him.[13]

North to the Netherlands

Some migrations took Amish families further afield—to the Netherlands, North America, and Eastern Europe. The movement north grew out of persecution and international diplomacy. In 1711 the Swiss Bernese government decided to rid its territory of Anabaptists by shipping them elsewhere. Already in 1699, Bern officials had asked the Dutch East India Company to take Swiss Anabaptists to islands in the Pacific Ocean.[14] The shipping company never responded, and so the Swiss drew up their own plans to export the Amish and

Mennonites to North America. The initial attempts to ship Anabaptists out of the Alps failed, but in the summer of 1711 the Bern government was gearing up efforts to try again, when sympathetic officials in the Netherlands intervened with the humanitarian promise of safe passage from Switzerland to Dutch territory. Once there, the refugees could decide where they wanted to go, the Dutch announced.[15]

An Amish couple from Kampen, the Netherlands, late eighteenth or early nineteenth century.

But problems troubled this scheme as well. First, the Swiss could round up only enough Anabaptists to fill four of the five ships they had contracted. Then, to the chagrin of the Dutch ambassador, the Mennonites nearly refused to ride on the same boats with the Amish.[16] Apparently the division of 1693 was still too sore. Finally, organizers persuaded the Mennonites to go along, though many jumped ship downriver and tried to make their way back to Switzerland. In August, the boats arrived in the Netherlands with an almost entirely Amish cargo. (The Mennonites who did stick it out to Dutch territory grumbled, complained, and eventually headed south toward the Palatinate.)

Arriving in Holland, the Amish were invited to settle in Prussia (now northern Poland), but decided to remain in the Netherlands instead. They formed several congregations, and with the aid of Dutch Mennonites established themselves in farming. The culturally refined Dutch found the traditional dress and untrimmed beards of the Amish quaint, if not odd. The Amish use of a Swiss-German dialect also set them apart in the Netherlands. An old story handed down from that time holds that Amish worship seemed so peculiar, that at times civil guards needed to keep curious Dutch crowds away from Amish church meetings.[17]

Wider horizons:
North America and Eastern Europe

While the Bern government continued trying forcibly to move Amish and Mennonites to North America, some Mennonites had been immigrating there voluntarily. Already a decade before the Mennonite-Amish division itself, a Mennonite couple named Jan and Mercken (Schmitz) Lensen had settled in Germantown, Pennsylvania, beginning the first continuous Mennonite community on the other side of the Atlantic. For the next 80 years or so, Mennonites—especially from the Palatinate and Switzerland—felt the pull of Penn's

A Voyage of Eighty-three Days

An Atlantic crossing could be filled with uncertainty and danger as storms and disease resulted in delay and death. In 1737, many of the earliest Amish families to settle in America arrived on the *Charming Nancy*. A journal apparently kept by one of that ship's passengers records these voyage details:

"The 28th of June while in Rotterdam [in the Netherlands] getting ready to start my Zernbli died and was buried in Rotterdam. The 29th we got under sail and enjoyed one and a half days of favorable wind. The 7th day of July, early in the morning, Hans Zimmerman's son-in-law died.

"We landed in England the 8th of July, remaining 9 days in port during which 5 children died. Went under sail the 17th of July. The 21st of July my own Lisbetli died. Several days before Michael's Georgli had died.

"On the 29th of July three children died. On the first of August my Hansli died and the Tuesday previous 5 children died. On the 3rd of August contrary winds beset the vessel and from the first to the 7th of the month three more children died. On the 8th of August, Shambien's Lizzie died and on the 9th Hans Zimmerman's Jacobli died. On the 19th Christian Burgli's Child died. Passed a ship on the 21st. A favorable wind sprang up. On the 28th Hans Gasi's wife died. Passed a ship 13th of September.

Landed in Philadelphia on the 18th and my wife and I left the ship on the 19th. A child was born to us on the 20th—died—wife recovered. A voyage of 83 days."

From S. Duane Kauffman, "Miscellaneous Amish Mennonite Documents," *Pennsylvania Mennonite Heritage 2* (July 1979): 12. On the diary's authorship, see the article's note 3.

Woods. In the eighteenth century, Pennsylvania was the destination of virtually all Mennonites who left Europe, and it would become the Amish destination, as well.

In 1681, Englishman William Penn had received a royal land grant and set out to create the colony of Pennsylvania as a "holy experiment." Penn was a member of the Religious Society of Friends (Quakers), a group that was itself a persecuted minority in England and Continental Europe. In Pennsylvania, Penn established a colony where religious toleration would be the order of the day.[18] He advertised especially in the Rhine Valley for immigrants to settle in his province, and Pennsylvania became one of North America's havens for marginalized religious minorities, including Quakers, Moravians, Schwenkfelders, Mennonites, Dunkers, and Amish, along with larger contingents of Lutheran, Reformed, and Presbyterian arrivals.

Exactly when Amish families first left Europe for North America is unclear. Perhaps none sailed until 1736—at least information on any Amish who emigrated before that time is sketchy. In 1737, the first significant emigration began when the *Charming Nancy* sailed for Pennsylvania with 21 Amish families aboard.[19] Once the Amish began to emigrate, they did so relatively quickly. Within about three decades, approximately 100 households made their way across the Atlantic. Amish immigration followed the general pattern of German New World immigration; most came to Pennsylvania during the peak years of Germans arriving in Philadelphia.[20] Some ships carried sizable groups of Amish, while others bore only a family or two.

No matter the method, a European exodus was expensive. In 1710, the generous Dutch Mennonites had established a Commission for Foreign Needs to help both their fellow Mennonites and the Amish with immigration costs. By 1742, though, one Mennonite pastor was complaining that the Dutch Commission was partial to the Amish. His own Mennonites were not getting as much financial assistance from the Dutch as some Amish received, he thought. Perhaps that was because the Amish needed less help than the Mennonites. The Dutch seemed more willing to offer aid to those families or groups who made an effort to help themselves. The Amish, suggested one Mennonite historian, "seem to have been better able to finance their own emigration" than were many Mennonites. Perhaps the "reason may well have been a more close-knit group structure."[21]

As some families sought the freedom promised by Pennsylvania, others set out for Eastern Europe on a similar search for places where they could live productive and unmolested lives. As with the dynamics of Atlantic migration, Amish movement to the east was a tiny part of a much larger people movement that took many German-speakers into lands ruled by Russian, Lithuanian, or Austrian nobles. In 1781, the Austrian emperor invited German farmers to settle in Galicia (now southeastern Poland). Three years later, some 20 Amish families were among the 3,300 German households who responded to the invitation.[22] Others moved to the neighboring Wlodawa area of what was then southern Lithuania. The Amish hailed from the Palatinate, Alsace, and Montbéliard and were accompanied by a number of Mennonite households from the same regions. Although the Amish and Mennonites wintered together after arriving in Galicia, by 1785 they were meeting separately for worship, with the Amish group under the leadership of a Catholic-turned-Anabaptist convert, Joseph Mündlein.[23]

In 1796, a few of the Amish joined some Mennonites in moving further east and joining a Hutterite community. Like the Amish and Mennonites, Hutterites traced their origins to the Anabaptist movement of the sixteenth-century Reformation, but Hutterites also had a distinctive communal lifestyle. Hutterite families lived on large rented estates where they held property in common, ate group meals, and performed community-assigned tasks and trades.[24] Though stemming from common religious roots, Amish and Hutterites expressed their faith in different ways, and the mixed community lasted only about a year. Perhaps the Amish were not prepared for the sort of strenuous Hutterite work ethic. In any case, the Amish claimed the Hutterites were interested only in material profit and left in disgust. Two young Amish women remained behind and married Hutterite men.

By 1801, these wandering Amish families had settled on estates in Russian Volhynia (now northwestern Ukraine), where they joined other Amish who had moved to the area from nearby Galicia or directly from Western Europe. During the next decades, in fact, almost all the Galician Amish relocated to Volhynia. The Volhynians adhered to the same church discipline as fellow church members in Western Europe, and they sang from the *Ausbund* hymnal. Correspondence from elder Mündlein, who had moved from Galicia to Volhynia, and the comments of area observers, indicate that the Volhynia churches followed customary Amish communion and footwashing practices, upheld the discipline of shunning, and maintained Amish clothing standards such as untrimmed beards for men and hook-and-eye fasteners instead of buttons on coats.

Persistent peoplehood

The Volhynian Amish experience illustrates the evolving nature of Amish life a century after Jakob Ammann first debated ministers in the Rhine and Swiss valleys. The church in Eastern Europe included households which had been Anabaptists for generations, as well as recent converts like Mündlein. Distinctly separate and identifiable in appearance, the Amish also were integrated to some degree into local economies through their leasing agricultural estates from landed nobles. Separated across hundreds of miles from fellow believers to the west, they corresponded and shared commitments to common church convictions.

A Baptismal Service, 1781

An eighteenth-century church discipline provides a window on the rhythms of church life, including a description of a baptismal service. According to the document, elders and ministers were to instruct applicants for baptism by beginning with the biblical account of creation. Next, the leaders told of the sin of Adam and Eve and their consequent expulsion from Paradise. The ministers were then to preach "the gospel of grace . . . with repentance and improvement of life, unto faith in the Holy Gospel."

Following this instruction, applicants entered a period of study during which the congregation was "admonished to diligently watch over" them "and support them by their good example." If the congregation agreed that the candidates were sincere in their confessions and repentance, the applicants could be baptized. Sermon texts were to include John 3, Acts 2 and Romans 6. The account continues:

"With these words the applicants are requested to come before the ministers and when they [the applicants] have fallen on their knees the story of Philip and the Ethiopian eunuch is told them, how he was reading the prophet Isaiah but did not understand it and how then Philip preached the Gospel to him, so that he desired to be baptized, and Philip baptized him. Then the applicant for baptism is asked: Do you believe from your whole heart that Jesus Christ is the Son of God? Answer, yes. Do you also believe that God raised him from the dead, and are you willing to be obedient to God and the Church, whether to live or die? Answer, Yes.

". . . The bishop [elder] places his hands on the head and a fully ordained deacon pours water on his [the bishop's] hands, whereupon the bishop calls him [the baptismal candidate] by name and says: On this confession of faith which

> thou hast confessed, thou art baptized in the name of God the Father and of the Son and of the Holy Ghost. Then the bishop gives him [the new member] his hand and raises him up, pronounces peace and says: The Lord continue the good work which he hath begun in you and complete it unto a blessed end through Jesus Christ. He then dismisses him in the name of God."
>
> Excerpted from "An Amish Church Discipline of 1781," *Mennonite Quarterly Review* 4 (April 1930): 140-48.

The Volhynian churches subscribed to a 16-point church discipline that elders and ministers from 19 churches had drawn up at a November 1779 meeting near the Palatinate village of Essingen. The Essingen agreement was one of several formulated by Amish leaders during those years, first at Steinseltz in April 1752, and then by representatives of 12 churches at Essingen in 1759.[25] The congregational nature of the Amish church meant that churchly decisions were not handed down from higher authorities, so much as they emerged from the consensus of leaders who discerned common problems and agreed on common responses. The decisions of these meetings, then, point to areas of contemporary discussion and debate.

The 1752 meeting clarified contested matters related to shunning and warned against pride in the form of fancy clothes and stylish grooming. Leaders also addressed conflicts stemming from leaseholding, counseling members to think of the welfare of the entire church and not just their immediate households. No one was to take on excessive debt, "thereby burdening the congregation or bringing hardship and shame to it," nor should competition among leaseholders undercut the ability of poorer families to obtain leases. Seven years later, the first Essingen conference revisited some of these issues, and also lamented that the practice of shunning "has been heeded poorly," and resolved "not to take God's discipline so lightly."

The 1779 Essingen discipline was more detailed and offers a window on the world of eighteenth-century Amish church life. Opening resolutions affirmed the confession of faith printed in the Anabaptist *Martyrs Mirror* and discussed the incarnation of Christ. Other statements outlined the ways Amish churches should relate to one another and urged ministers to make fraternal visits to other congregations as a means of maintaining accountability among a scattered people. There was no room for "pride or arrogance" among the ministry, "but in lowliness and humility" they were to use "caution" and "introduce nothing new or unusual, so that they not be led astray from simplicity in Christ." Economic decisions were to be made with the welfare of the whole church in mind and preference in employment given to fellow church members. The Essingen conference also urged care for widows and orphans. Finally, a number of resolutions outlined inappropriate conduct, condemning smoking and snuff tobacco, shaving beards, and wearing silks, printed fabrics, or pointed high-heeled shoes "made according to worldly styles."

Migrating Amish copied and recopied the Essingen discipline, taking versions of it with them into Eastern Europe and on to North America. Its mix of congregational accountability, meaningful church discipline, and attention to a simple lifestyle made it a key document in Amish circles and pointed to common aspects of Amish identity. Much had changed in the social and religious scene since the Reformation, and even since Ammann's 1693 reform movement, but the elements of Essingen pointed to persistent and practical peoplehood.

No doubt the 1759 and 1779 ministers' gatherings convened in Essingen because it was the home of the respected elder Hans Nafziger. Nafziger seems to have understood the challenges facing his church. On the one hand, he was aware of the welcome and toleration in some quarters for those Amish

In 1782, Daniel Joder was leaseholder on the Vogelstocker Estate, near Speyer in the Upper Palatinate.

deemed economic assets. At one point he optimistically exuded that, "Our articles of faith . . . have become so clear and well known that the mighty of this world have taken a change of opinion," citing the openness of the Austrian emperor to Amish settlement in Galicia.[26]

Yet Nafziger also knew that the world did not fully accept him or his convictions. Around 1780 he had been arrested for baptizing two young women who had not been raised Amish, having been taken from an Amish widow and raised in a state orphanage. After coming of age, the two returned to live with their mother and soon asked to join her church. When word of their baptisms reached their former guardians, local officials moved to banish the sisters and punish Nafziger. Although the elder spent some time in prison, the potential punishments were never carried out due in large part to the good reputation that Nafziger and his church had with the area's state church bishop and other imperial authorities.[27] If painfully aware of their outsider status, Amish such as Nafziger also knew that states sometimes had an interest in curbing persecution.

Nor did the challenges facing eighteenth-century Amish all come from without. Conflict within the church troubled Nafziger and other leaders, who engaged in remarkable amounts of travel as they mediated churchly disputes. Some of the sharpest occurred among Swiss Amish settlers in the Netherlands, and German elders made no less than four extended pastoral visits there in the 1760s and 1770s.[28]

As senior leaders in other communities died, Nafziger and others undertook additional trips to provide pastoral oversight or to ordain successors. "[As to] how it is going otherwise in our congregations," he admitted at one point, "we must lament with Paul the Apostle that we have come short of the glory that we should have before the Lord. But the ban and avoidance is still kept fairly strictly, but the young ministers are yet in need of much teaching."[29]

Nafziger's correspondence with churches from Eastern Europe to North America suggest the sort of common concerns that united a people now spread far beyond the Alsatian villages and Swiss valleys where they had begun a century before. His 1788 and 1790 letters to minister Christian Schowalter who had immigrated to Lancaster County, Pennsylvania, include news about crops and the weather, the Reformed church family who now leased the farm where Schowalter once lived, and events from the Russian-Turkish war and the French Revolution. Nafziger passed on news from the Volhynian Amish and kept the Amish in America up-to-date on recent European ordinations. Despite geographic separation, he hoped Schowalter was "still one with us in the articles of faith, baptism, the Lord's Supper, footwashing, ban and avoidance, solemnization of marriage, in keeping to doctrine and congregational practices according to the old customs."[30]

Nafziger's hope was not in vain. Across the Atlantic, the convictions the old elder held so dear had, in fact, persisted, even as that new environment was also shaping the tradition in distinctive ways.

4.
Settlement and Struggle in the New World: The Amish in Eighteenth-Century Pennsylvania

"In this country is a very good living."
— Amishman Hans Lantz

Putting down roots

The Amish who arrived in North America did not share a singular experience. During the decades before the American Revolution, some 70,000 German-speaking Europeans came through the port of Philadelphia, and the Amish were one small part of this larger people movement. While some Germans who rode this immigrant wave had no religious affiliation, the vast majority were Lutheran or Reformed, with smaller numbers of Catholics, Moravians, and various Pietist and Anabaptist groups. English onlookers quickly labeled all these German newcomers "Pennsylvania Dutch."

These Pennsylvania Dutch (or Pennsylvania German) settlers soon developed a common dialect—also known as Pennsylvania Dutch—which along with their other customs and folkways set them apart from their British-rooted neigh-

During the eighteenth century, Amish immigrants to North America entered through the port of Philadelphia. This scene was carved by Aaron Zook.

Ruins of the building used by the Chester County, Pennsylvania, Amish as a place of worship in the late eighteenth and early nineteenth centuries.

bors. For example, Pennsylvania Germans were more likely than other immigrants to settle in communities composed of fellow ethnics, and their clothing styles, architecture, and patterns of food preparation were also distinct and identifiable. Pennsylvania German settlement concentrated in southeastern Pennsylvania and spread into the Maryland and Virginia "backcountry." Rather than being attracted to land near county seats or market towns, Pennsylvania Germans tended to gravitate to townships where fellow church members lived. Immigrant Amish life was one piece of this larger Pennsylvania German pattern.[1]

While it is difficult to claim absolutely who the first Amish immigrants were or where they lived, the first clearly identifiable Amish settlement was in what later became central Berks County, Pennsylvania. In 1736, the Detweiler and Sieber families—perhaps the first of the approximately 500 Amish arrivals in the 1700s—put down roots there. Hans Sieber and another early immigrant, Jacob Beiler, quickly bought land in the Northkill Creek and Irish Creek areas of Berks County. This original settlement may have had nearly 200 residents at its height, and by 1750 it included families with such common twenty-first century Amish surnames as Fisher, Hershberger, Hertzler, Hochstetler, Kauffman, King, Lantz, Miller, Speicher, Troyer, Yoder, and Zug (Zook).[2]

Other Amish households took up land in Lancaster County, launching a small community sometimes labeled the Old Conestoga settlement. It persisted through most of the eighteenth century before breaking up as its families moved to other locations. Some Amish households may also have lived in northern Lancaster County's Cocalico region for a time, and later in the far eastern part of the county near Cains.

Although Lancaster County later was home to one of America's largest Amish populations, most Amish church members lived outside of its boundaries during the colonial period. More families lived in places like Berks County's Cumru Township (along Maiden Creek) and on the Berks-Lancaster border along the Conestoga Creek. Others settled in the Tulpehocken Valley in a settlement that extended from Berks into what later would become Lebanon County. By 1767, Amish newcomers, along with households who had been in North America for some years, were heading west to Somerset County, Pennsylvania, where in the eighteenth century they generated three distinct Amish congregations. And in 1791, Amish families were living in central Pennsylvania's newly organized Mifflin County.[3]

While the frontier drew some Amish, others headed east. By 1768, a church had organized closer to Philadelphia, in Chester County's Great Valley. The Chester County group constructed a schoolhouse, but then took the unusual step of using the building for Sunday morning church services.[4] While European Amish in some places may have used meetinghouses even as early as the Ammann-Reist division, most commonly the Amish had worshiped only in members' homes or barns.[5] Perhaps out of frugality or necessity, or perhaps to emphasize that people—and not the building—were really the church, the Amish rejected special physical structures for worship. Though not a large settlement, the Chester County Amish community was well known, since it was along the route followed by new arrivals traveling from Philadelphia. Into the nineteenth century, the Chester church offered hospitality and aid to fellow Amish immigrants moving west.[6]

In the later 1700s, a few Amish also may have been among those Pennsylvania Germans who followed "the Great Wagon Road" from Pennsylvania south into Virginia and North Carolina. Records of settlers with typical Amish surnames in those states are suggestive, but inconclusive. In neither place did on-going Amish congregations form, so if some Amish did end up in the Shenandoah Valley or western North Carolina, they very likely eventually blended with Pennsylvania Dutch-speaking neighbors, perhaps intermarrying with them and joining one of the German-speaking churches in those regions.[7]

Due to their relatively well-organized and -financed immigration to America, the Amish were prepared to purchase land in the New World. Some bought heavily and then resold to their children, to other Amish families, or to non-Amish neighbors. When describing the land holdings of early settler Christian Beiler, one twentieth-century Amish historian simply concluded, "All in all, Christian had so many land grants that it is doubtful if we can name them all."[8] A survey of land records turns up non-commercial transactions, too; along with farm purchases Amishman Christian Rupp was one of five Lancaster Countians receiving a deed for land to build a community school.[9]

Land transactions also point up other patterns and tendencies among Amish families, especially when compared with the experience of other Pennsylvania German immigrants, such as the Mennonites. For example, in contrast to many Mennonite immigrants who purchased unimproved properties, Amish immigrants often bought partially cleared land from non-Amish owners. Despite the benefit of taking over some-

Lewis Riehl

While some Europeans saw North America as a land of possibility and promise, others who immigrated did not do so freely. When Lewis Riehl was about eight years old, he was playing and exploring in a European harbor where ships were preparing to sail for the New World. Someone persuaded young Riehl to board a ship, and once the boy was on deck would not allow him to leave. Riehl discovered too late the intent of the captain to carry him across the Atlantic against his will and sell him in Philadelphia. A Chester County, Pennsylvania, family paid the cost of Riehl's transit in exchange for his labor as a redemptioner. According to Riehl family tradition, the farmer who owned Riehl treated him badly, and as soon as he finished his required years of service he left and found a welcome among the Chester County Amish living around Malvern. Riehl later joined the Amish church and married Veronica Fisher. Eventually Lewis and Veronica left the old Chester County settlement and helped form the Mifflin County, Pennsylvania, Amish community.

See David Luthy, "New Names Among the Amish, Part 3," *Family Life* (November 1972): 22.

what-improved farms, these Amish were generally buying cheaper, thinner soil in Berks, Lebanon, and Chester counties, rather than the more productive Mennonite-held acres in central Lancaster County. Even in Lancaster's Old Conestoga settlement, where for a time Amish and Mennonites lived side-by-side, tax records show the Mennonites to have been generally wealthier than the Amish.[10]

For the most part, though, eighteenth-century Amish did not settle especially close to Mennonites, many of whom had preceded them to North America. While the Mennonites had strong communities in Philadelphia, and in Montgomery and Lancaster counties, the Amish initially settled elsewhere and only later moved to Lancaster in great numbers. For their part, the large Mennonite communities in Philadelphia and Montgomery County had little contact with the Amish. In a 1773 letter to fellow church members in the Netherlands, Philadelphia Mennonites wrote, "As to the Amisch, they are many in number; but they are not here near us, and we can give no further information concerning them except only this, that they hold very fast to the outward and ancient institutions."[11]

The church in a new world

Holding fast to those "ancient institutions" was hardly accidental. While many Amish immigrated to better their financial standing—and Amish migration within Pennsylvania during the eighteenth century often continued this pattern of economic self-help—the ability to practice their faith unmolested was an important motivation for crossing the Atlantic. The formal side of that practice, though, was less well organized than it would be later. Challenges of frequent migration, dispersed settlement, and transportation marked colonial life and meant that Amish worship services—like those of many denominations at the time—were infrequent.

Nor were resident church leaders immediately available in all places. While the ranks of early Amish immigrants may have included ministers or deacons, no firm record exists of an Amish bishop (elder) in North America until Jacob Hertzler arrived in 1749 and lived in Northkill.[12] Providing stability for fledgling congregations swept up in competing political and religious opinions in a new environment, Hertzler apparently assumed his role in a winsome way. Family lore holds that the old bishop was "very sociable and talkative." Even in his old age he preferred walking rather than riding horseback,

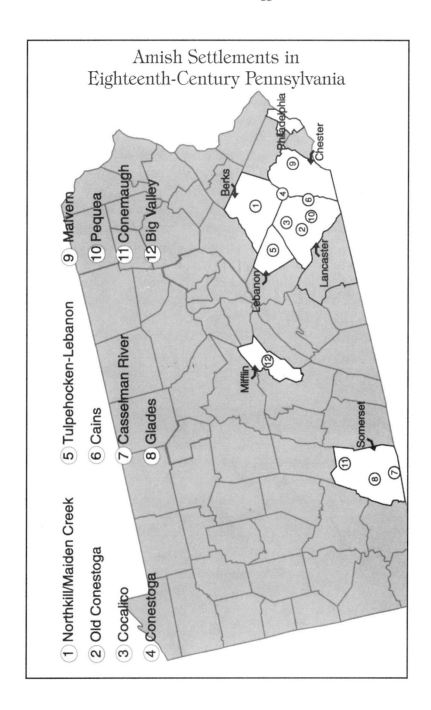

Amish Settlements in Eighteenth-Century Pennsylvania

1 Northkill/Maiden Creek
2 Old Conestoga
3 Cocalico
4 Conestoga
5 Tulpehocken-Lebanon
6 Cains
7 Casselman River
8 Glades
9 Malvern
10 Pequea
11 Conemaugh
12 Big Valley

trekking many miles on foot to visit and encourage others.[13] The coming of European-born leaders, and the ordination on American soil of resident ministers and deacons, eventually provided each settlement with church oversight. Bishops performed baptisms and marriages, served the Lord's Supper, and meted out church discipline. Ministers assisted with preaching and teaching, and the deacons administered aid to the needy and kept almsbook records.

The religious life of Pennsylvania's Amish was embodied in daily activity as much as around formal Sunday worship services. Apparently most families were farmers, although several household heads, like Lebanon Valley's Hans Gnage and the Old Conestoga community's Michael Garber, were millers. Jacob Beiler of the Northkill settlement was a tanner—an occupation that he might have coupled with seasonal farming. And Hans Blank of Lebanon Valley (and later eastern Lancaster County) was said to have been a folk-physician who had converted to the Amish church in Switzerland.[14]

For those who farmed in Lancaster County, wheat was the chief cash crop of the eighteenth century.[15] Amish estate inventories and wills drawn up in several settlements also point to flax (linen) and apples as typical farm crops, with the apples often converted to distilled cider. These wills also made specific provisions for Amish widows, with the children who took over farm management directed to supply their mother with ample produce from garden and field.[16]

Fitting in and standing apart

How much were colonial Amish settlers like their non-Amish neighbors, and how much did they stand apart? Wills and estate inventories do not suggest a notable presence or absence of particular household goods or equipment. With little visual evidence from the time it is hard to know exactly how distinctive dress may have marked the church's members. English colonists often remarked on the peculiar dress of

The home of immigrant Nicholas Stoltzfus (c. 1718-1774), built about 1770 along the Tulpehocken Creek in what was then Cumru Township, now Wyomissing Borough, Berks County, Pennsylvania. Son Christian Stoltzfus and his family lived here until 1804, when they moved to Lancaster County. This home is being restored by the Tri-County Heritage Society, Pequea Bruderschaft Library, and Stoltzfus descendants.

Pennsylvania Germans of all religious persuasions. Undoubtedly the Amish demonstrated a commitment to simplicity in appearance, but the form that such plainness took may have been somewhat less striking in their ethnic context.

When it came to westward migration the Amish appear not to have been much different from their colonial neighbors, German or British. Amish immigrants often were among the first to settle in the areas in which they chose to live, whether in Berks County or what became Lebanon County. In Somerset County, Amish communities probably put down roots by

1767—two years before the region officially opened for settlement.[17] Moving into frontier areas, in some cases to locations where Native American populations had only recently been driven away, the Amish participated in the larger story of European land occupation that marked the era.

In large part the Amish could acquire land as readily as they did because they were not like many of their colonial neighbors in an important respect. The Amish had immigrated as free people with the ability to control the terms and conditions of their work. During the eighteenth century, however, only about a quarter of all those who came to British North America did so as free labor.[18] The Amish may not have realized how relatively unusual their status was, but that status was crucial to their communities' growth and economic success.

If the Amish position as free laborers was notable, so too was their refusal to own slaves. Slavery was a legal part of Pennsylvania life until 1780, and even after that year only a gradual program of emancipation freed human property. No records exist of any Amish family ever owning slaves. Probably the refusal to own African-American workers stemmed as much from the Amish insistence on simplicity as it did from Christian humanitarianism. Studies of colonial Pennsylvania slave-owning practices show that slaves were often not so much an economic necessity in Penn's Woods as a status symbol that announced their owner's financial success. Among a people who shied away from ostentatious clothing and home furnishings, the ownership of human ornaments of wealth was naturally taboo.[19]

Some Amish families did purchase redemptioners, however.[20] Redemptioners typically possessed marketable skills but did not have cash to finance their immigration. Instead, they crossed the Atlantic on credit and then paid their passage by selling their labor for a negotiated number of years. Amish farmers probably bought redemptioners because their labor, unlike that of slaves, was not a sign of unnecessary expense.

Occasionally a redemptioner even joined the Amish church as a result of contact with Amish employers or neighbors. A testimony to the practice of mutual aid, Amish church almsbook records also show that successful Pennsylvania Amish sometimes paid the immigration costs of European Amish families, thus sparing the newcomers the prospect of becoming redemptioners.[21]

Frontier fires

As frontier settlers the Amish soon found themselves in the midst of the politics of provincial warfare. Pennsylvania became an important battleground for competing claims of British and French imperial designs. The English, taking land from the Atlantic coast westward, and the French, claiming territory from the Great Lakes southeastward, clashed over rights to the Appalachian Mountain region. After 1756, the ensuing military conflict that became known as the French and Indian War (or Seven Years War) spread death and destruction even into eastern Pennsylvania. Many Native American tribal

Jacob Hochstetler stops his sons from shooting at hostile Indians surrounding the family's cabin in this carving by Aaron Zook.

The Hochstetler Incident

One of the most popular and well-worn stories in Amish family history is the attack on the family of Jacob Hochstetler. The Hochstetlers lived in Berks County, Pennsylvania's Northkill settlement, a region that suffered a number of such incidents from 1755 to 1758.

Folk tradition holds that during the night of September 19, 1757, Jacob Hochstetler, Jr., opened the family's cabin door to see why their dog was barking so intently. Thereupon he was shot in the leg by a group of Indians stalking the house. The wounded boy and his two brothers, Christian and Joseph, all reached for their hunting guns in order to defend the family, but their father Jacob would not allow them to shoot and made the boys put the weapons away. His commitment to non-retaliation and Jesus' teaching to "turn the other cheek" would not permit him to see his sons resort to violence.

The Hochstetlers instead hid in the cellar under the house, but the attackers set fire to the cabin itself. Trying to escape through a cellar window opening, the family was caught. The Indians killed Jacob Jr., his mother, and sister and took captive Jacob Sr. and sons Joseph and Christian. Separated from his sons, Jacob was taken into French-controlled western Pennsylvania. The Native American group that had captured the Hochstetlers evidently was working closely with the French, and the attack likely was provoked by international politics and regional military strategy rather than by anything the Hochstetlers themselves had done, despite a family legend that Mrs. Hochstetler had earlier angered local Natives by turning away a number of their hungry.

The following spring, Jacob Hochstetler's captors allowed him to hunt in the woods alone, and Hochstetler fled. After 15 days he made his way by canoe and raft to Shamokin, Pennsylvania, and eventually back to an Amish community.

Four years later his two sons were still captives, and he issued an appeal to the province's lieutenant governor, asking for help in finding them. Eventually both were freed and reunited with their father.

Family tradition carried the Hochstetler story through the generations in an embellished form, but the general outline of the events, deaths, captivity, and escape match what surviving government documents from the time report.

The traditional tale is told in Rev. Harvey Hostetler, ed., *The Descendants of Jacob Hochstetler, the Immigrant of 1736* (Elgin, Ill.: Brethren Publishing House, 1912), 26-45. Contemporary reports documenting the incident are found in Richard K. MacMaster, et al., *Conscience in Crisis: Mennonites and Other Peace Churches in America, 1739-1789, Interpretation and Documents* (Scottdale, Pa.: Herald Press, 1979), 122-27.

nations sided with the French and attacked settlements within the English colony's domain. Thus, Pennsylvania's Berks County, and what became Lebanon and Dauphin counties to the west, felt the pressures of international conflict.[22]

Frontier Amish were not immune from the resulting violence, and at least one household, the Hochstetlers, suffered the death and captivity the war brought. Other families may also have been affected. One Hans Lantz of the Northkill Amish settlement wrote that his family had "been obligated to flee" their home "on account of the war." The Lantzes had returned only after the English "gained the upper hand . . . [and] fought back the French and the Indians."[23]

Fear of attack from French-inspired bands perhaps balanced the fear of losing religious freedom to the English. After the Pennsylvania government declared war on the Delaware and Shawnee nations in the spring of 1756, the once-pacifist province moved to initiate a militia and fund military defense. The "peace churches"—Religious Society of Friends (Quakers), Mennonites, Amish, and German Baptist Brethren (Dunkers)— appealed for exemption from this program. In lieu of direct participation most proposed to supply material aid to frontier war refugees or provide commissary services to the militia. The measure was short-lived, though, as political feuding in Philadelphia sank all attempts to extend the life of the militia act and the legal pressures on conscience eased.

After 1763, hostilities in Pennsylvania died down, but the mid-century conflict had tested Amish identity and resolve. Despite the attacks, Amish communities did not dissolve. The Northkill settlement, hit hard by the fighting, remained the largest Amish congregation into the 1780s. Even so, it was the availability of better soil elsewhere—not Native American hostility—which led to its extinction as families abandoned Berks County. Moreover, even after the war, Amish settlers continued to move into areas known to be subject to violent attack. The militia law could have tested the Amish resolve to be a nonresistant people, but both sides seemed open to compromise, and the matter passed without incident. By 1776, however, a new and revolutionary war would test the Amish church more severely.

The threat of revivalism

Significant threats to the vitality of the Amish church came not from generals or raiding parties, but from preachers associated with the powerful and wide-ranging evangelical revival movement then spreading across the north Atlantic world.[24] During the mid-eighteenth century, the Amish church lost members to competing Christian groups who charged the Amish with dead formalism and tried to infuse their communities with a more experiential religion. The religious toleration and equality among churches in Pennsylvania created a sort of spiritual open market in which pastors and evangelists spread their wares and sold their products as freely and easily as any merchants. Not only were the Amish reticent to broadcast their faith verbally, but their particular understandings of salvation and church made them prime targets for proselytizers.

The Amish believed that Christians experienced salvation in everyday living. This was not salvation earned by individuals; it was the free gift given by God's grace. And that gift was realized as one's life was transformed day-by-day into the image of Christ. *Nachfolge Christi*—following Jesus daily—was one way in which Amish forebears, the Anabaptists, had described the Christian life. To the Amish mind, being faithful to Christ's commands was a visible indication of faith. The Amish did not downplay Christian conversion, as such—in fact Amish writings stressed the need for regeneration, or the new birth, which would result in a new way of life. They believed they could see quite clearly a marked difference between the Christian and non-Christian life. But that difference—when lived out—was sharp enough to authenticate itself without needing to be confirmed by an extraordinary conversion experience.

The revivalism of many evangelical churches stood in some contrast to Amish faith understandings. For many revivalists, salvation was primarily an instantaneous experience that followed a deep and inner personal struggle, culminating in an emotional release interpreted as forgiveness. Not that the revivalist impulse put no emphasis on ethics or the Christian's daily life, but for many evangelicals these things were secondary. Instead, they believed that the singular, emotional experience of conversion was the only sure sign of one's being right with God.

The Amish view of the church was also different from that of many evangelicals. The Amish thought of church in community terms. Church members were mutually accountable to each other, even in matters of personal lifestyle. Baptism symbolized commitment both to God and fellow believers, while the Lord's Supper was a sign of the local church's unity in matters large and small. Typically the revivalists' emphasis on individual salvation weakened the importance and authority of the church. Communion and baptism became rites between the individual and God; that the larger congregation was somehow involved seemed almost incidental. Then too, accountability took on a different shade. If a singular conversion experience had validated one's faith, what business did the church have in addressing issues of pride, wealth, or a worldly lifestyle that might surface later in a believer's life?

To some revivalist-oriented Methodists, Baptists, and (later in the century) United Brethren, the Amish were stuck in a formal traditionalism. Their church service seemed "cold" to circuit-riding preachers and itinerant evangelists who sought to bring a "warm" spirituality to the Amish. How many Amish abandoned their tradition for revivalist religion is unclear, but alarmed observers thought the numbers were significant. In one well-known case Abraham Drachsel (Troxel), Jr., an Amish bishop in what became Lebanon County, Pennsylvania, made "too much of the doctrine of regeneration." His congregation silenced him from preaching, and he left the Amish. Apparently a sizable portion of his congregation followed him, and one Amish historian speculated that defection to other churches led to the demise of the Lebanon Valley Amish settlement.[25]

The German Baptist Brethren (also called "Dunkers," today the Church of the Brethren) posed a larger challenge to the Amish. While sharing many of the revivalists' spiritual emphases, the Brethren stood much closer to traditional Amish understandings of church than did other evangelicals, and such Brethren similarities may have made their church especially inviting. Like the Amish, the Brethren preached in German, emphasized plain dress (including untrimmed beards for men), practiced the footwashing rite, and were nonresistant. In some areas, vigorous Brethren preaching drew many Amish members or members' children into the Brethren camp.[26]

Perhaps one of the reasons some Amish families moved west to Somerset County was to escape the influence of eastern revivalists, but popular evangelists won converts there, too.

Evangelists were eager to win Amish followers, but the Amish themselves were slow to put divine faith into human words. They preferred to let their lives speak and allow their responses to life stand as their own witnesses. Events in Pennsylvania soon tested that Amish response and challenged a clear witness.

Tories, rebels, and pacifists

The storm of the so-called French and Indian conflict had hardly cleared a dozen years when new clouds of war gathered. The outbreak of what came to be the American Revolution had a profound impact on the young Amish communities as they became caught up in political and military turmoil.[27]

To many Americans living in seaport towns and cities, the trade policies and taxes of the British Empire seemed both unfair and intolerable. To many southern planters and a few frontier farmers, the government of King George III was burdensome. But for perhaps as many as one-fifth of the 13 colonies' citizens, the British crown was the object of loyal devotion. For these folks, scattered along the Atlantic seaboard, the patriots in Boston and Philadelphia were nothing but illegal insurrectionists who deserved death as traitors. Those loyal to the government of London received the name *Tories*, and they fought for king and empire.

For the Amish and other Christian peace churches, the political choice offered by the patriots on the one hand, and the Tories, on the other, was incomplete. The peace churches believed they represented a third option: peaceful neutrality. They insisted that Jesus had commanded Christians to live in love with everyone, issuing a clear call to discipleship that put even politically-sanctioned military violence off-limits. Thus the Amish (and other pacifists) could not support actively either side in the bloody battle for control of the colonies.

Yet the Amish also taught that Christians were to be subject to government in all matters that did not conflict with con-

Amish buggies outside a Somerset County, Pennsylvania, meetinghouse (white building) and horse barn (unpainted building). Amish have lived in the area since 1767. They are one of the only groups of Old Order Amish who worship in church buildings.

science. To their non-Amish neighbors, such teaching probably made the Amish peace stance seem somewhat sympathetic toward George III.[28] As the war dragged on, other issues complicated the political picture. Since 1727, in order to settle in the English colonies, all German immigrants had signed a declaration of loyalty to the British crown. While some may have signed the document without much thought, the declaration was for the Amish a matter of ethical concern. If they had promised loyalty to London, their Christian integrity required them to keep that pledge, even if their neighbors now insisted that the monarch lacked all legitimacy. And what of taxes? The Amish always had paid taxes to proper authority, but during the Revolution two groups—patriots and Tories—both claimed to be the sole authority to which tribute was due.

Wartime events did not wait for theological reflection. Already by mid-1775, energetic Pennsylvania revolutionaries organized Committees of Observation and Safety and Committees of Correspondence, which served as local patriot watchdog groups. The Committees tried to force residents to join local militias and stop buying British goods. Using social intimidation and physical force, the Committees attempted to make Pennsylvanians fall in line and support the revolutionary cause. Those who refused to participate were labeled "Tories." Neither the patriots nor the Tories accepted the peace church position of neutrality. As one diary entry lamented, "If one objects with the merest word, one is told 'You are a *Tory!*' . . . And those on the other side say, 'You are rebels.'"[29]

On July 1, 1775, as the war's first weeks rapidly evaporated any middle ground between patriots and Tories, a small group of Mennonites, Amish, and Brethren met with the Lancaster County Committee of Correspondence. Minutes of that meeting show that Christian Rupp and Michael Garber, "Representatives of the Society of people called Amisch Menonists," were among those present. Rather "than by taking up of Arms, which we hereby declare to be against our Consciences," the Amish and other petitioners asked if they could instead contribute money to a general fund "to assist the Common Cause." They were aware that the war had brought "Calamities & Misfortunes" to many Americans, they announced, and wished to offer humanitarian aid.[30]

The Committee agreed and the churches set out to collect funds in lieu of military service. Where records have survived, it seems that the Amish and Mennonites did contribute to the fund, even though the Committee kept the purpose of the collection unclear. As historian Richard MacMaster has pointed out, many peace church people "thought they were giving for nearby poor families or to help refugees from British-occupied Boston; in fact, most of the money went for military expenses."[31]

Not all Amish were so accommodating to patriot Committees. In the fall of 1779 in Berks County, Amishman Isaac Kauffman was tried, convicted, and jailed as a Tory. Earlier that year a militia officer had demanded to use Kauffman's horse. Kauffman refused and retorted, "You are Rebels and I will not give a horse to such blood-spilling persons." Both Kauffman's opinion and his refusal to hand over his animal clearly revealed to the court that he was "a person of evil and seditious mind and disposition." Despite having "eight young Children" and later apologizing for his "improper Expressions," Kauffman's sentence was the forfeiture of half of his land and goods as well as imprisonment for the duration of the war.[32]

The weariness of war

Already in 1777, the Amish were among those Pennsylvanians who refused to deny their past pledges to George III or to take new oaths of allegiance to the revolutionary government. They lost the right to vote as a result. Beginning the next year, all who were not sworn supporters of the patriot state were assessed double taxes. On one Berks County tax list from 1779 a patriot wrote the word "Tory" after the names of nine Amish heads-of-households. On that list Amish families represented more than a quarter of all Tories in the county. Oral tradition among the Amish has kept alive the story that several of these Amish tax-list-Tories spent time in jail and were freed only when a sympathetic Reformed Church pastor interceded on their behalf.[33]

The Amish community in Chester County witnessed the war's combat most directly. The September 1777 Battle of Brandywine probably involved British and American troop movements across Amish farms. Several Amish families lost livestock to foraging Crown soldiers returning to Philadelphia. George Washington's men from nearby Valley Forge took all of Amishman Christian Zook's fences for lumber—and, legend holds, his wife's freshly baked bread.[34]

If patriot neighbors thought that pacifist Amish were Tories in disguise, perhaps a few almost were. Amishman Hans Lantz praised George III in a private letter, and then confided: "I also hate and despise with all my heart treachery, rebellion and assassinations. . . . I am also heartily disposed . . . to prevent such as much as possible." Either way, Lantz hoped that the king's "throne might be well fortified with fairness and be handed down so that he may have eternity for his faithful service and have his reward from God."[35]

An Amish Folktale:
"Strong" Jacob Yoder (c. 1726-1790)

"Once upon a time, so the story runs, a certain strong man in Virginia who had heard of this 'Strong' Yoder had a desire to meet him and test his strength. He left his home on horseback and journeyed to Pennsylvania. When he came into the community he met a neighbor of 'Strong' Jacob's and inquired about him. He said that he was the strongest man in his own community, and he had come to whip this man, who was his rival. The neighbor told the stranger that Yoder was a peaceable man and that he had better let him alone. But the Virginian went on, arriving at 'Strong' Jacob's home after dark. The man made all the noise he could on the porch. When 'Strong' Jacob opened the door, the stranger, to get the advantage of 'Strong' Jacob, took hold of him, but Yoder was more than his equal and at once thrust him onto the floor, holding him and calling for a rope. He tied him securely, dragged him beside the fireplace, and let him lie there until morning, then released him and sent him home. The stranger was convinced that he had found a man who was superior to him in physical strength, and went home a wiser, though disappointed man."

From C. Z. Mast and Robert E. Simpson, *Annals of the Conestoga Valley in Lancaster, Berks, and Chester Counties, Pennsylvania . . .* (Elverson, Pa. and Churchtown, Pa.: C. A. Mast and Robert E. Simpson, 1942), 267.

For some young people, patriot sympathies or the social pressure to conform to the revolutionary party proved so strong that they cast their futures with the patriot Committees. A number left—or simply never joined—the Amish church, and family traditions have preserved stories of sons who went off to battle and never returned.[36] The separation in some homes must have been poignant as an older generation who had fled the militarism of Europe watched younger family members follow the sound of the muster drum.

The war carried political implications for peace church people beyond the death and destruction they may have witnessed or experienced. The patriot takeover of Pennsylvania left them disenfranchised until 1790 and socially marginalized in new ways. Some Quakers who once had been politically active withdrew from government for good, and a few Mennonites later moved to Canada where they saw less civic instability. Amish churches apparently lost members to the appeal of revolutionary rhetoric that promised the "New Order of the Ages" in republican rather than religious form.[37] On one level the war drained members and potential members from the fellowship, but on a deeper level the conflict challenged Amish identity: how American was this church going to be? Was freedom in the New World really the freedom to reject what had been preserved in spite of European persecution?

Precarious position

As the Amish completed their first century as a distinct people, their existence was little surer than it had been in 1693. In North America the Amish barely maintained their numbers after more than a half-century of settlement. The challenges of establishing new homes, responding to revivalist overtures, and the new wealth and freedom of mobility that had resulted from immigration had each taken a toll. Patriotic war, too, arrested Amish church growth. Genealogical studies show that no Amish immigrant family retained all of the children in the church. In fact, probably less than 40 percent of the first generations continued in the Amish tradition, and, by the end of the eighteenth century, surnames such as Reichenbach, Schenck, and Schowalter, among others, had disappeared entirely from Amish ranks. Although some 500 Amish adults and children had arrived in Pennsylvania before the Revolution, and most had large families, by 1800 there were likely fewer than 1,000 in the new United States.[38]

Several decades earlier, an Amish immigrant had written to friends in Europe advising them to come to America because "in this country is a very good living."[39] Many Amish had, in fact, survived and prospered in colonial Pennsylvania, even though that survival and prosperity had carried its own temptations. At times, living in America had meant becoming American, with all its revivalistic and patriotic trappings. Still, the Amish had persisted, and after 1800 they would welcome a new wave of European immigrants eager to join that "good living" in America.

5.
A Time of Testing:
The Amish in Europe,
1790-1860

> *"Our dogmas and principles are simple . . . 'Love God and your neighbor.'"*
> — Amish leaders to the French Interior Minister, 1809

Toleration and civic responsibility

In the early years of the nineteenth century, the Amish community near the Palatinate town of Kircheim-Bolanden met for Sunday services in a second-floor room of an abandoned Roman Catholic monastery known as the Münsterhof. Several hundred yards south of this place of worship ran the so-called Emperor's Road, linking Paris and Berlin. In 1813, French Emperor Napoleon I and his beleaguered army used this road as they retreated from their disastrous attack on Russia. Apparently those French forces included several Amish soldiers by the name of Virkler—at least family tradition preserves the memory of Virkler sons marching into Russia with Napoleon and surviving the return.[1] As they struggled back to France, these Amish boys may have passed the old Münsterhof cloister and its surrounding Amish tenant farms.

That possibility is more than coincidence; it points to important developments in European Amish life during these years, and it raises provocative questions. Why were Amish men participating in the French military? What did the nearly incessant European warfare in those years mean for rural western Europeans, especially socially marginal religious dissenters? Military conflict, the demands of the state, and the currents of popular culture all left their mark on men like the Virklers and churches like the one at the Münsterhof. At least one member of the Virkler family, Rudolph, eventually left for America and its promise of freedom of conscience, and within about 50 years, the Münsterhof congregation itself had died out.[2] Social and political pressures only fueled a wave of emigration that in turn further sapped congregational strength. These were not easy years for the European Amish.

Until the early 1800s, Amish, Mennonites, and other religious and ethnic minority groups frequently experienced discrimination—even persecution—from civil and some church authorities. Here and there, to be sure, a tolerant noble or an aristocrat in need of reliable tenant farmers would offer a safe haven for unwanted people, but Mennonites and Amish always received such limited freedom as an exceptional gift, never as a civil right. Tolerance and liberty of conscience were privileges dispensed at the goodwill of local lords and could be revoked at any time.

After 1789, the unfolding French Revolution profoundly changed western European political thought. That upheaval not only overthrew the French king and powerful noble elite, but also introduced influential and novel ways of thinking about how people and governments relate to one another. A major tenet of the Revolution was its new view of *citizenship*— a view that spread after 1800 especially to other French occupied and allied countries. In this new understanding, people were not *subjects* who had peculiar obligations and received uneven privileges based on their ancestry or religious affiliation. Instead, citizenship was universal. Everyone living within a state's borders could claim equal rights and had to bear equal responsibilities. Ideally, the government would not deny rights to the Amish simply because they were members of a minority religious group. In this way the French Revolutionary idea of citizenship opened the door for social acceptance that went beyond toleration. But while the Amish potentially were freed from future discrimination and persecution, they also were freed to engage in a process of acculturation and assimilation that accompanied such civic acceptance.[3]

The French revolutionary government did make one distinction for its Amish and Mennonite population, granting them exemption from military involvement. A document signed by the Revolution's infamous and powerful leader Maximilien Robespierre directed all local French officials "to exercise the same kindness and gentleness towards them [the Amish and Mennonites] as is their character, and to prevent their being persecuted."[4] But Paris did expect some type of extra tax or noncombatant work from the nonresistants. Before such details were worked out, however, the revolutionary government was itself overthrown by one of its own military heroes.

Napoleon Bonaparte's rise to power about 1799 and his crowning as emperor in 1804 changed the lives of nearly all western Europeans. Not only was the next decade filled with the destruction of Napoleon's many military campaigns, but the new emperor pushed the Revolution's idea of citizenship to its logical conclusion. All citizens would receive the same civic rights and the same civic responsibilities, regardless of religious affiliation. For the Amish, that decision meant that they no longer were exempt from military service or other civil duties.[5] Napoleon's military and political tactics required more than small, professional armies could accomplish; he needed a large fighting force that he could raise only through universal conscription. Eventually Napoleon came directly or indirectly to control every area of Europe in which the Amish lived, so virtually all the

An Amish farm near Salm, in the French Vosges Mountains. In the nine-teenth century, Amish from this area immigrated to Illinois and Ontario.

Amish had to face this newly-assigned citizenship duty.

The Amish response to this new situation was mixed. Undoubtedly some were glad to say good-bye to their second-class status, and according to one observer, some Alsatian Amish even reluctantly agreed to wear the tricolor cockade—symbol of the French republic—after wearing such "was made a duty."[6] Many liable for military service hoped to avoid direct participation in violence by hiring a draft substitute or joining a noncombatant regiment (though such regiments ceased to exist in 1807 as combat troops assumed those duties, as well).

If little systematic evidence exists to document the Amish response to universal conscription, the reaction of fellow Mennonites along the Rhine may give some clues. In 1803 and 1805, Mennonites met in general conference to discuss the challenges of living in Napoleon's Europe. The Mennonites rejected military participation and civil-office holding; soldiers were not to receive communion, the gathering declared. While upholding traditional teaching, the conference's tone was so defensive that one may surmise members were in fact rejecting customary practice and participating in armed force.[7] The situation could have been the same among the Amish, considering Amish family lore that preserves the memory of sons who were involved in the military.

Negotiating with Napoleon

For their part, Amish leaders made a concerted effort to win freedom from French military demands, presenting several petitions to the highest ranks of government.[8] In the summer of 1806, church leaders gathered at the home of Hans Steiner to discuss how to proceed. Two years later they commissioned elders Christian Engel and Christian Güngerich to carry a petition to Paris, and the two men arrived there early in 1809. Congregations in Lorraine declared January 29 a day of prayer and fasting for the success of the mission, and the two elders were able to offer to the interior minister a document contending that "their religious principles expressly forbid them to bear a lethal weapon against their brothers and enjoins them to abandon their goods rather than to preserve them at that price." The Amish were productive citizens, the petition went on to state, who meant no harm to the orderly functioning of society. But that commitment only added to the "perplexity they encounter when they try to reconcile their duty with their religion."

In May, still waiting in Paris for some response to their appeal, Engel and Güngerich wrote again to the interior minister "that our dogmas and principles are simple and received of all Christians. 'Love God and your neighbor' . . . are the basis of our worship and doctrine." The elders tried to impress the seriousness of their case by asserting that "an invisible but invincible power keeps us attached to our religious precepts and most importantly the rule of not staining our hands with the blood of our neighbors." While authorities ignored this initial overture, the Amish did not give up, especially since their young men continued to be drafted.

Then in June 1811, 15 leaders gathering in Bildhäuserhof drew up a second petition, which four ministers carried to Paris and this time presented to the minister of religion. The

An Alsatian Amish couple, early nineteenth century.

petition did, in fact, make its way to the State Council and the Emperor himself, but in April 1812 both rejected the appeal as a dangerous loophole in the notion of universal citizenship. They announced "that the tolerance the government shows to opinions that are not harmful to society cannot go so far as proclaiming, with a decree, exemptions that one can too easily predict may be abused." The judgment was clear: eligible men would continue to be drafted. Amish leaders sent yet a third petition in 1814, but before it worked its way through bureaucratic channels, Napoleon was overthrown and the restored monarchy ended conscription.

Men of conscriptable age had not been the only ones to suffer through the upheaval of the French Revolution and the subsequent decade of Napoleonic campaigns. Joseph and Barbara (Rupp) Roth and their family lived in Alsace where Joseph was a successful miller. In 1802, the Roths had to leave their home and hide in nearby woods for more than a week as the battle lines neared their home and soldiers dealt heavy damage to their mill. Twelve years later, Napoleon's forces returned and stopped at the mill to demand money. Finding nothing, the troops beat Joseph, ruined the milling machinery, and broke all of the building's precious glass windows. Soon thereafter Joseph and Barbara died, leaving five orphaned sons to live with relatives.[9]

The violence and social disorder of the Revolution did not endear the cause to many Amish, even if they understood the dynamics of power it had unleashed. "One may say that the mighty have to be afraid of the common people," Essingen elder Hans Nafziger wrote in 1790 to a fellow minister in Pennsylvania, "otherwise their life is not safe from the common rabble. There is such an uprising and unrest between the mighty and the common folk, the like of which I have never seen in my lifetime." Johannes Oesch was more blunt. A leaseholder in the southern Palatinate—a hotbed of radical sentiment—Oesch found his farm surrounded by revolution-minded peasants and confided that "One should not wish to live a life ruled by people of this sort."[10]

Farming fame

Perhaps in many cases the resentment toward Amish lease-holders that local peasants felt during the French Revolution was rooted in the fact that these Anabaptist outsiders seemed to have too close and too successful a working relationship with land-owning nobility. Resentment boiled over near Landau where neighbors attacked the Mühlhofen estate farmed by

Early nineteenth-century drawing of a French Amish farmer.

Amish leaseholder Daniel Holly. Local lore credited Holly with amazing strength, able to carry a donkey across a stream, grab an enraged bull by its horns, or single-handedly free a loaded hay wagon that was jammed in a barn door; yet neighboring peasants ran Holly off the estate in December 1792 and burned his house. Holly fled north to a farm rented by an uncle.[11]

Close relations with the land-owning elite could also provide a means of escape. In 1802, widow Katharina (Imhof) Stalter of Zweibrücken, hoping to leave the war-torn Rhine Valley, wrote

"Expert in All Lines of Agricultural Industry"

A French journalist offered this description of Alsatian Amish in 1819: "The entire number of souls may be twelve or fifteen hundred . . . . I do not think that there is a single family living in any of the towns. They are small farmers being found especially as tenants on the estates of noblemen. Through their industry, intelligence, and experience as farmers they have become expert in all lines of agricultural industry. This circumstance as well as their reliability and punctuality in meeting all their financial obligations have made them much sought after by noblemen as farmers on their estates . . . ."

"To their credit be it said that, unlike many others, they pay their debts, not in worthless assignats [government-issued land bonds], but in good coin. They do not use tobacco, nor play cards. To [popular] music they are strangers. They do not go to law. They take care of their poor and come to the rescue of their members who have financial reverses for which they were not responsible personally. On the whole they are rather illiterate, but honest, temperate, industrious, and of good moral character."

Excerpted from C. Henry Smith and Cornelius Krahn, *Smith's Story of the Mennonites, fifth ed.* (Newton, Kans.: Faith and Life Press, 1981), 213.

to the former Zweibrücken duke who was now Elector of Bavaria. Katharina reminded the elector that after revolutionaries had ousted him from Zweibrücken, her late husband, Heinrich, had visited him, and the duke had promised to remember that kindness. Prompted by Katharina's letter, the elector paved the way for the Stalters and other Amish households to obtain leases in Bavaria, leading to the establishment of the first Amish communities in that kingdom.[12]

In Bavaria and elsewhere the continuing appeal of Amish tenants stemmed from their growing reputation as skilled farmers. Travelers, government agents, and early scientific observers all remarked on Amish husbandry and the way it stood at the forefront of western European farming practices in the 1700s and 1800s. As one French scholar has explained, in an ironic way the very outsider status of the Amish fitted them for their role as agricultural innovators. Because they rarely were able to own land, Anabaptist farmers invested their earnings in livestock and other productive assets rather than real estate. They also experimented with breeding cattle—the Graber family of Montbéliard enjoying notable success in this regard—and emerging veterinary medicine techniques. As leaseholders with only a limited number of acres under contract, the Amish also needed to find creative ways to expand productivity. They turned to improved methods of clearing land, draining swamps, and fertilizing tilled ground with animal manure and gypsum. The Amish also maximized their resources by pioneering new methods of crop rotation. Traditional rotation patterns sought to renew soil by systematically allowing fields to lay fallow (unplanted) for a year, a process that left up to a third of one's acreage out of production at any given time. In contrast, the Amish planted every field each year, but devised an order of rotating crops so that the succession of plants themselves replenished the soil. Finally, Amish farmers were successful in part because they used family labor extensively. By the early nineteenth century, in fact, the term Anabaptist nearly became synonymous with good farming.[13]

So common was this popular association that in 1812 a new French farming almanac appeared under the title *L'Anabaptiste ou Le Cultivateur Par Experience (The Anabaptist, or The Exper-*

The cover of one of the Klopfenstein almanacs showing an Amish farmer.

ienced Farmer], dedicated to promoting innovative agriculture. The almanac's publisher produced the booklet with the cooperation of French Amishman Jacques Klopfenstein, a successful farmer who had received national recognition from Napoleon's Imperial Society of Agriculture for his progressive farming methods. By connecting the almanac with the name of this influential farmer, the publisher hoped to increase the booklet's circulation and popular appeal.[14]

But Klopfenstein also symbolized Amish assimilation in the powerful currents of Napoleonic political culture. Each year for more than a decade, local politicians appointed the successful farmer and almanac-sponsor to his town's governing council. Perhaps not surprisingly, the Klopfenstein farming almanac also included articles supporting the French emperor and his military program. The cover of one of the early issues even included a rural landscape in which the sun in the sky was replaced with the imperial coat of arms.

Leaving the church or leaving the continent

During the first half of the 1800s, some of Jacques' extended Klopfenstein family immigrated to America, but most remained in French territory where they underwent a process of gentrification and eventually joined the socially respectable state church. These two forces that pulled at the Klopfensteins—immigration or acculturation—tugged at many European Amish. The final fall of Napoleon in 1815 did not end the influence of French Revolutionary thought or slow the tendency of the state to usurp the moral authority of the church. The years of upheaval and war had also ruined some of the tolerant nobles who earlier had granted the Amish privileges and freedoms in exchange for tenancy. Moreover, the small political states which rose from the ashes of the French Empire had all been brought up on the revolutionary ideals of universal citizenship and the need for standing armies maintained through universal conscription.

"My Children and I Like it Very Much"

In 1840, Johannes and Barbara (Gerber) Güngerich and their children immigrated from Kutzenhausen to Tazewell County, Illinois. In December of that year, Johannes penned a lengthy account of their trip to relatives in Europe, detailing both the difficulties and rewards of the experience. In portions of the letter not reproduced here, Johannes favorably compared life in America with what he had known as a leaseholder in Europe, reported that he had no intention of returning to Germany, and encouraged others to follow.

"To report to you further about where we live, what we are doing, and how our journey went. First, we departed from LeHavre [France] on the eighth of May . . . . We sailed for four days and had good weather, after that we had a little storm . . . [lasting] four days; our ship was running three feet higher on one side than on the other and rising and falling nine or ten feet front and back. We had to tie everything down that was breakable and when we ate, we had to hold up the bowls. . . . During this storm, on the 16th, my wife gave birth to a little daughter, her name is Barbara, her place of birth is the sea. She is a healthy, strong child, everything went well, and the mother and child stayed healthy for the whole trip. . . .

"We spent 48 days on the ocean to New Orleans. . . . [On board] we had a large room—there were 70 people in our group—and all had plenty of room. We did well and brought over the same number of people we started out with: two died and two were born. . . .

"We arrived Friday evening in [New] Orleans and on the next morning we made our declaration to the government, to say what goods we had with us; a man came to search through to see if it was really as we had declared. . . . [The next leg of the journey by river boat] "left at four in the afternoon for a small city called Badarusch [Baton Rouge], about forty hours away from [New] Orleans. Sunday at one o'clock the axle of the paddle wheel broke, and the paddle wheel . . . broke into pieces, and a piece tore a hole down under the ship and it began to sink. . . . [The ship made it to the river bank where] "they tied it up quickly with the ropes and anchor chains, otherwise it would have fallen right back. The people were all rescued . . . . [T]here were many property owners, French and English people, who came with horses to ride and with wagons or carriages to console the people. . . . We got back our large trunk with the money and our best clothes and linens, the other things lay in the water for eight weeks. When we had been there for two weeks, many people got sick, and several died. Cousin Nicki Gerber and his wife also died in this place, five days apart. My two sons and the oldest girl were also sick, and when they were well again, I had my wife and children travel ahead to the area where we now live, and I stayed until I got my things back again.

"I have bought land now—250 acres, 150 is tilled land, in all four corners good flat land, with not a stone to be found, neither small stones nor large, and you can plant what you want . . . . My children and I like it very much in America."

Source: Hermann Guth, *Amish Mennonites in Germany: Their Congregations, The Estates Where They Lived, Their Families.* (Morgantown, Pa.: Masthof Press, 1995), 314-18.

While the Amish church had never been static, these early nineteenth-century years may have been especially trying, given the tempting new social mobility afforded by universal citizenship and the experience of military conscription. And while the state churches had lost much of their political power and influence, the official denominations still offered a measure of social status to their members. Genealogical records for the Waldeck and Wittgenstein communities in Hesse show that people of non-Amish backgrounds joined the Amish congregation there during the early nineteenth century. But the same records indicate that the reverse was equally as true—prosperous Amish families married into and requested membership with the official state churches.[15] Some signs of change may have been subtler as shifts in attitudes and social adaptation pointed to potential acculturation. In 1844, the Ixheim congregation near Zweibrücken constructed a meetinghouse.[16] The move was not without controversy, and in fact it divided the local church. But the presence of the issue itself may have signaled a change in self-understanding among some Amish. A physical church building could represent a move away from a traditional Amish understanding of church as the people of God—pilgrim and mobile as their meeting places—and toward a more Protestant idea of church as an institution and a location where preaching and the sacraments are found. Meanwhile, sometime after 1830, Amish in Hesse began playing pianos in their homes. The use of musical instruments marked another way in which those Amish were adopting popular cultural practices into their own communities.[17]

In some ways, of course, the Amish remained a distinct people. Singing from the *Ausbund* during worship services kept fresh the memory of a martyr past. The social component of church discipline—shunning—underscored the Amish sense that Christian discipleship was practical and demanded integrity in even the routine interactions of life. Holding a literal footwashing service as a part of communion (after the pattern of Jesus and the disciples in John 13) reminded members of their role as servants. Into the 1800s, footwashing still marked the Amish church's communion practice as different from that of neighboring Mennonites, who continued to criticize the rite.[18]

But cooperation marked other aspects of Mennonite and Amish relations, especially in devotional literature. In 1780, an Amish elder and a Mennonite minister cooperated in publishing the Anabaptist history book *Martyrs Mirror*, while the prayer book *Die Ernsthafte Christenpflicht (Devoted Christian's Prayer*

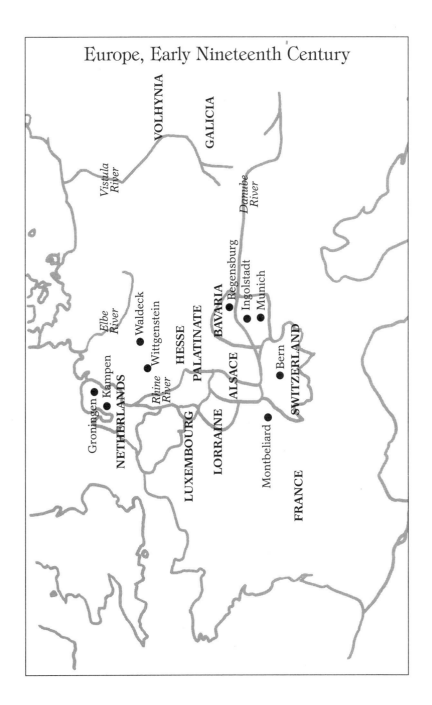

Europe, Early Nineteenth Century

Book] was popular in both groups, as was *Christliches Glaubens-Bekentnus* (an edition of the Dordrecht Confession with a collection of prayers and songs) that had been published in 1664 by a Dutch Mennonite elder.[19] Many Amish congregations also began using a Mennonite catechism commonly known among the Amish as the "Waldeck Catechism."[20] Another Mennonite-written book that was well loved in Amish circles was *Die Wandlende Seel (The Wandering Soul)*, which recounted biblical history as its narrator traveled through time and conversed with biblical characters.[21] And common in both Amish and Mennonite homes was a collection of Psalms put in German verse by Reformed pastor Ambrosias Lobwasser.

In some places, in fact, cooperation between smaller Amish congregations and nearby larger Mennonite ones was so thorough that the Amish were actually absorbed into the Mennonite community. Of the Amish churches in the

Amish living near Millbank, Ontario, descend from nineteenth-century immigrant families.

Netherlands, for example, the group at Kampen merged with the neighboring Mennonites in 1822, and the Groningen Amish did the same in 1824.[22] By 1838 in Eastern Europe, the Volhynian Amish—though still notably conservative in dress and traditional in custom—had joined with neighboring Swiss-descended Mennonites.[23] Meanwhile, the Amish in Bavaria were using their old *Ausbunds* less often, and in 1843 produced a new songbook to replace the old Anabaptist hymnal.[24]

The next year the household of Daniel and Elise (Beller) Oesch moved to Luxembourg and launched a church there that nurtured a distinct Amish identity. But the Luxembourg experience was becoming the exception rather than the rule.[25] For many more Amish, the future of the church seemed to lay across the ocean.

A new wave of Amish emigration

Emigration from Europe had slowed during the years of Napoleon's many campaigns and Great Britain's "War of 1812" with the United States. After about 1815, however, as sea travel became more regular and safe, immigration to North America increased. Between 1820 and 1860, more than five million Europeans left for Canada or the United States, and some 27 percent were German-speakers.[26] Typically these immigrants were seeking to improve their economic lot, fleeing debt, or seeking adventure.

These motives surely influenced some Amish to venture across the Atlantic. For example, some Swiss Amish and Mennonites left their Jura Mountain farms following crop failures in 1816 and 1819. In the Rhine Valley, meanwhile, opportunities for estate-leasing narrowed as the population of maturing Amish children outstripped such tenant possibilities and forced some young adults, especially after 1830, to look for land abroad. In a few cases, Amish leaseholders left for North America after accumulating too much debt. Such was the situation of Jakob Nafziger near Darmstadt and Josef Stalter, Jr. of

---

Amish Immigration from Europe to North America

c.1736-1770: About 500 people. Settled in eastern Pennsylvania. In the years that followed, a few of the immigrants themselves and many of their descendents moved westward.

1804-1810: Several families. Most eventually settled in the Midwest.

1817-1860: About 3,000 people. Almost all settled in Ohio, Illinois, Indiana, Ontario, New York, Iowa, or Louisiana. A few stayed in Pennsylvania temporarily or permanently.

1860-1914: Fifty or more families and many single individuals. Some settled with relatives in established Midwestern communities; others went to the far West, typically without retaining Amish or Mennonite identity.

Zweibrücken, both of whom emigrated in 1849.[27] For those facing financial difficulties, kin already in America might lure relatives with images of America's golden opportunities. As one letter from a settler in Bureau County, Illinois, reported to those in the Old Country, "Cattle you can have as many as you want [in Illinois]. . . . On one small piece of land you make a great deal of hay. You can live a great del more comfortable herr than in Germany [sic]. The land is much more productive."[28]

For other Amish emigrants, faith commitments and convictions also figured into the mix of motives. The pressures and promises of universal citizenship prompted some parents to consider leaving, especially those in France after King Charles

X restored military conscription in 1829. Again, Amish ministers sent a petition of protest, asserting that they desired to be good citizens and asking if they could make some civic contribution other than organized violence. They hinted that if the state offered no alternative they might well "go into exile" and emigrate. Since "they all consider themselves happy to be French . . . . there is not one who would not leave the realm with despair in his heart, but you know, my lord [interior minister]," the petition continued, "how powerful religious conviction is."[29] In the end, this appeal got nowhere since a popular revolt soon ousted the government of King Charles. Conscription, however, remained a tool of succeeding French and Rhine Valley German states. If some Amish and Mennonites were willing to make peace with war, others considered anew the possibility of emigration for conscience sake.

Families such as Andreas and Elizabeth (Eiman) Ropp left when their sons began to reach draft age.[30] Others, like Daniel and Elizabeth (Bauman) Bender sent away their son only; at age 15 Wilhelm Bender sailed alone from Europe to avoid conscription.[31] Nor did all emigrants completely avoid the military. Joseph Wuerkler was actually drafted in the renewed French conscription act of 1829, but escaped the army and fled to America.[32]

The wave of Amish emigration crested in the 1820s-1850s. While a few families and individuals had left during the opening decades of the nineteenth century, most emigrants sailed after 1817. Probably some 3,000 people packed their bags between then and 1860.[33] The rapid loss of members and leaders during these years weakened the church that remained in Europe. At times, nearly an entire congregation from Bavaria or Hesse left together as a large group.[34] Several Amish communities in those regions were so diminished that they eventually disbanded.

Those leaving Europe took church letters with them, signs of their intent to join or begin a congregation in North

Aux Gouttes, the Graber farm in Pays de Montbéliard, France. The former sheep shed, on the left, also served as the meeting place for the Amish church.

America—and perhaps as a way to vouch for their integrity when they asked established U.S. and Canadian Amish for financial aid in the process of settlement. In 1827, Peter Oswald carried a document signed by two ministers and indicating that Oswald "has been received as a brother through the covenant of baptism, and since that time has also conducted himself as a brother to the best of our knowledge." Oswald ended up in Holmes County, Ohio.[35]

But what sort of North American society beckoned these immigrants? Change had affected both sides of the Atlantic since the first Amish had sailed for Penn's Woods a century earlier. While Napoleon had been raising armies in Europe, he was also selling more than 830,000 square miles (2.15 million square kilometers) of Louisiana Territory to the young United States. Opportunities for white settlers to obtain land in

America now stretched far beyond eastern Pennsylvania. The former Thirteen Colonies had become an assertive and expansive nation whose restless population pushed relentlessly westward. Canada was changing, too, as its expanding population began demanding limited self-rule from Britain, and a mild nationalism swept through the provinces when they held their own against the Americans in the War of 1812. The challenge of discerning what it meant to "love God and your neighbor"— as Amish elders had summed their practical theology in 1809— would remain as lively a concern in Canada and the United States as it had in Europe.

6.
Prosperity and Promise in North America, 1800-1865

> *"We had everything in abundance."*
> — Amish bishop David Beiler

Fresh frontiers

In 1800 the Amish faced an uncertain future. In the preceding decades the American Revolution had challenged the church's place in American society, while the influence of revivalism had drawn youth away from their parents' faith. Scattered geographically and few in number, the church existed in a new nation that was itself undergoing rapid transformation.

By 1800 the oldest Amish communities in Berks County, Pennsylvania, had mostly disappeared as their members moved to better soils in Lancaster County or farther west. The Lebanon Valley settlement, meanwhile, lost so many members to other denominations that it, too, was practically extinct before the nineteenth century began. Even the Chester County church that seemed healthy in 1800 had crumbled by 1830 as most of its members moved away. And in central and north-eastern Lancaster County where two Amish congregations persisted, membership remained small until about 1840.[1] If troubled church life in the east had led some families to move west, hoping to establish stronger congregations, they were not always successful. Of three church settlements in southwest-

Elizabeth Zug (1786-1855) lived in Lancaster County, Pennsylvania, near the village of Eden.

ern Pennsylvania's Somerset County, only one survived. The freedom of the frontier and the influence of revivalists took their tolls there as well.

While some Amish moved west to preserve a more traditional church and family life, others had different ideas. Amishman Joseph Schantz moved to the border between Somerset and Cambria counties where in the fall of 1800 he took the novel step of chartering a town on part of his farm. Schantz (anglicized as *Johns*) laid out lots—including space for a public school and church buildings—and then proceeded to sell them to non-Amish buyers. Even when he later moved to another farm some miles away, the civic-minded Amishman remained a noted local public figure. Although he had chosen the Native American designation Conemaugh for his town, the new residents changed its name to *Johnstown* 21 years after the Amishman's death.[2] Such was the worldly civic activity of one Amishman who left the east.

But by that time, Somerset County was itself becoming "the east," as white settlers—Amish among them—pushed relentlessly westward into the Ohio River Valley. In 1809 the family of preacher Jacob Miller moved from Somerset County, Pennsylvania, to Tuscarawas County, Ohio. The Millers' nephew Jonas Stutzmann accompanied them but settled nearby in Holmes County. Four years later, other Amish from Pennsylvania located just to the north of them in Wayne County, Ohio.[3] In time, many families that descended from immigrants of the 1700s would establish settlements in the Midwest, such as the community in Logan and Champaign counties, Ohio, that was populated by households from Mifflin County, Pennsylvania's "Big Valley."[4]

New arrivals

These American-born Amish hardly had begun putting down roots in new western settlements when hundreds of European Amish immigrants began arriving on North

David Mast, Farming Entrepreneur

James L. Morris was a storekeeper and civic leader in Morgantown, Pennsylvania, whose colorful diaries reported the activities of his neighbors, including members of the Conestoga Amish community. A series of Morris' diary entries point to the agricultural experimentation of Amish deacon David Mast. As a means of replenishing soils poor in phosphorus and potassium, Mast's use of ground animal bone later became common in southeastern Pennsylvania.

September 12, 1845: "This David Mast is one of the most enterprising men of our neighborhood and as an agriculturalist he has scarcely his equal. To a knowledge of the various theories he adds an extensive practice and is not too timid to indulge in experiments."

October 15, 1845: "David Mast purposes manuring the Watts farm (which is very poor) with bone dust. He has offered $5.00 per ton for all the bones that can be collected and wants 30 or more tons. This is the first attempt in this neighborhood to use bone manure."

June 10, 1846: "David Mast whom I mentioned last winter as having erected a bone mill, strewed or sowed a quantity of bone dust upon poor forest land on which he sowed oats. A small patch of land was left unstrewn and the difference is remarkable. On the land on which the bone dust was applied, the oats is [sic] equal to any in the good valley land, while on the other it is merely 'forest oats.'"

Morris diary quoted in Grant M. Stoltzfus, "History of the First Amish Mennonite Communities in America," *Mennonite Quarterly Review* 28 (October 1954): 256. Original Morris "Diary, or Daily Notes of the Weather together with the Events of the Neighborhood, etc., etc.," in 3 vols., is housed at the Historical Society of Berks County, Reading, Pennsylvania.

American shores. Eventually totaling some 3,000 people, the nineteenth-century Amish newcomers were fleeing the political and military consequences of life in post-Napoleonic Europe or looking simply to improve their economic lot in life. The first ripple of what would become a wave of nineteenth-century Amish immigration was the Christian Augspurger family of Hesse, who scouted land in Ohio in 1817. Returning to Europe, the Augspurgers rallied more families to join them and in 1819 returned to Ohio's Butler County where they founded a community composed of European immigrants.[5] Groups of nineteenth-century arrivals settled not only in Butler County, but also in places like Stark County, Ohio (1823); Waterloo County, Ontario (1824); Lewis County, New York (1831); Fulton County, Ohio (1834); and Allen and Adams counties, Indiana (1840s). A few immigrants moved to older, established communities such as those in Lancaster and Somerset counties, Pennsylvania, or joined American-born Amish to form new settlements in places as far west as Johnson County, Iowa (after 1840), or Hickory County, Missouri (about 1855). In Wayne County, Ohio, the new immigrants remained on the edges of the older Amish settlement.[6]

Many of the Amish who came to North America after 1817 arrived not in Philadelphia, as had their eighteenth-century predecessors, but through the port of New York. After 68 days at sea, Catherine (Schertz) Dettweiler and her children landed in New York and took a boat to Albany, where they caught a canal barge to Buffalo. From there they sailed across Lake Erie to Cleveland, took another canal to Cincinnati, and then traveled by riverboat down the Ohio River and up the Mississippi and Illinois rivers to Peoria.[7]

Others sailed from Europe to New Orleans, then took steamboats up the Mississippi, Ohio, or Illinois rivers to Midwestern destinations. Through the years, a few newcomers stayed on in New Orleans and established a small Amish congregation near the city. Some of the members, such as the families of Christian

"White" Jonas Stutzmann (1788-1871)

In 1809, Jonas Stutzmann became the first Amish settler to live in Holmes County, Ohio. Two hundred years later he remains one of the most unusual of that community's residents, best known because he wore white for much of his life.

Stutzmann moved with relatives from Somerset County, Pennsylvania, to Ohio. Three years later he married Magdalena Gerber, and after her death, a woman named Catherine. Jonas had eight children who lived to adulthood.

In 1850, Stutzmann published a 30-page booklet of writings entitled *First, Second, and Third Appeals to All Men to Prepare for the Approaching Kingdom of God Upon Earth*. The collection is the first known piece of original material published by an American Amish author. Of the three "Appeals," the first was dated July 19, 1849, and the second and third both November 22, 1849. Highly unusual were the book's contents. Stutzmann announced that he had received revelations from God warning all people to repent since the return of Christ was imminent. Church leaders were to stop observing communion and instead earnestly repent and purify themselves for the coming Kingdom of God.

Using a numerology derived from apocalyptic passages of the biblical book of Daniel, Stutzmann predicted Christ's second coming to be 1853. "God has deemed me worthy, his humble servant, to reveal unto me clearly and distinctly that the time of the fulfillment of his plan with mankind is at hand," Stutzmann wrote. "He revealed this unto me not for my sake only, but that I proclaim it before all men, so that everyone may prepare himself." So sure of Christ's return was Stutzmann that he built a chair for Jesus to sit in when Jesus arrived. It was nine inches larger than a standard-size chair.

"White" Jonas' booklet was in English, perhaps because he hoped to communicate with a wide readership. Stutzmann

included his address in the book, and urged all who were waiting for the predicted return of the Lord to write to him. In
1852, he published a pamphlet, this time in German, that
expanded on several of his visions.

One of "White" Jonas' visions affected his choice of clothing and gave him his nickname. "According to what I have
seen in the spirit," he wrote in *Appeals*, "there are but three
colors for the children of God, viz.: the fallow [beige], gray,
and white—the colors of eagles and sheep." For the rest of his
life Stutzmann wore only white clothes. Some said he also was
obsessed with cleanliness. Even after his predicted date for
Christ's return passed without incident, he continued to wear
white until he died.

Although the Amish rejected Stutzmann's apocalyptic
teaching, he remained a member of his church all his life, and
most of his children joined the Old Order Amish. Some of
Stutzmann's convictions were typically Amish, including his
rejection of expensive clothes, dancing, and church buildings
that replaced private homes as the meeting places for worship.
Said one Amish historian, "His peculiar views and dress were
not seen as a threat to anyone, for he never had any followers."
His unusual life grew out of honest conviction, not a spirit of
rebellion.

For more information, see Gregory Hartzler-Miller, "'Der Weiss' Jonas
Stutzmann: Amish Pioneer and Mystic," *Mennonite Historical Bulletin* 58
(October 1997): 4-12, and David Luthy, "'White' Jonas Stutzman, Family
Life (February 1980): 19-21.

Oswald and bishop Joseph Maurer, remained in Louisiana only
a short time before continuing on to Illinois. But others never
left, including preacher Christopher Maurer who served this
church from the time of his 1846 arrival from Alsace until his
death in 1872. One way the Louisiana Amish stayed connected
to their northern compatriots was through the visits of the

remarkable Ohio bishop Peter Naffziger, who twice walked from Ohio to New Orleans to minister to the small city congregation and bring news from fellow believers in the north. The Louisiana group seems to have dissolved in the latter 1800s.[8]
The new wave of European immigration also produced the first permanent Amish presence in Canada.[9] In 1822, Christian Nafziger arrived in New Orleans on the first leg of a journey to locate land for members of his Palatinate congregation. Nafziger traveled by foot from Louisiana to Lancaster, Pennsylvania, where fellow Amish informed him of available acres in Canada. Arriving in Ontario, he negotiated the purchase of a large tract in Waterloo County and returned to Europe to share the news of his good fortune. On his return trip, Nafziger's ship stopped in England where, according to family lore, the Amishman had an audience with King George IV, who certified the Canadian land deal. Beginning in 1824, European Amish families settled in Waterloo County, and by 1837 they were taking up lands in neighboring Perth County, as well. Soon the settlement also gained new members from Pennsylvania, with members of both groups coming to the aid of the other when needed.[10]
The process of immigration and adjustment was a challenge for all newcomers, but those with ethnic or religious group connections frequently benefited from the help of family networks or the practice of mutual aid. Amish arrivals were no different. Even as "an old man of nearly eighty years," Illinois Amishman Christian Ropp clearly remembered the welcome that the Chester County, Pennsylvania, Zook family had offered the tired Ropps when in 1826 they had arrived in Philadelphia.[11] Individuals without money enough to pay for passage might also receive aid, as young Wilhelm Bender learned when Amishman Peter Kinsinger paid Bender's fare and arranged for him to work for bishop Benedict Miller in Somerset County, Pennsylvania, where some years later Bender and Miller's daughter Catherine married.[12]

Another recipient of her church's generosity was Jacobina (Schwartzentruber) Nafzinger. Widowed during her 1827 Atlantic crossing, Nafzinger and her six young children and two brothers landed in Baltimore but made their way to Philadelphia. When Chester County Amishman Christian Zook heard of the family and its dire situation, he went to Philadelphia to find them.[13] After three months with the Zooks, the Nafzingers settled in Lancaster County where other Amish families helped to take care of and support Jacobina's children.[14]

According to Louis C. Jüngerich, assistance of the sort Nafzinger received was commonplace. An immigrant himself, Jüngerich arrived in Pennsylvania from Hesse in 1821, and then penned numerous letters to European relatives, giving exacting detail on how to finance trans-Atlantic travel. Writing in 1826 to his uncle Christian Iutzi, Jüngerich confirmed that the Amish church "works actively" to assist those "arriving in this country. Entire families often can find shelter with them, as was the case with [Amishman] Johann Brennemann and a hundred more. Members of the congregation paid their passage and picked them up from the ports of entry. Within a few years, the newcomers reimbursed members of the congregation and earned enough more besides to make a start for themselves." New arrivals are "fortunate" to be "taken in by such people," Jüngerich concluded. Prompted by such descriptions, Christian and Maria (Sommer) Iutzi's family immigrated in 1832 and settled in the Butler County, Ohio, Amish community.[15]

A restless people

Like their neighbors in nineteenth-century North America, rural Amish populations were remarkably mobile. Caught up in an emerging market economy that left land values fluid and increased competition, Amish households were among the thousands that packed up and moved each year, often in a quest for affordable and productive land. Even non-farmers such as blacksmith and locksmith Christian Beck of Fulton County, Ohio, or schoolteacher Christian Erismann of central Illinois, were tied to agricultural economies since they lived in predominantly rural communities.[16]

Bishop Isaac Schmucker spent most of his adult life in northern Indiana as leader of that area's change-minded Amish churches.

The travels of bishop Isaac Schmucker illustrate Amish mobility and the factors that prompted movement. Schmucker was born in Lancaster County in 1810. He moved with his parents to Mifflin County, Pennsylvania, and later lived with his wife Sarah Troyer in Wayne and Knox counties, Ohio. In late 1841 the Schmuckers became one of the first Amish families to locate in what became the large church community in northern Indiana's Elkhart and LaGrange counties. A decade later he was living in central Illinois, but in another year ill health in the family caused the Schmuckers to return to Indiana.[17]

The northern Indiana settlements typified the processes of migration that produced so many Midwestern Amish settlements. The churches in LaGrange and eastern Elkhart counties, for example, were composed of households from Pennsylvania and Ohio, drawn to new and potentially more profitable western locations. In fact, a small group of eastern Amish land scouts had explored possibilities in Iowa and Illinois before choosing northcentral Indiana in 1840. Many of those who followed were young families with small children. Among the original Elkhart County Amish settlers, the average age of male family heads was 33, and of females only 28, at the time of their arrival. With the exception of one family of means, the households averaged about as much wealth per person as their non-Amish neighbors.[18]

At the same time, just a few miles to the southwest, another settlement emerged from different migration paths. Here, near what would later become the town of Nappanee, Indiana, recent European arrivals and American-born Amish from the east intermixed, connected by an intricate web of family ties and neighborly connections from Pennsylvania, Ohio, and Ontario.

The forces of migration that took families north and west sometimes brought them back south and east. For three years after their 1829 arrival from Europe, the family of Christian Ebersol, Sr. lived near Lancaster, Pennsylvania, and then moved to Waterloo County, Ontario. After settling in Ontario, one of the Ebersol boys returned to Lancaster where he married Elizabeth Stoltzfus—a descendant of 1766 immigrants—and remained in her community. Nevertheless, the Ontario and Pennsylvania Ebersols kept up family contacts through the years, traveling to visit one another by horseback and railroad.[19]

Young people might also move in search of adventure. For about 15 years, one Andrew Baechler traveled extensively, working in the gold mines of California, Idaho, British Columbia, Montana, and even across the Pacific in Australia. In 1867, Baechler finally settled among fellow Amish in central Illinois.[20] Others, like Indiana bishop Schmucker, may have pulled up stakes in part to escape conflict and church difficulties in their home communities.[21] Some reasons for migrating were more personal and preferential. In 1832, the Andreas and Elizabeth (Eiman) Ropp family left Ontario for Butler County, Ohio, because "it was too cold in Canada." The Ropps had come from Alsace and later ended up in central Illinois.[22] Widowhood seems to have forced Magdalena Augspurger and her children to leave Butler County, Ohio, for Davis County, Iowa, where they homesteaded in that area's small Amish community. In 1854, Augspurger purchased 160 acres of government land for a fraction of the price it would have cost her to expand her holdings in Ohio.[23] Earlier, in 1846, another Butler County farmer, bishop Joseph Goldsmith, had also moved to Iowa in search of cheaper land after financial difficulties forced him to sell his Ohio property and relocate on more affordable farmland in Iowa's Lee County.[24]

Some families bought and sold land without immediate plans to move. In 1837, for example, 10 Amish men from Wayne County, Ohio, each purchased land in Adams County, Indiana, but none settled in the area until at least 1841, and a few resold their acres without ever living on them.[25] Complex transactions, land speculation, and the occasional dishonest

About 1844, European-born Amish immigrants Henry Stahly (1810-1894) and Magdalena Ehrisman Stahly (c. 1812-1879) settled on land that later became the town of Nappanee, Indiana. Photo taken about 1875.

agent sometimes combined to cheat families out of money and property, as happened to the Susanna (Nafsinger) Raber family in Hickory County, Missouri. The Rabers paid for 200 acres of land that turned out not to have been for sale.[26] Regardless, migration continued, at times depleting eastern settlements. Only a small cemetery remained in Knox County, Ohio, after the entire Amish community in that place scattered to Illinois, Iowa, or other places in Ohio.[27]

While most Amish searched for what was considered good farmland, others settled on soil deemed useless. Fulton County, in Ohio's northwestern corner, contained the so-called "Black Swamp," an area avoided by most Europeans. In 1834 a sizable group of Amish immigrants arrived in the swamp—so wild a place it took them 11 days to travel the last 20 miles. Clearing and draining the land, the Amish developed some of the richest fields in the state.[28]

Stress and struggle in the church

The forces of migration had changed not only the size, but also the geographic center, of the church. By 1851, for example, the area with the largest Amish population was not the old Lancaster community in southeastern, Pennsylvania, with its four Amish church districts, but rather central Illinois with eight congregations.[29] This growth in size and distribution was not without tensions. For example, although Amish families— immigrants and old-line households—were instrumental in forming new settlements and organizing churches as they went, the relationship between church and family was not always clear. In many places, extended family networks were prominent and potentially competed with churchly authority.

One way the church strengthened its authority was by holding parents accountable for the actions of their children. As an Anabaptist church, the Amish practiced adult baptism, and individuals made a voluntary choice to join the church as adults. If that choice ultimately meant surrendering one's autonomy to the accountability of the larger church, it was to be based on an informed decision made by a teen or young adult. Since young children and many teens were not members of the church, they were not under church discipline, and parents often avoided being too heavy-handed in enforcing church expectations lest they undercut their principled commitment to adult baptism. Parental permissiveness, then, could stand in tension with churchly expectations.

During the early 1800s, however, church leaders took steps to discipline members who tolerated their children's deviant behavior. No one was to be forced to become a Christian, but neither were parents to encourage children in sin by winking at it. In 1837, the Somerset County church declared it would

Native Americans, First Nation Canadians, and the Amish

The westward migration of Amish families was part of the larger story of European appropriation of North America, and as such, it was also the story of disinheritance for the continent's Native Peoples. In some cases, the Amish moved onto land from which the Indians had been expelled only recently. In Elkhart and LaGrange counties, Indiana, for example, U.S. troops forced Natives to leave in 1840, and the first Amish arrived in 1841. In one case, central Illinois Amishman John Engel assisted with the army's job of native removal when he served as a teamster during the Black Hawk War of 1832 in which the Sauk tribe was brutally defeated. Engel's experience was highly unusual among the Amish.

Historian Russell Krabill has noted that no documentation exists to show "how the Amish felt about taking over the land which had been taken from native peoples." Krabill suggested that perhaps the Amish, like other white settlers, "were so busy carving out their homes in the wilderness that they did not give it much thought."

After 1840 in Lee County, Iowa, however, the small Amish community there disbanded when its settlers discovered that they were living on land reserved for Indian peoples. Yet Amish family tradition suggests that even while they lived in Lee County, the Amish got along well with Native neighbors. After serving visiting Indians pumpkin butter, one Lee County Amish woman received a gift of bear claws.

In Ontario, First Nation Canadians got along so well with one of the Schwartzentruber families that the Indians often took young Michael Schwartzentruber on hunting trips and taught him how to use a bow. And apparently in the early days of the Wayne County, Ohio, Amish settlement, both Native and Amish farmers lived peaceably, side-by-side, along the

Sugar Creek. While documentation of such encounters is slim, it may be significant that nearly all the stories involving Native Americans passed down through Amish families are ones of goodwill.

Steven R. Estes, *Living Stones: A History of the Metamora Mennonite Church* (Metamora, Ill.: Metamora Mennonite Church, 1984), 30-32; Orland Gingerich, *The Amish of Canada* (Waterloo, Ont.: Conrad Press, 2002), 33; Rich H. Meyer, "Why Don't We Tell the Beginning of the Story? Native Americans Were Here First," *Mennonite Historical Bulletin* 60 (July 1999): 1-8; Russell Krabill, "The Coming of the Amish Mennonites to Elkhart County, Indiana," *Mennonite Historical Bulletin* 52 (January 1991): 3, 4; David Luthy, *The Amish in America: Settlements That Failed, 1840-1960* (Aylmer, Ont. and LaGrange, Ind.: Pathway Publishers, 1986), 115, 116, 227, 263, 328, 356, 380, 381, 472.

no longer permit parents to dress their children in fancy clothing, as some parents had been doing. Neither should parents turn a blind eye to youthful courting practices where teens "take the liberty to sleep or lie together without any fear or shame." If such happened "with the knowledge of the parents," the Amish concluded, the "parents shall not go unpunished." Parental authority would have to yield to church standards; increasingly the bishops and ministers, not the fathers and mothers, had the final word.[30]

Those Somerset County decisions were concluded at a regional meeting of Amish leaders held in 1837. Other meetings of ministers had been held in 1809, 1826, and 1830 in Pennsylvania, and in 1827 and 1831 in eastern Ohio.[31] At such gatherings, ministers resolved to stress personal humility and reaffirmed their commitments to the social implications of church membership and its disciplinary corollary, shunning the unrepentant. Assembled ministers also denounced expensive furniture, fancy porcelain, decorative dishes, and other signs of popular refinement.

The Amish also debated a series of doctrinal matters involving baptism and the fraternal relationship of Amish and

Mennonites.[32] After 1850, the practical question of how to administer baptism caused a stir in Amish circles. Traditionally the Amish had held baptismal services, like worship services, in private homes. But some Amish began to argue that because Jesus was baptized in the Jordan River, their own baptismal candidates also should kneel in a stream or river while the bishop poured water on their heads. Debate ended when the church compromised and allowed both methods. No bishop would be compelled to use a method with which he was uncomfortable, and very few adopted the innovative stream-baptism style.[33]

Other debates involved interaction with religious competitors. In 1843, Stark County, Ohio, minister George Jutzi had to contend with the ideas of an itinerant preacher associated with William Miller, the nationally-prominent figure who champi-

Apostolic Christian Church

Occasionally associated with the Amish, the Apostolic Christian Church has its own distinct history. The church traces its beginnings to 1832 when Swiss Reformed theology student Samuel Froehlich questioned some of his church's doctrinal teaching and found himself excommunicated.

Froehlich then traveled throughout Switzerland and met with disaffected Christians—including some Mennonites—eager for church renewal and revival. Two Mennonite ministers disappointed with the spiritual life of their own people joined Froehlich and other supporters at Langnau. Froehlich's group espoused the typical Mennonite teachings on adult baptism (but by immersion) and nonresistance to violence. Additionally, they practiced social shunning as a form of church discipline. Deeply important to the Froehlich group was a strong sense of inner Christian repentance, conversion, and sanctification.

> After 1847, persecuted and harassed, members of the Froehlich group—eventually named the Apostolic Christian Church—began immigrating to the United States, settling first in Lewis County, New York, which was home to a sizable Amish settlement. Especially in New York, and later in Illinois and Ohio, the Apostolic Christians attracted Amish who saw their own tradition as focused too much on human effort and not enough on divine grace. Yet the similarities between the two churches were also clear to observers who nicknamed the Froehlich group "New Amish," both because many of its members once were Amish and because many of the group's key doctrines seemed to mirror Amish practice.
>
> In 2000, the Apostolic Christian Church had a membership of about 23,000 in 79 congregations. Typical Amish and Mennonite surnames are still found in some Apostolic Christian churches.
>
> For more information, see Perry A. Klopfenstein, *Marching to Zion: A History of the Apostolic Christian Church of America, 1847-1982* (Fort Scott, Kans.: Sekan Printing Company, 1984); and Donald B. Kraybill and C. Nelson Hostetter, *Anabaptist World USA* (Scottdale, Pa.: Herald Press, 2001).

oned the idea that Christ would return in 1844 and bring an end to human history. Jutzi refuted the notion and also critiqued Methodist revivalist techniques that Jutzi thought played on emotionalism.[34] Other church groups targeted the Amish in particular as candidates for proselytism. A Swiss evangelical movement—later named the Apostolic Christian Church—drew converts from several Amish settlements.[35] In some areas, in fact, the new group received the designation "New Amish" after scores of former Amish church members joined them. The Lewis County, New York, Amish settlement especially was shaken by Apostolic Christian inroads. After 1847, the Amish there lost not only a majority of their members, but also four preachers and a bishop to the local "New

Amish" fellowship. A few families remained Amish and with the resolute leadership of bishop Michael Zehr maintained their church in the face of strong opposition.[36] Apostolic Christian congregations also sprang up in Woodford County, Illinois; Wayne and Fulton counties, Ohio; Davis County, Iowa, and elsewhere. In each case many Amish joined them.

Some inter-religious interaction could be positive. After 1850, for example, Waterloo County, Ontario bishop Peter Litwiller was "known to frequently engage in religious discussion" with his neighbor, Father Eugene Funcken, spiritual overseer of the area's Roman Catholic population. Litwiller and Funcken became good friends, and the priest tolled his church's bell when the Amishman died, and then wrote an appreciative account of Litwiller's life for the local paper.[37]

Cultures in conflict

While these doctrinal debates and religious encounters were important in themselves, the larger context in which they took place was perhaps even more significant for the identity of the church. The first decades of the nineteenth century were years of profound cultural change in the United States, and the Amish were not immune from the accompanying social upheaval.

This transformation revolved around popular notions of refinement and respectability. Typically, Americans of earlier generations had valued plainness in dress, decor, and deportment. Patriotic luminary John Adams, for example, counseled against the unnecessary expense of painting barns and other demonstrations of frivolity and waste. Nor was Adams alone. While a relative handful of Southern planters imitated the British aristocracy, most white Americans made a public virtue of avoiding ostentation. In such an environment, Amish simplicity—even given its Pennsylvania German peculiarity—was a variation on an American theme. Between about 1790 and 1850, however, there was a remarkable cultural shift in the

Amish Church Structure and Leadership

The Amish church in North America was congregational in organization; that is, each congregation was formally self-governing, and there were no national or regional denominational structures. Prior to 1862, gatherings of Amish leaders occurred on an occasional basis and never presumed to include every community. Locally, each church had its own leadership, defined in four recognized offices:

1. *Völliger Diener* (fully approved minister) or bishop. The bishops provided spiritual leadership for the local congregation and, along with the preachers, took their regular turns in preaching Sunday morning sermons. Bishops also conducted baptisms, marriages, and ordinations. If congregations expelled unrepentant members or received them back into fellowship, it was the bishop who carried out these pronouncements. In Europe this office typically was known as Aeltester (elder); the term bishop was a later English designation.

2. *Diener zum Buch* (minister of the Book/Bible) or preacher. Preachers assisted the bishop in preaching and teaching. Sometimes preachers were simply called ministers.

3. *VölligerArmendiener* (fully approved minister to the poor) or full deacon. The full deacon performed all the duties of a deacon (see below), plus a number of additional ones. Full deacons assisted with baptisms and in some places took a regular turn in preaching. More common in Europe, the office of full deacon was rarely used in North American churches.

4. *Armendiener* (minister to the poor) or deacon. The deacon looked after the physical welfare of the congregation. Deacons maintained the "alms fund" and distributed money to the needy in the church. In some places deacons also read aloud the scripture in Sunday morning worship. In addition, deacons assisted bishops in performing baptisms, administering communion, and dealing with matters of church discipline.

In many European communities, church members elected leaders by a simple plurality of votes. Preachers and deacons were chosen from among the male members of the congregation, bishops from among the preachers, and full deacons from the ranks of deacons. Leaders received no formal training and no salary.

In America, the common means of choosing leaders involved not just the voice of the church (voting), but also drawing lots. After church members had voted for candidates to fill a particular position, all those who had received (usually) two or more votes would draw lots. Each candidate chose a book from a group of specially prepared Bibles or hymnbooks, one of which included a slip of paper. Whoever drew the book containing the paper was considered chosen of God and ordained. (The Lewis County, New York, Amish used the European process of simple election, instead of drawing lots, much longer than most other communities.)

Ordination was a lifetime responsibility; if a man moved, his ordination moved with him. Thus, some Midwestern Amish congregations might end up with three or more bishops, if bishops from several areas migrated to the same place. Typically, though, each congregation had one bishop, two preachers, and one deacon.

A congregation met for worship every other Sunday. The "in-between" Sundays were spent attending other Amish congregations that were having church that week, or visiting family. Church services included singing, prayers, and Bible reading, as well as two sermons. In addition, each ordained man present offered a response, or "testimony," to the biblical correctness of the sermons.

Twice a year, before the spring and autumn communion services, each congregation had a counsel meeting. During counsel, members were to be reconciled with anyone in the group with whom they had a disagreement. Communion would take place only if all members were at peace with one another. Congregations also addressed lingering or new questions of appropriate lifestyle and daily Christian conduct. Only if all members reached consensus could they commune on Sunday, a tradition that strengthened congregational unity and accountability.

Commonly, churches worshiped in private homes. When a congregation grew too large to meet in members' houses, the church divided into two smaller groups. Such divisions always occurred geographically, and eventually congregations came to be called districts since members living in a given area made up a given congregation. In much of the literature on Amish church life, the term "district" is used in the way "parish" or "congregation" is used in other Christian denominations.

For a great deal more information, see Paton Yoder, *Tradition and Transition: Amish Mennonites and Old Order Amish, 1800-1900* (Scottdale, Pa.: Herald Press, 1991), chps. 3-6.

United States which affected not only how people lived, but how they thought about how they lived. Americans began to aspire to living in a style that they called *refined*. In about a generation or two, gentility triumphed, and being respectable came to mean something other than plain and simple.[38]

In an ironic way, the fact that white America was relatively free from social class and rank distinctions meant that suddenly the possibility was open for anyone to be an aristocrat. In a society that prized individual liberty, the race was on to the top of the social ladder. Publishers issued exacting guidebooks (based on the old manuals of Renaissance-era nobility) to instruct Americans on how to talk, walk, eat, laugh, and write a letter like a gentleman or a lady. Genteel activities demanded genteel surroundings, including houses with carpets, mirrors, and display objects such as dishes that one did not use, but had only "for show." Ordinary people worked long and

hard to give the appearance of not working at all. Refined people read novels, had more clothes than they could wear, and
found creative ways to demonstrate that they possessed excess
wealth. This refinement of America, as one historian has called
it, combined with a market economy to produce a budding
consumer culture and joined with popular revivalism to promote a religious endorsement of progress, betterment, and
good taste.

In the wake of this realignment of public virtues and values,
the Amish commitment to separation from the frivolity of the
world took on new significance. The Amish were not interested simply in preserving a European heritage; instead, they
struggled to define themselves in a rapidly changing cultural
context. Lancaster County bishop David Beiler was sensitive to
the implications of the shifting popular mood. Writing in the
wake of refinement's triumph, Beiler bemoaned the emphasis
on fancy carriages, stylish clothing, and expensive household
furnishings that tempted even Amish families. Beiler longed
for the good old days when "Christian simplicity was practiced
much more, and much more submission was shown toward
the ministers."[39] Now Amish youth clamored for months of
education each year. Beiler thought that they should be satisfied with knowing how to read and write—anything more
would surely lead to a competitive spirit and pride. Beiler
feared that the Amish were also being enticed by the lure of
gentility, patterning their lifestyle after fashionable society
rather than the simple teaching of Scripture and the example
of the humble Jesus. The world into which Beiler had been
born in 1786 had changed dramatically in the course of several decades and left him on the defensive because of his interest in simple things.[40]

At one point Beiler seemed to pin some of his church's
mounting interest in genteel habits on more recent Amish
arrivals. These "many foreign immigrants with strange man-
ners and customs" clung to the promise of progress more than

Nineteenth-century immigrants formed the so-called "Swiss Amish" settle-ments in Allen and Adams counties, Indiana. The Swiss Amish drive only "open buggies" without enclosed tops, such as this one in Allen County.

the steadying anchor of tradition, in Beiler's opinion. It was true that some nineteenth-century immigrants were decidedly change-minded and open to the prospect of refinement. A group of Hessian Amish arriving in Butler County, Ohio, in 1832—some of whom moved to McLean County, Illinois, five years later—was especially known for its genteel sensibilities. Hessian men wore buttons on their coats, and some families even had pianos in their homes, while their leaders appeared flexible with matters of doctrine and discipline.[41] Yet the picture was more complicated than Beiler may have imagined. Change-minded bishop Isaac Schmucker, for example, had been born into a Lancaster County family that had arrived before the American Revolution, while bishop Christian Ropp, a recent immigrant of 1826, remained a leading conservative voice throughout his life in Illinois. Then, too, most of the so-called "Swiss Amish" who immigrated to America as late as the 1850s and settled in Allen and Adams counties, Indiana, remained quite plain and tradition-minded.[42]

Yet Beiler had identified an important impulse that animated much of the struggle in the Amish church during his lifetime. The church's response to an American culture that suddenly prized and promoted the refinement of people and their surroundings would pull the Amish in at least two directions. For some, the invitation to gentility was a welcome overture from the larger society, a sign that not only toleration, but also acceptance was possible for a people once religiously marginalized. For others, the refinement of America gave new meaning to the importance of humility, separation, and the wise authority of tradition—rather than the forces of the popular marketplace—to guide life. As historian Paton Yoder summed up the situation, by the mid-1800s, most Amish were sorting themselves into change-minded and tradition-minded camps. That divide would prove exceedingly critical.

Innovation and involvement

The practical side of this difference in orientation worked its way out in the symbols and substance of church and community. Signaling a shift in their understanding of *church*, some Amish began constructing church buildings, often called *meetinghouses*. While these structures were quite plain and simple, they marked and invited important changes. No longer would the church simply be a pilgrim group of people gathering in private homes. No longer would the congregation remain at the host family's house after services for a meal and afternoon fellowship. Now church could be a place to go to and to leave at selected times during the week. In 1853, the Amish around Rock Creek near Danvers, Illinois, erected the first permanent Amish meetinghouse.[43] The neighboring Partridge (Metamora),

Illinois, Amish church put up a structure the following year. In 1855, the Amish in Logan and Champaign counties, Ohio, built the first of several meetinghouses in their settlement, and the Haw Patch (later Topeka), Indiana Amish constructed a church building the next year. In the decade that followed, more change-minded Amish churches erected meetinghouses.

The Logan County Amish also became the first to sponsor an ongoing Sunday school program. During the early 1800s, Sunday schools had become widespread among American Protestants.[44] Many of these Sunday schools were "union schools," supported jointly by several local denominations. An innovative form of Christian education, Sunday schools would

The South Union Amish Mennonite meetinghouse, Logan County, Ohio (constructed 1876). In 1863, Amish Mennonites in this area launched the first permanent Sunday school among their people anywhere in North America.

increase biblical knowledge, supporters claimed. But, opponents warned, Sunday schools also segregated and compart-
mentalized religious education by separating children from
parents and used uniform materials written by unknown,
inter-denominational authors whose generic messages were
calculated to offend no one. Awarding high marks or even
prizes to those who performed well in Sunday school promoted the worldly ideals of competition, pride, and earned status.[45]
None of these aspects of Sunday school made the idea popular
with tradition-minded Amish.

In the 1850s, some Amish children from Logan and
Champaign counties had attended union Sunday schools. As an
alternative, in June 1863, bishop Jacob C. Kenagy and preacher David E. Plank opened the first permanent Sunday school
among the Amish.[46] Earlier Plank had visited a local union
school from which he drew his ideas and inspiration. The new
school, held in the Amish church house, was not without opposition. Several church members claimed that Sunday school, in
session in the afternoons during those early years, disrupted
family visiting that otherwise occupied Sunday afternoons.
Others were unsure of the doctrinal content of the school's first
materials. Still, the Sunday school had the support of most of
its progressive-minded members.[47]

The nearby Champaign County Amish congregation, under
the leadership of preacher John Warye, soon established a
Sunday school, as well. An equally progressive group, the
Champaign church permitted members to drive more expensive enclosed carriages instead of the common open buggies
used by most Amish at the time. But even progressives drew
the line at some point. When two young Pennsylvania
Amishmen visited a Sunday service in Champaign County and
began to show off their harmonic skills during a congregational hymn, "Warye rose to his feet, struck the pulpit desk with
his fist, and commanded the congregation to stop and after his
stern rebuke, 'Net Bass singa!' [No bass singing!], he permitted

the congregation to proceed."[48] Worshipers were to think about what—not how—they were singing.

For conservative-minded Amish who saw the changes in temperament and tone that accompanied the adoption of meetinghouses and Sunday schools, there seemed cause for concern. How much could the church borrow from secular models of organization and efficiency and still remain faithful? Conservatives correctly sensed that adopting styles and patterns from the surrounding culture—be they fashionable clothing trends or more systematic and bureaucratic Christian education programs—were not without serious implications for other aspects of community life. Biblical teachings on humility, simplicity, and submission to the wisdom of elders did not fit easily with the assertive American notion that bigger was better and new meant improved.

Conservatives noticed that progressives did not stop with innovations in church life; openness to change seemed to breed interest in the secular goings-on of larger society. Increased business contacts among enterprising Amish sometimes blurred the line between the church and the world. Mississippi River steamboat-owner and -operator Henry Detweiler managed to balance his social and business life with his Amish church's lifestyle expectations for a time. Eventually, though, Henry and his wife Magdalena Bachman were excommunicated because of their infrequent church attendance, unable to fulfill their duties in both their church and their work.[49] And in other Amish settlements, such as Wayne County, Ohio, keeping after the world's fads and fashions led some Amish to pose vainly and to pay for photographs of themselves.

Despite the growing rift between tradition-leaning and change-minded church members, the Amish remained at least nominally united, with those on both sides generally recognizing one another and sharing communion together. An exceptional case was the small Mifflin County, Pennsylvania, group under the leadership of bishops Samuel B. King and "Long

Christian" Zook. After 1849, the King and Zook group broke fellowship with the larger Amish church (except for a small group in Lawrence County, Pennsylvania, with which they maintained contact). The exact disagreement between King's congregation and other Amish is no longer clear; however, the King group (later known as the "Byler Amish") represented notably conservative Amish convictions.[50]

Did the Mifflin County schism foreshadow deeper divisions? Certainly innovations in church life and involvements in worldly business had pulled some Amish towards the social mainstream. Though conservatives like David Beiler might warn and protest against too much accommodation with "the world," there was no doubt that some Amish were identifying more closely with broader American culture—including its system of political power and authority.

Democrats, Whigs, Republicans, and Amish

Popular politics emerged as something of a national pastime during the first half of the 1800s, as democratization promised finally to fulfill Americans' aspirations for liberty and equality. Political parties, organized on a local level after about 1830, served as a channel for civic-minded Americans to involve themselves in their communities. Tree-stump speeches, torchlight parades, and bonfire rallies became standard campaign fare as family, friends, and neighbors debated the merits of candidates who promised to secure the republic's future.

Although much of the political enthusiasm appealed to English-speaking citizens, it also beckoned ethnic immigrant communities like the bilingual (German dialect and English) Amish, promising an acceptable means of acculturation and Americanization. Yet important convictions might have discouraged Amish involvement in politics. Anabaptist sensibilities concerning the separation of church and state, for example, along with a lingering Amish suspicion that governments were agents of persecution and harassment, made many Amish wary of such entanglements. The 1837 Amish ministers' meeting held in Somerset County, Pennsylvania, had declared public office-holding, jury service, and voting, taboo. The boastful and haughty nature of electoral politics smacked of competitive pride, if not outright untruth.[51]

Yet undeniably, some Amish had always been involved in public life. In a rare move, Chester County bishop Christian Zook likely issued a printed handbill during the War of 1812, urging the Amish and other nonresistant churches to elect public officials committed to peace and ending the war.[52] More common was direct participation in local government. While it

Bishop Jacob Zehr (1825-1898) and Elizabeth Ehresman Zehr (1830-1902) at their home in Woodford County, Illinois. Jacob immigrated from Bavaria to Illinois in 1848; Elizabeth immigrated to Ohio as a five-year-old girl.

is impossible to know exactly how many Amish became involved in this way, enough did to alarm conservative church leaders in several states.[53] One civic-minded Amishman was Christian Ebersol, Jr., an immigrant of 1829 who lived most of his adult life in Lancaster County, Pennsylvania, where he remained a rather traditional and conservative member of his church. But Ebersol was also active in community affairs. He served as his township's first road supervisor and later as one of its public school directors. Since the township had for a time refused to support common schools, Ebersol's early involvement shows his having had more confidence in public education than many of his non-Amish neighbors.[54]

Not only Ebersol—a product of nineteenth-century Amish immigration—but also the descendants of earlier eighteenth-century arrivals became involved in civic life. In Mifflin County, Pennsylvania, Amish church members held a variety of local posts. Already in 1797 Abraham Yoder served as a township road supervisor. The next year Christian Lantz and Christian Zook were named public overseers of the poor. Historian S. Duane Kauffman has discovered about three dozen Amishmen who filled local government offices in Mifflin County through the 1840s.[55] While the Amish generally avoided law enforcement offices that required the use of violence, they served as township supervisors, overseers of the poor, school directors, assessors, auditors, tax collectors, and, in one case, county commissioner. Most notable was Shem Zook, who not only served multiple terms in at least five different township and county offices, but also took an interest in political party machinery. Zook was one of several Mifflin County Amish active in the Anti-Masonic and Whig political parties, both of which represented conservative business interests. Local lore preserves the legend that the Pennsylvania Railroad, so impressed with Zook's political savvy, asked the Amishman to run for governor after Zook successfully negotiated an important track right-of-way.[56]

In the 1840s and 1850s, the McLean County, Illinois, Amish were involved in local civic life, as well. Members held posts as township, road, and school supervisors, and one Joseph W. Zook even served as justice of the peace. Most of the Amish active in Illinois politics supported the conservative Whig party, but the Hessian Amish lined up behind the Democrats. After the Republican Party formed in 1854, it drew heavy McLean Amish support.[57] Maverick Illinois Amish schoolteacher Joseph Joder was an ardent Republican and abolitionist. Come election day, every "freedom-loving citizen," Joder wrote, was to "come forward to the ballot box and silently decide in favor of freedom." Among Joder's many non-Amish associates was a young lawyer named Abraham Lincoln. A number of Illinois Amish interacted with Honest Abe, including McLean County preacher Christian Farni and his brother bishop Peter Farni. In the 1850s, the Farnis became entangled in a St. Louis-based investment scheme that collapsed in the financial panic of 1857. During the ensuing legal wrangling and bankruptcy proceedings, Lincoln offered legal advice to the brothers and on one occasion appeared in court on their behalf. For his part, Christian wrote to Lincoln and promised support in the approaching 1860 electoral contest.[58]

Yet it was Lincoln's very election to the presidency that in some ways marked the limits of Amish civic participation. With Lincoln in the White House, sectional conflict seemed all but inevitable, and Civil War broke out within weeks of his inauguration. How far would Amish involvement in American politics extend? Before 1861, some Amish had been active in both their church and their state without noticing the underlying tension between the two. But when the state assumed the authority to decide life and death on the battlefield (much as it had assumed the authority to authorize human slavery), the ultimate claims of government could no longer be ignored. Would civic-minded Amish, who had identified with the American nation through their political participation, now fulfill all their duties as citizens?

Uncivil war

The April 1861 shooting between Charleston, South Carolina, and Fort Sumter marked the beginning of the violent and bitter struggle between the North and the South. Nearly all the Amish lived in northern Union states, and many had sympathies for the ruling Republican Party. Moreover, the Amish had never been friends of slavery—although virtually none had taken an active part in the abolitionist movement, either. How would they respond to a divided nation that had exhausted compromise and demanded its citizens choose sides?

Some Amish families ended up as fractured as the country. In Woodford County, Illinois, for example, two sons of Amish bishop Johannes and Barbara (Gerber) Gingerich chose different paths. While Peter Gingerich refused military induction, in 1862 his older brother Christian enlisted in the Union army. For men such as Christian, the Union cause was clearly justified, and moral duty seemed to demand joining in the fray. But for Peter and many others, killing was not justified even as a means to a greater good.[59]

Christian was not alone among his people in marching with the Yankees. In 1862, 28-year-old Emmanuel Hochstetler joined the 22nd Iowa Volunteer Infantry and later died of wounds received at the battle of Vicksburg.[60] Meanwhile, some immigrant Amish accustomed to military service in Europe may not have seen the American war as a matter of conscience. Amishman J. Emile Strubhar, in fact, joined the Northern army so as to more quickly become a U.S. citizen after the hostilities ceased. Already at home in the American social and political milieu, Valentine Nafziger of Hessian Amish background served in the military both during and after the war, and then joined a national veterans' organization.[61]

It is probably impossible to know how many Amish men joined the regular fighting forces of the Union army, but most seem to have used the legal means available to avoid such service.[62] State and later federal draft laws typically allowed men

Allen County, Indiana, ministers Peter Graber and Jacob Graber, along with laymen Daniel Grabill, Daniel Stoll, Victor Delagrange, Peter Stoll, and John Stoll, signed this notarized January 1865 request for Peter Graber, Jr.'s exemption from the Civil War draft.

the option of paying a commutation fee (often $300) or hiring substitutes to muster in their place. Paying the commutation fee was "the most well-defined and consistent response of the Amish church to the draft laws of the war period," according to historian Paton Yoder, but in some cases, young Amishmen hired substitutes to fill their draft calls.[63] Yet not all Amish leaders approved of the practice of using substitutes. While admit-

---

Bishop Jacob Schwarzendruber Speaks Out During the Civil War

During the Civil War, state and federal conscription law allowed draftees to hire substitutes to serve in the draftee's place. Evidently some Amish young men used this provision to avoid induction, but not all Amish were comfortable with the ethics of such an arrangement. Bishop Jacob Schwarzendruber of Johnson County, Iowa, expressed his opposition in a letter composed in late spring 1865, after the war's conclusion:

"Concerning the draft, or buying volunteer substitutes or paying volunteers to send them out to fight, I hold that it is wrong according to God's Word and the teaching of Jesus and the apostles . . . .

"Are we then still nonresistant according to the teachings of Jesus and the apostles who have proclaimed to us the perfect will of the Father? . . . 'Whoso sheddeth man's blood, by man shall his blood be shed,' for God made man in his image [Genesis 9:6]. So we do not want to go ourselves or to pay others that they would go. How is this right before the eyes of God? . . . The Saviour's teaching is not as we have done, that we should be permitted to buy substitutes or help pay for people and let them go to kill others.

"Are we then still nonresistant? Jesus says* in Luke chapter 3 verse 14 to the soldier, 'Do violence or injustice to no man.' Dare I then pay someone to do injustice? Matthew 5:7, 'Blessed are the merciful for they shall obtain mercy,' and this is before the righteous judge, and how unmerciful things go in war with those who have never harmed us, and are also created after the image of God. Do we do right then voluntarily to support the war with money and to vote for those who want to make war? All vengeance is forbidden to the follower of Jesus . . . . Jesus says 'Love your enemies, bless them that persecute you, do good to them that hate you, pray for those who despitefully use you and persecute you, then we shall be the children of the heavenly Father.' . . . [In Acts 7:60] Stephen prayed for those who stoned him, and what do we do? We send people to fight. Are we then still nonresistant? . . ."

*The quotation is from John the Baptist. Schwarzendruber viewed the entire New Testament in harmony with and reflecting the teachings of Jesus.

Excerpted from Harold S. Bender, ed. and trans., "An Amish Bishop's Conference Epistle of 1865" *Mennonite Quarterly Review* 20 (July 1946): 222-29.

ting that substitution was not unknown in his congregation, an Amish bishop in Iowa criticized the practice as hypocritical.[64] And years after the war was over, John S. Stoltzfus of Lancaster County, Pennsylvania, still kept as a tragic reminder the uniform that his draft substitute had worn before dying in battle.[65]

Even for those not liable for the draft, community pressure to join in the war's spirit was a challenge. In Wayne County, Ohio, public coercion to contribute money to a so-called "Voluntary Fund" for the war was intense. While Wayne County's nonresistant Mennonites contributed heavily, the Amish there were less willing to give and better resisted the community's pressure.[66]

For other Amish, the war's deepest impressions came not so much from the conscription of men and money as from the stark realities of the war itself, realities that left deep memories which became often-repeated family tales. After stealing a wagon load of wheat from a Hickory County, Missouri, farmer, Southern troops forced teenage Christian Raber of the area's local Amish community to haul the grain some 30 or 40 miles in Raber's father's wagon. A frightening experience, it was not Raber's last run-in with troops. During the war's later years, an intoxicated Union soldier stopped the wagon which young Raber and a friend were driving. Not satisfied with the answers that the Amish boys gave his questions, the soldier shot and killed Raber's traveling companion. Shocked and shaken, Raber drove the 12 miles home with his friend's body. The soldier was later acquitted of wrongdoing and given an honorable discharge.[67]

Soldiers commandeered Amishman Christian Petersheim of Aurora, West Virginia, and forced him to haul supplies for weeks, while his family wondered whether he was dead or alive.[68] And the Amish of Davis County, Iowa, never forgot the fall 1864 morning when Southern sympathizers from nearby Missouri rode through their community, stealing and looting from barns and homes. Such was war, even among neighbors.[69]

"Who is there that has not deserved it?"

The American Civil War was the bloodiest conflict in United States history. Beyond the physical and financial toll, some contemporaries saw in the war great moral meaning. On March 4, 1865, at his second inauguration, Abraham Lincoln reflected on the war and concluded that perhaps God was teaching America a lesson through all the death and destruction. In the form of war, the sin of tolerating slavery had visited its curse upon the Union, the president suggested.

Three months later, Amish bishop Jacob Schwarzendruber of Johnson County, Iowa, expressed somewhat similar thoughts in a letter to fellow Amish church leaders. Schwarzendruber saw God using the war to test the faithfulness of the church. "The war in this country is a permission or a sending of God to punish the people because of their sins," the bishop wrote, unknowingly repeating the president's idea. "And who is there that has not deserved it?"

The lesson for the Amish was clear to Schwarzendruber. His church had become more worldly and progressive, too much involved in an American culture which included injustice and war. As a result, the Amish were now in part responsible for the nation's tragic calamity. "Our people should all keep themselves apart from all party matters in political things," he warned, "where brother votes against brother and father against son." Entangled in the war machinery, the Amish church had "departed from the example of Jesus and the martyrs," he feared.[70] Conservatives like Schwarzendruber believed that the tragedy of the Civil War demanded repentance and reform.

Half a continent to the east, in Lancaster County, Pennsylvania, 76-year-old bishop David Beiler had already seen God's judgment in the war's events. "Perhaps with war and strife and bloodshed," Beiler thought, Providence was teaching the Amish church to live more simply and obediently. The first half of the nineteenth century had been a time of material and social prosperity, Beiler was sure. But, he wondered, in having "everything in abundance according to natural things," had some Amish "become forgetful of the great goodness of God?" Looking back over some six decades, he saw a struggle in his church that reminded him of the schism between the American North and South. Just as two different sections of the nation had years before chosen divergent social, economic, and political paths, so too had change-minded and tradition-minded Amish set out on apparently incompatible means of relating to the world.[71] Now the nation had divided. Could the church hope for more?

Beiler's observations were to the point. The Amish in North America, both the descendants of the eighteenth century immigrants and the new arrivals of the 1800s, had prospered abundantly. Their prosperity stemmed in a large part from their own beliefs and practices: simplicity, community, mutual aid. But American prosperity had also led them to a fork in the road, with one path pointing toward greater integration into North American society and the other pointing toward some type of critical distance. For many Amish, the choice became especially acute in the 1860s, the very decade in which the United States painfully struggled to remain united. The Amish church also struggled during those years—and ultimately divided.

7.
Years of Division,
1850-1878

"In many places patience has grown cold."
— open letter from a group of Amish ministers, 1861

The context of conflict

As the church approached mid-century it seemed to some observers to be on a collision course with central tenants of North American culture. While many Amish had left Europe in part to avoid the pressures of political conformity, and most found the fairly open and tolerant social atmosphere of North America appealing, the question of how much their new environment would shape them became unavoidable. In this respect, the Amish were no different from other minority groups that struggled to maintain old values and embody traditional practices in new settings. For the Amish the stakes were especially high since their notion of faith was one that placed a premium on practical expressions of faithfulness—expressions that often took specific forms, and which might appear from the outside simply to be ethnic folkways. Instead, this emphasis on the observable fruits of discipleship often highlighted their distance from mainstream values.

Especially for those living in the United States, the tension could be sharp. Commitments to self-determination and individual freedom of choice, for example, had become articles of faith for most Americans, and much of popular culture rested on the assumption that defending such freedom was at the heart of national identity. The unchecked celebration of human progress and individual achievement had propelled Americans to conquer a continent, produce secular self-government, and place profound hope in the abilities of technology to free individuals for lives of autonomous fulfillment. For the Amish, on the other hand, accountability to church and family limited individual choice, separation from the world entailed less-than-full participation in politics, and simplicity and modesty cautioned against always striving for bigger, better, and newer.

But if this posture placed one at odds with larger society, not all Amish agreed on what that meant for their church. Indeed, for some the promise and prospect of American culture was attractive, and adaptation to it was welcome. They viewed change not as an exercise in wholesale assimilation, but as a necessary means of remaining relevant. After 1850 especially, tension between the push for change and the pull of tradition became acute. Increasingly that tension resulted in conflicts that threatened to split local congregations and divide the entire fellowship.

The third quarter of the nineteenth century was a time of remarkable disagreement, dissension, and schism among the Amish. While the church was still nominally united in 1850, 25 years later the controversies had produced permanent divisions. The events of those years marked subsequent Amish history, and the results remain visible today. Those Amish who resisted the claims of American progressivism and modernization maintain a distinctive integration of faith and life that is still identifiable. Those who chose the path of adaptation and social relevance eventually blended, for the most part, into larger American society.

While these years are critical for understanding Amish history, the debate and discussion that marked them can be difficult to describe. Part of that difficulty lies in the fact that no single Amish division took place during these years. Though there were key moments of conflict, the formation of competing parties worked its way out at different times in different places. A process of "sorting out," one historian has suggested, would be a better way to describe the alignment of churches into change-minded and tradition-minded camps. If by 1860, for example, the Amish in northern Indiana had broken into progressive-leaning and more tradition-guided factions, the Ontario Amish did not split until the 1880s, and the church in Iowa divided only in the 1890s.[1]

Also important for understanding the debate within the Amish church after mid-century was the Amish idea of church order, or *Ordnung*.[2] *Ordnung* embodied the teachings and practices of the church, defined members' lifestyle and conduct, and served to unify the highly congregational Amish. Without a hierarchy or systematic, scholarly theology, it was the practical order of life—the ordinary application of faith in daily life—that held Amish churches together. The Amish *Ordnung* included general principles such as modesty and simplicity, and specific directives such as wearing certain patterns of plain clothes and avoiding costly, showy household furniture. *Ordnung* was not a written code or rulebook, but rather a traditional way of going about life, one that continued slowly to evolve over time and often allowed for gradual, considered change.[3]

During the mid-nineteenth century, though, the purpose and function of church order became unclear. For some Amish, church order was something with which to tamper only very carefully and cautiously. For others, *Ordnung* was a more dynamic principle that guided change and certainly did not prohibit innovation. For conservative-minded Amish, the *Ordnung* gave physical expression to biblical teachings and virtues. For the progressives, those teachings and virtues could be expressed in a number of different ways in an ever-changing world; *Ordnung* really only embodied biblical ideals that in turn guided change. Different views of order and change necessarily led to a division in the Amish church. With a common *Ordnung* as the church's only organizational glue, disagreement on the purpose and use of *Ordnung* naturally led to fracture.[4]

Clouds of controversy gather

Around 1850, several common problems surfaced in Amish communities in northern Indiana, eastern Ohio, and central Pennsylvania, and ripples of their dissension at times disturbed the shores of more placid Amish communities. While these early debates were hardly enough to split the church, each one pointed to growing tensions that eventually would divide the whole fellowship. As precursors for the coming schism, these difficulties were significant.

Already in the late 1840s, trouble surfaced in northern Indiana, where Amish households had been living since 1841 after arriving from Ohio and Pennsylvania. Those who settled in eastern Elkhart County—many of whom had Ohio roots—were less conservative and tradition-minded than most of those in neighboring LaGrange County—many of whom hailed from Pennsylvania. When the Elkhart-LaGrange church grew too large to meet comfortably in its members' homes, it separated into two county-defined church districts, and the factions became even more distinct.[5]

Under the progressive leadership of bishops Isaac Schmucker and Jonas D. Troyer, the Elkhart County Amish toyed with more expensive clothing, more formal education, and holding local public offices. Such practices were prime examples of the desire to fit into their host society. How better to be accepted as fellow citizens than to dress and work like one's neighbors and become involved in civic life? To the more tradition-minded LaGrange Amish, such innovations smacked of compromise and an undermining of the Christian values of simplicity, humility, and community decision-making. As con-

Amish 1860

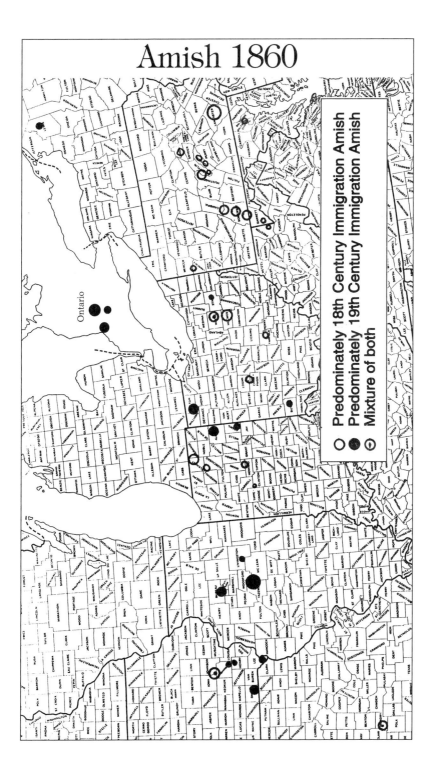

Predominately 18th Century Immigration Amish

Predominately 19th Century Immigration Amish

Mixture of both

Ontario

servative LaGrange County Amishman John E. "Hansi" Borntreger interpreted the events of the late 1840s, "Most of the church members were in harmony with their [conservative] ministers, but several preachers . . . and part of the church . . . had much to say in opposition, causing the faithful ones much concern and grief."[6] Borntreger believed that the liberals had drifted from their biblical foundation and had simply "started a new church according to their own opinions."[7]

The differences in northern Indiana had not yet produced schism. Both groups still recognized one another as Amish and hoped that the other would see its way to reconciliation. Even Borntreger himself occasionally attended the worship services of his more progressive Amish neighbors. Yet, in retrospect, the seeds of division had been planted. The differing perspectives obvious in each group could hardly be ignored or expected to disappear. To the change-minded Amish, selective innovation was a means of making the church relevant and appealing in a new and constantly changing world. For the Amish opposed to such adaptation, easy and individual change represented a lack of commitment and faith. Was not the church to be different from "the world" in its public life?

Controversies in Pennsylvania and Ohio mirrored in some ways the Indiana conflict. In the two eastern states the disagreement began over the proper mode of baptism. Some argued for baptism in a stream, while others held to a traditional baptismal rite performed as part of an indoor church service. While eventually those on both sides of the issue compromised and recognized either mode of baptism as legitimate, the division in those communities persisted, largely because the baptism dispute had been a surrogate for other issues and attitudes. Those who championed stream baptism also tended toward a more progressive, innovative church life, while those who favored baptism among fellow church members in a home were more cautious about the church's attempts to catch up with and adapt to its surrounding culture.

For example, Mifflin County stream-baptism advocate Shem Zook was also involved in politics, writing and publishing, and big business contacts with major railroad companies. Similarly, the Wayne County proponent of stream-baptism was bishop Jacob D. Yoder, who engaged in shady business deals, raced mules, traded in horses, and held a deviant interpretation of the biblical story of Adam and Eve.[8]

Clearly, conservatives thought that they had something to worry about when change-minded Amish introduced new things. Even a new form of baptism—which the conservatives never rejected categorically—appeared to be merely the first step toward wholesale involvement in society and, in the case of bishop Yoder, even questionable doctrine. Tampering with *Ordnung* that regulated baptism had an unsettling effect on other practices. Stiff resistance to change on the part of some Amish grew out of a realization that people cannot easily make selective changes; choosing to adapt in one area of life often leads to unforeseen and undesirable changes in another.

Even though the Indiana, Ohio, and Pennsylvania controversies of the 1850s did not result in outright breaks in fellowship between conservatives and progressives, the tension between the camps grew. While the change-minded and tradition-minded Amish recognized one another as Amish, they also recognized that they could not much longer overlook the growing gap which stood between them. As Lancaster County's David Beiler observed in 1862, "The split appears to be becoming almost irreparable."[9] It was during this time of uncertainty and confusion that conservatives proposed an innovative idea.

Diener-Versammlungen

Two conservative-leaning bishops proposed that the church address the knotty questions before it by assembling a comprehensive gathering of Amish leaders—a *Diener-Versammlung* (ministers' meeting)—that would address problems irritating particular communities, as well as point the direction for a con-

The 1863 and 1868 Diener-Versammlungen *were held in this Mifflin County, Pennsylvania, barn owned by Christian B. and Rebecca (Zook) Peachey.*

tinental sense of unity in belief and practice among North American Amish. Ideally the meeting would set the tone of future church activity and, its tradition-minded proponents hoped, slow the onslaught of change. Working in the best tradition of Amish community, local churches could come together around a clear and united witness of practical Christian humility, simplicity, and peace. In short, a *Diener-Versammlung* could reassert the importance of practical *Ordnung*.

Already in 1851 David Beiler had written to a fellow Holmes County, Ohio, bishop that Beiler had "often thought that a church-wide ministers' meeting" could be a blessing. Such a gathering would serve not only as a forum for discussion, but more importantly as a setting in which the whole church could "take the Word of God as the plumbline" and come to unity.[10] In the past, infrequent regional ministers' meetings in Europe and America had resolved disputes and renewed church life and commitment, and at time even produced written guide-

Rachel Zook (1837-1916), Israel Zook (1833-1919), and Phoebe Zook (1842-1917), children of well-known Amish layman Shem Zook. Rachel and Phoebe watched the proceedings of the 1863 Ministers' Meeting from the hayloft of the Christian Peachey barn.

lines listing agreed-upon principles and practices.[11] Apparently Beiler thought that a continental meeting held the same potential. Dissension and division might dry up if Amish from across the United States and Canada met to reaffirm common convictions. In the same vein, Holmes County bishop Frederick Hege also suggested that a general ministers' conference could settle local problems, such as those that had sprung up in his part of Ohio. Like Beiler, Hege was a tradition-minded man.[12]

A North American gathering was a novel solution to the problems facing the mid-century church. No previous ministers' gathering had ever been so comprehensive in scope. Nor had an assembly ever set out to address the broad question of the church's general direction and future. Yet while Amish conservatives initially floated the idea, it fell to a somewhat progressive Amish deacon—eastern Lancaster County's John Stoltzfus—to call the first ministers' conference. Although Stoltzfus never broke with the tradition-minded camp while he lived in Pennsylvania, John and his wife Catherine Holly later moved to Tennessee where he allied himself with change-minded Amish. On March 8, 1861, Stoltzfus issued an "Open Letter to Amish Church Leaders," in which he suggested that a continental conference of Amish leaders meet and "put together and achieve [an agreement] suitable to the peace and forbearance of the Gospel."[13]

Another document, perhaps representing a formal response to Stoltzfus on the part of other leaders, recorded the feelings of fellow ordained men. "It is now the case," the second letter stated, "that in many places patience has grown cold, so much so that neglect and division have crept in."[14] The document proposed an initial meeting later that same year in Holmes County, Ohio. Apparently response to this suggestion was positive, though the assembly did not actually convene until the next year, and then in a different location. These letters had implied that such a continent-wide ministers' meeting should become an annual event, and for 17 years it nearly was.

In June 1862, the first of these comprehensive ministers' meetings convened in Wayne County, Ohio, with 72 leaders in attendance.[15] More than half were from Ohio, but participants came from five other states, as well. Scores of lay members— more than 400 in 1862, according to deacon Stoltzfus—also attended the sessions but did not vote or participate in discussions. The number of attendees and observers was too large to allow for meeting in a private home, so the group convened in the barn of Amishman Samuel Schrock. Many attendees arrived by train, taking advantage of the good network of rails in the northern United States.

From the start, the ministers' conferences tended to favor the change-minded Amish agenda. Both the first year's moderator, bishop Jonathan Yoder from McLean County, Illinois, and assistant moderator, bishop John Esh of Juniata County, Pennsylvania, were well-known Amish progressives. The remarkable layman Shem Zook of Mifflin County, Pennsylvania, served as the first recording secretary. Not only did leaders affiliated with the progressive camp attend in greater numbers (about 50 of the 72 registrants could be considered change-minded), but conservative Holmes County bishop Levi Miller charged that not all the tradition-minded church districts had been informed of the meeting, and thus had been left out.[16] Miller's charge was only partly true; conservative David Beiler and other Lancaster County bishops and ministers, for instance, stayed away from the meeting on purpose. Although Beiler had originally suggested the ministers' meeting, he soon sensed that it might simply become a vehicle for bringing more change into the church, rather than creating a unified front against it.

The proceedings of the *Diener-Versammlungen* were fairly informal. Sessions opened with sermons, these being the highlight for many participants who otherwise had little opportunity to hear preachers from other states. Issues or problems brought to the conference received floor discussion and debate.

Special committees took up important questions and formulated written responses that they then presented to the larger group. The first two annual meetings used an informal consensus method to approve or reject committee findings, but by 1864 the ministers'-meeting was employing a system of majority votes.[17] One limitation of the conference's power was its inability to enforce decisions. Because the Amish retained local congregational authority, churches that disagreed with a particular ministers'-meeting decision could simply ignore it.[18]

The first meetings were somewhat successful in restoring peace to tension-filled Amish communities in northern Indiana, Ohio, and central Pennsylvania. Several local conflicts seemed to move toward resolution—or so attendees thought at the time. Although the change-minded and traditional Amish within those settlements eventually went separate ways, immediately after 1862 some Amish were optimistic that the annual meetings might bring harmony to strained relations. Said the 1863 proceedings: "there is hope for healing."[19] On the practical question of defining the roles of deacons and full deacons—an issue hotly debated in Logan and Champaign counties, Ohio, and Mifflin County, Pennsylvania—the first ministers'-meetings established helpful guidelines.[20] Moreover, the annual gathering was united in its response to the liberal Hessian Amish of Butler County, Ohio. So long as the Hessians insisted on using worldly musical instruments, other Amish—traditionalists and progressives alike—could not hold them in close fellowship or assist them in ordaining new leaders.[21] Neither would ministers'-conference participants approve of joining state militias, holding membership in secret societies such as the Masonic Lodge, or posing for photographs, since picture-taking was a sure sign of vanity and pride, and might even be a form of graven images prohibited by the Ten Commandments.[22]

Despite the hard line that the annual meetings took with the Hessians and some other expressions of popular culture, many

The *Diener-Versammlungen*

The Amish *Diener-Versammlungen* (ministers' meetings) met annually from 1862 until 1878 (except 1877). Below are the location, moderator, and registered attendance for each meeting. In addition to the registered bishops, ministers, and deacons, the gatherings drew up to 1,500 interested Amish laymen and women who came to hear visiting preachers or simply observe the proceedings. Full deacon (later bishop) Samuel Yoder of Mifflin County, Pennsylvania, was the only leader who attended every gathering.

The *Diener-Versammlung* was held in May or June, and, except for the 1864 meeting, all were held around Pentecost. Bishop Abner Yoder of Somerset County, Pennsylvania (later moved to Johnson County, Iowa), was the only moderator who eventually sided with the Old Order Amish; all other moderators chose the Amish Mennonite path.

1862	Wayne Co., Ohio	Jonathan Yoder	72
1863	Mifflin Co., Pennsylvania	Abner Yoder	42
1864	Elkhart Co., Indiana	John K. Yoder	71
1865	Wayne Co., Ohio	unknown	89
1866	McLean Co., Illinois	Samuel Yoder	75
1867	Logan Co., Ohio	Elias Riehl	42
1868	Mifflin Co., Pennsylvania	John K. Yoder	34
1869	Holmes Co., Ohio	Samuel Yoder	27
1870	Fulton Co., Ohio	John P. King	40
1871	Livingston Co., Illinois	Samuel Yoder	56
1872	LaGrange Co., Indiana	John P. King	56
1873	Wayne Co., Ohio	Samuel Yoder	41
1874	Washington Co., Iowa	John K. Yoder	28
1875	Tazewell Co., Illinois	John P. King	38
1876	Fulton Co., Ohio	Samuel Yoder	30
1877	not held		
1878	Woodford Co., Illinois	John K. Yoder	43

conservatives were disappointed in the tone and outcome of conference discussions and committee reports. On the question of social shunning, long a New-Testament practice in Amish churches, some ministers'-meeting resolutions and committee reports seemed to waffle.[23] The conferences also refused to forbid political participation.[24] Moreover, the suggested way to bring peace in most disagreements was to ask conservatives to be more tolerant.

"It seems to me that each was allowed to have his own opinion," David Beiler concluded after hearing reports of the early conferences. Perceptively Beiler saw that the peace achieved by the ministers' conferences was really "a conciliatory spirit without coming to the point which was and is the real reason for the differing views." The annual meetings addressed symptoms without dealing with deeper underlying disagreements between the conservative and change-minded worldviews and assumptions about the *Ordnung*. "If we wish to destroy a weed," Beiler said, drawing on agricultural imagery, "we must pull it up by the roots; otherwise it will just keep growing." Certainly "if the causes of offense are not put away, then, according to my opinion, no real unity can be restored."[25] The tension between the two wings of the Amish church was building, not lessening, in the wake of the early Amish ministers' meetings.

A breach in 1865
Originally proposed to restore harmony in the church, the Amish ministers' conferences seemed simply to point up the gulf that separated members. With the change-minded group in control of the national forum, many conservatives felt ignored by the *Diener-Versammlungen* which they had begun attending in good faith. In 1864, a group of tradition-minded Amish leaders met in Lancaster County to try its hand at resolving the tensions in their state's Mifflin County churches. That gathering fared no better than the national conference,

Too Much Money in the Offering?

In order to cover conference expenses, the later Amish Mennonite ministers' meetings collected donations from attendees. In 1873, the man charged with collecting and counting the contributions was surprised by the size of one donation. Several months later, Amish Mennonite leaders ran the following advertisement in the Mennonite periodical *Herald of Truth,* which many Amish Mennonites read:

"Notice.—At the collection taken at the Amish Conference held this year, near Orrville, [Wayne County] Ohio, a twenty dollar bill was thrown in. Bro. Jacob King, who received it thinks the giver probably made a mistake. If so it will be returned to the claimant giving satisfactory evidence that he was the giver."

From *Herald of Truth,* 10 (September 1873): 152.

but it did demonstrate that conservatives were keen to work together in addressing church conflicts; they were not ignoring the problems at hand.[26]

Disturbing to conservatives was that year's national meeting. The gathering announced its opinion and settled a disagreement between northern Indiana conservatives and progressives before all the tradition-minded leaders from Ohio had arrived.[27] Conservatives felt betrayed.

The following year, tradition-minded Amish leaders made a final and rather bold attempt to put their views before the larger Amish church. The 1865 ministers' meeting met again in Wayne County, Ohio, home to a sizable progressive Amish community. Just to the south in Holmes County, most of the Amish were of a more tradition-minded stripe. Several days before the start of the official *Diener-Versammlung,* 34 conservative-leaning leaders gathered in Holmes County. Representing

Amish churches in Ohio, Indiana, Ontario, and western Pennsylvania, they drew up a document akin to the summary *Ordnung* statements that had come from regional ministers' gatherings in decades past. The Holmes County statement served as a type of manifesto of the tradition-minded Amish position, and conservatives took a firm stand against all that they believed to be "destructive to our salvation and contrary to God's Word." Popular attitudes and widely accepted social customs which tempted the church, they warned, in truth "serve to express pomp and pride." Worse still, they "lead away from God."[28]

The church's call in a self-indulgent culture was clear, the conservatives insisted. Among other things, members needed to separate themselves from worldly carnivals, the pride and wasted expense of "speckled, striped, flowered, clothing," and from "unnecessary, grand, household furnishings" and "pompous carriages." Activities that unraveled community fabric, introduced inequality, or stymied the practice of mutual aid—commercial property insurance or operating large-scale businesses "according to the ways of the world," for example— were taboo for the tradition-minded group. Conservatives also addressed church practices, warning against lax discipline and the singing of catchy, popular hymns with spiritually shallow lyrics.[29]

There was no doubting the purpose of the statement; it defined the terms under which the tradition-minded Amish were willing to work. "[A]ll those who affirm such with us and demonstrate with works and deeds," the authors announced, "we are willing to recognize as brothers and sisters and resume fellowship with them." Though blunt and specific, the document ended on a note of grace and invitation. Spiritual renewal—not a list of prescribed practices—was what conservatives intended their call for separation from sin to inspire. Such renewal involved the enabling grace that God offered disciples, and so the writers concluded that "the gate is portrayed for us as straight and the way as narrow, but it is not therefore ever closed, but stands open for all repentant souls, and as the Savior says in Luke 14:33, 'Whoever does not forsake all that he has cannot be my disciple.'"[30]

With their position in hand, nearly all of the 34 signatories headed north to the 1865 annual meeting in Wayne County. The conference registered the highest attendance of any with 89 leaders present. About 40 percent of those assembled were tradition-minded Amish, the most significant representation they would ever achieve. Curiously, the printed minutes of the 1865 meeting are the most sketchy of any of the conferences' proceedings, so it is difficult to reconstruct the exact order of events. Apparently the ministers' meeting took up the conservatives' paper near the end of its business session and did little with it. While no formal response on the part of the Holmes County conferees to the tone and agenda of that year's larger gathering survives, it appears they were bitterly disappointed with the reception they received at the national meeting.[31] After 1865 only a handful of conservative Amish leaders ever attended another annual conference. Ignored out of their church, the traditionalists withdrew from the activities of the Amish majority who were increasingly comfortable with change. (While it is impossible to say exactly how many Amish sided with the conservatives, they eventually numbered about one-third of all districts.)

Symbolically, then, the year 1865 stood as a point of public separation between change-minded and tradition-minded Amish. Not that a single schism split the church all at once on that date. Indeed, in some places the informal process by which churches sorted their affiliation took years and was not especially rancorous. For example, conservative-leaning and progressive-minded Amish in Ontario and some parts of Iowa remained largely united until the 1880s and 1890s. Only then did the differences between the two camps become gulfs large enough to actually divide the churches. In 1877, division came

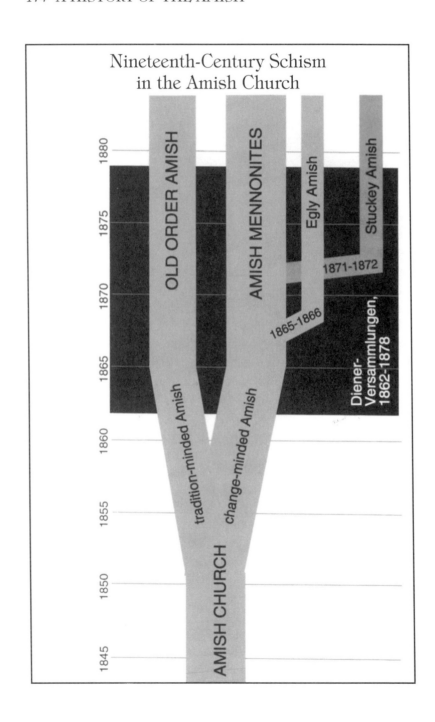

Nineteenth-Century Schism
in the Amish Church

OLD ORDER AMISH

AMISH MENNONITES

Egly Amish

Stuckey Amish

1880

1875

1870

1865

1860

1855

1850

1845

tradition-minded Amish

change-minded Amish

1871-1872

1865-1866

Diener-
Versammlungen,
1862-1878

AMISH CHURCH

to the Lancaster County, Pennsylvania, Amish settlement, but most of the members sided with the conservatives.[32] In central Illinois, nearly the opposite situation transpired: all the Amish congregations there chose the course of change.

Because the conservatives had defined their concerns in terms of a traditional understanding of *Ordnung* (the "old order"), others eventually labeled them Old Order Amish.[33] Meanwhile, many in the change-minded group had been constructing closer relations with neighboring Mennonites, many of whom had an affinity for the relatively tolerant and open Amish progressives. As a result, the Amish majority coming out of the *Diener-Versammlungen* embraced the designation "Amish Mennonite." While these labels were not immediately or universally recognized, after the 1865 ministers' meeting, the terms "Old Order Amish" and "Amish Mennonite" accurately pointed to two paths that Amish churches were choosing in their interaction with the wider world. After the Wayne County ministers' conference, the change-minded group (Amish Mennonite) and the conservatives (Old Order Amish) were going separate ways.

Later ministers' meetings

Twelve more national gatherings followed the 1865 meeting, and except for 1877 they were annual affairs. During these later years attendance varied from 75 to 27 registered bishops, ministers, and deacons, though the assemblies continued to draw large crowds of lay members eager to hear the preaching of visiting ministers. After 1865, however, the nature of the conferences changed in a significant way.

The ministers' meetings had begun as mass consultations aimed at bringing unity and a sense of common purpose to the Amish. With the exit of the conservative wing of the church after 1865, the gatherings took on a more formal, deliberative—perhaps even legislative—flavor. More rules of order came into play, and references to precedents established in past proceedings became more common.[34] In 1867, for example, the conference "decided that all proceedings of former meetings which were brought to a conclusion remain in force." Moreover, "no minister who is a member of the meeting shall have the right to make any changes afterward."[35] The Amish Mennonites still addressed issues on a case-by-case basis, but they did so in a more formal way.

The Old Orders, in contrast, had outlined a clear set of explicit prohibitions and expectations in 1865, but they handled the

---

Excerpts from the Proceedings of the Amish *Diener-Versammlungen*

1863: "Should likeness [photographs] be permitted?" [Answer:] "It was decided almost unanimously that they [the delegates] want to reject this thing [photography]."

1866: "May a person who, for the sake of worldly income, produces intoxicating beverages . . . be considered a useful member of the congregation?" [Answer:] "It was looked upon as improper, and would not throw a good light on the church. We would do much better to stay far away from it and stay away from such drinking places and rather to avoid such and avert the bad consequences which follow. For at such places chains, nets, and snares are set up in order to catch innocent souls."

1867: May church members contribute to the building of Civil War monuments "which cost thousands of dollars, and benefit neither the dead or the living, and lead only to idolatry"? [Answer:] "There are always poor and needy among us to whom we can be helpful and in that way make better use of that which we have."

1868: "We declare service in the army to be contrary to the Gospel . . . [It] must be forsaken with true penitence and sorrow, and also by leaving off and renouncing everything connected with it . . . [including] pensions. . . . if there is need, it is the duty of the church to support the poor . . . ."

1870: On frequenting "shows" and "fairs": "It was shown clearly, and with power that, according to God's Word, to frequent such places . . . would give an evil appearance and that, according to the words of Jesus, one cannot let his light shine to good works if he takes part in and supports them. . . . In fact, these [amusements] might be compared to the fair or vanity fair in the City of Vanity, described by John Bunyan [in his book *Pilgrim's Progress*] . . . . All were therefore admonished to avoid all such evil appearance . . . ."

1875: "According to God's Word is it right for a brother to . . . borrow money on low interest and then loan it out again with high interest?" [Answer:] "We consider it to be unjust . . . ."

Excerpted from Paton Yoder and Steven R. Estes, trans. and eds., *Proceedings of the Amish Ministers' Meetings, 1862-1878* (Goshen, Ind.: Mennonite Historical Society, 1999).

application of their *Ordnung* in the more informal and personal setting of local congregations. For its part, the Amish Mennonite pattern was taking its cues from the values and methods of larger society that championed bureaucracy and prized formal, large-scale systems of authority. Amish Mennonites were combining a more tolerant attitude toward individual conduct with a more rigid vision of structure and organization. While they neither surrendered church discipline nor established elaborate denominational hierarchies, they had clearly moved farther in that direction than had the Old Order Amish, who maintained a tradition-guided, but informally-managed, church life.

The change-minded Amish Mennonites did not embrace every aspect of American national life. In the wake of the Civil War, should nonresistant Christians contribute toward the building of war monuments and memorials? The 1867 *Diener-*

Versammlung said no.[36] The next year, the Amish Mennonite gathering responded to inquiries for church membership from a veteran who was receiving a government pension. The ministers' meeting decided that the applicant could become a church member only if he broke all ties with the military, including his pension, and the church was to cover his living expenses if he was disabled.[37] And what of Grange membership? The Grange was a popular Midwestern-based farmers' union that fought for rural rights and promoted social recreation in farm communities. Given its potential to replace the church as one's primary community and source of identity, Amish Mennonites rejected Grange membership.[38]

The ministers' conferences continued to address issues peculiar to the Amish church as well, such as approaches to church discipline, modesty in dress, and the extent to which members could grow wealthy by patenting inventions.[39] Moderation guided answers to such queries. Yet even after 1865, things did not always run smoothly for the change-minded Amish Mennonites. Even without Old Order voices presenting alternative answers to ministers'-meeting issues, unity was at times still out of reach.

Division among the Amish Mennonites

It soon became clear that the problems and conflicts in the Amish church had not resulted simply from the presence of protesting conservative-minded folks. Indeed, nearly as soon as the Old Orders opted out of the national forum, the change-minded Amish Mennonites who remained engaged in the annual gatherings began to disagree among themselves over what type of changes they could or should embrace. With the absence of the voices of tradition, change-minded leaders were free to press each other on just how much change each had in mind.

One division among the Amish Mennonites occurred already in 1865 and involved the thought and practice of a

European-born, renewal-minded bishop named Henry Egly who lived in Adams County, Indiana.[40] Sometime in the 1840s, while suffering a lengthy illness, Egly experienced a powerful spiritual awakening. The force of Egly's personal conversion convinced him that his was an experience God wanted everyone to have. After his 1854 ordination as a preacher (he had been a deacon since 1850), Egly stressed the importance of

Bishop Joseph Stuckey (1826-1902) of Danvers, Illinois.

each individual having an inner, experiential encounter with God as a prerequisite to forgiveness and salvation. Only those who had such an experience could be baptized, Egly said. Then too, Egly was critical of the spiritual tone of some Amish congregations. It seemed to Egly that some people relied on their parentage or church membership for salvation, rather than on personal conversion. Was not baptism without true conversion the same as infant baptism that the Anabaptists had rejected long ago?[41]

To some Amish, Egly's teaching was another version of Protestant revivalism that stressed emotionalism and ignored biblical injunctions for obedience. And if overstated, some feared, Egly's emphasis on a conversion experience would weaken similarly important teachings on discipleship. Salvation by grace through faith was a fundamental doctrine for the Amish, but they feared that an inordinate preoccupation with the process of becoming a Christian detracted from an emphasis on what being a Christian meant. Did not the New Testament speak more about living the Christian life than about the exact method one followed to get there? While the larger Amish church did not dismiss Egly's personal testimony nor deny that he may have had a close encounter with God while ill, they did resist his teaching that everyone should come to faith in the same way that he did.

About half of Egly's congregation heartily endorsed his leadership, to the chagrin of the rest of the group. In January 1858, the congregation called on three Amish leaders from Holmes County, Ohio, to mediate the conflict. Instead of chiding Egly, as some in the congregation had hoped would happen, the Ohio delegation ordained Egly a bishop![42] The tension thereafter only increased, since Egly, as a bishop, now oversaw baptisms and refused to baptize those whom he felt had not experienced a proper conversion. Some of those he rejected protested that he was not taking their claims of Christian faith seriously. In response, Egly argued that baptism without prop-

Farmer Peter Short (1826-1904) hosted the 1876 Ministers' Meeting in his Fulton County, Ohio, barn.

er conversion was no baptism at all, and he even offered to re-baptize those who subsequently experienced dramatic encounters with God's grace.[43]

By the spring of 1865, conflict in the congregation peaked. Egly refused to discipline a church member whom he claimed was not really a church member in the first place because she had not been baptized in "the knowledge of godly repentance" as he understood it.[44] Egly's ideas were receiving a hearing outside of Adams County, too, especially in communities in Ohio, Illinois, and Indiana where immigrant family networks tied Amish to supporters in Egly's church.[45] To these sympathizers, Egly was a true reformer. While the ministers' meeting of 1865 tried to address some of Egly's concerns, the gathered ministers seemed to be tired of his criticism and pointed statements.[46]

That fall, Egly's own congregation was so divided they could not celebrate communion, and the situation degenerated into a stubborn stalemate and split the church.[47] The next year, Egly met with supportive Amish throughout the Midwest, forming a loose network of like-minded church districts, popularly labeled "Egly Amish." While Egly continued to stay abreast of events in the Amish Mennonite world, he never attended another annual ministers' conference. Nor did other Amish Mennonites show much interest in interacting with the Egly Amish. Both sides seem quietly to have agreed to go their separate ways.[48]

The dynamics behind the so-called "Egly division" were complex. Egly had come to America from Europe in the nineteenth century, but he was not change-minded in the ways that many of his fellow recent Amish arrivals were. Much of what Egly stressed and taught was quite traditional. Egly's followers maintained clearly conservative dress standards and for many years worshiped only in the German language. Yet Egly also mixed popular American evangelical sentiments with his Amish tradition. As a church leader, he exercised considerable personal authority over his congregation, downplayed congregational discipline and corporate decision-making, and demanded individual experiential conversion of a particular type—all common traits among evangelicals of the day. Additionally, Egly was open to popular social reform movements such as alcohol temperance. Egly's mixture of Amish traditions, American evangelicalism, and popular reformism blended to form a distinct spirituality that appealed to some Amish Mennonites searching for a personal faith in a strange land.

That Amish found Egly's brand of Christianity attractive illustrates the diversity among the change-minded Amish population. Even if they were relatively open to the winds of popular culture blowing across the North American landscape, different breezes caught the attention of different churches and individuals. For some, change had meant meetinghouses and greater individual choice in the display of wealth and status. For others, change primarily meant reorienting one's religious world to include emphases from American evangelicalism and social reform. Fresh winds bearing the American virtue of tolerance and broad-mindedness could split the Amish Mennonite ministers' meetings, too.

Joseph Stuckey

In 1872, a second division transpired within Amish Mennonite ranks. Again, specific doctrinal differences were involved, but the debate centered on the nature of the church, the role of community, and the autonomy of individuals. The person around whom controversy eventually swirled was McLean County, Illinois, bishop Joseph Stuckey.[49] The popular and respected Stuckey had become a minister in 1860, and his ordination as bishop came only four years later.

Stuckey was typical of the progressive Amish church leaders in central Illinois. While Old Order appraisals of Stuckey would have characterized him as liberal, he was in certain ways cautious about change. He was cool to portrait photography and at least initially expressed caution about Sunday schools as new and unnecessary innovations.⁵⁰

Yet clearly Stuckey stood with the change-minded Amish Mennonites. Dress standards in Stuckey's Rock Creek (later

Amish schoolteacher Joseph Joder (1797-1887), McLean County, Illinois. Joder's universalism caused a stir among the Amish Mennonites.

named North Danvers) congregation were matters of individual discernment, and members took their grooming cues from
store windows more than from traditional understandings of
adornment and cautions against pride. Some of the Rock Creek
Amish men wore buttons on their coats, styled their hair, and
sported neckties. Change was not limited to attire. The Rock
Creek Amish also used their old Reformation-era *Ausbund*
hymnal less and less often, and one family loaned an organ to
accompany the singing in a community Sunday school (held in
a local schoolhouse) to which many of the families sent their
children.[51]

Specific tensions, though, surfaced around Stuckey's practice of allowing Amish who had been disciplined in other
churches to join the more tolerant congregations under his
oversight without first making amends with their home
churches. In so doing, the McLean County bishop was under-
cutting church discipline and unity, some change-minded
Amish Mennonites charged, by disregarding the opinions and
decisions of fellow churches. Traditionally, Amish leaders
acknowledged the discipline of other congregations, even if the
other group's standards differed from their own. This pattern
of reciprocal respect was central to the Amish balance of local
congregationalism with a broader sense of unity. Stuckey's
action might even open the door to a consumer approach to
church membership, whereby those not liking what they
found in one church could simply shop around and find a
group that matched their tastes.[52]

The events that sparked the break between Stuckey and his
fellow Amish Mennonites involved both doctrine and discipline and centered on schoolteacher and poet Joseph Joder. A
member of Stuckey's church, Joder had studied Latin, Greek,
and Hebrew, and otherwise cut a rather unusual profile as a
nineteenth-century Amishman.[53] One of the peculiar features
of Joder's theology was his belief in universalism, the conviction that all people, no matter how they live their lives, will

share equally in eternal salvation. There is no place for hell or future consequences for evil in the universalist scheme of thought—heaven is the destination of all humankind.

Forms of universalist thought have been present through church history, though the Christian tradition generally has regarded universalism as heresy. In the mid-nineteenth century, however, universalism was a relatively popular religious teaching in America where it seemed to comport well with national affirmations of liberty, equality, and democracy. Universalist circuit riders spread the teaching throughout the Midwestern United States and founded Universalist churches. By 1850, there were large Universalist congregations in the Illinois cities of

---

Joseph Joder's Controversial Poem

Amish schoolteacher and poet Joseph Joder caused a sensation with his poem *"Die Frohe Botschaft" (Glad Tidings)*. Written in German in 1869, the lines of verse drew criticism from many quarters of the Amish Mennonite church. Joder's opponents claimed that the poem advocated *universalism* (the belief that there is no such thing as hell or punishment for the wicked).

The poem was on the whole an affirmation of the Christian doctrine of salvation by grace through faith alone. Interspersed with traditional orthodoxy were several stanzas that supported a universalist perspective. Controversial portions included these lines:

Stanza 2: "Such teachings/As we frequently hear/Of eternal torment in hell/Cannot possibly be the truth:/They deny God's goodness/And make His spirit harsh."

Stanza 15: "It is not at all reasonable [to believe]/That in the future the torment of hell/Should last forever./Only insanity can so delude us/As to believe or hear/What God's word does not teach."

Stanza 16: "It [the idea of eternal punishment for the wicked] is pure fable,/A heathen suggestion;/Lack of understanding honors only/The darkness in the corner;/Sectarian presumption/Builds up hatred and quarreling."

Stanza 26: "Love flows forth from God/And works its way into the whole of creation,/Makes everything like unto itself,/Until the whole earth/Shall become one universe,/A Heavenly Kingdom of Peace."

When Joder's bishop, Joseph Stuckey, did not discipline Joder quickly enough for promoting these universalist beliefs, other Amish Mennonites censured Stuckey.

Translated by Jennie A. Whitten and published in Steven R. Estes, *A Goodly Heritage: A History of the North Danvers Mennonite Church* (Danvers, Ill.: North Danvers Mennonite Church, 1982), 296-300.

Peoria and Champaign. Perhaps Joder learned of the doctrine through these churches, through universalist publications, or through his own private Bible study. Even before Joder's case captured Amish Mennonite attention, universalism had provoked controversy when Illinois preacher Daniel Holly left his ministry among the Putnam County Amish and joined the Universalists. Nearby, in the late 1850s, Amish lay member Moses Ropp was excommunicated for his universalist views.[54]

Joder's writing, however, formed the celebrated confrontation between the Amish church and universalism. Joder had written several poems that could have been interpreted as defenses of universalism, but he had penned them in English and they attracted little attention among the Amish. In 1869, though, Joder authored 26 stanzas of verse under the title "Die Frohe Botschaft" *(Glad Tidings)*. This new poem was both in German and more explicitly universalist. It did not escape the notice of other Amish church leaders.[55]

Copies of the poem showed up at the 1872 ministers' meeting. Since some fellow ministers long had been suspicious of what they considered Stuckey's lax discipline, the assembly that year decided that the public presence of universalism in Stuckey's congregation demanded direct attention.[56] Several months later, a delegation of three Amish Mennonite leaders visited Stuckey and asked him why he considered Joseph Joder a member of the church when Joder's heretical views were so widely known. Stuckey admitted his church had not excommunicated Joder, nor was he yet ready to do so. Stuckey's statements could have been interpreted to mean that he agreed with Joder—although Stuckey later denied this. At that point, the delegation, symbolically representing other Amish Mennonite leaders, withdrew fellowship from Joseph Stuckey and the Illinois congregations that supported him.[57]

Stuckey might have argued that in the congregationally-structured Amish church, he could not single-handedly excommunicate anyone without the support of the congregation, and the congregation wanted to exercise more patience with Joder. Eventually, in 1873, Stuckey and his church did refuse to allow Joder to join them in observing communion, but only after they found Joder incorrigible.[58] Joseph Stuckey represented a fairly tolerant approach to church administration. Patience was important for Stuckey and the Amish who looked to him for leadership.

At several previous ministers' meetings, Stuckey had posed questions that seemed to imply he was unsure whether strict discipline really brought people to repentance. Only God could turn unbelief and disobedience around, he seemed to have said in 1867; the church's role might be patient and loving, waiting for God to work instead of jumping to excommunication and shunning. Rather than bringing erring members back to the church, tough discipline might drive some people further away.[59]

Stuckey was not alone in his approach to church discipline. Several other Illinois congregations allied themselves with Stuckey and collectively became known as the Stuckey Amish. Stuckey also maintained some informal contact with several

relatively liberal Amish congregations that remained independent of the larger Amish Mennonite fellowship represented by
the *Diener-Versammlungen*. These more liberal churches included two in Iowa under the leadership of immigrant bishop
Benjamin Eicher and preacher Philip Roulet, and two others in
Butler County, Ohio.

In one sense the "Stuckey Amish" represented the limits of
change-minded Amish Mennonite tolerance. While rejecting
the Old Order option, most Amish Mennonites were not willing to accept the sort of individual latitude that Joseph Stuckey
allowed. By the late 1870s, then, the Amish Mennonite majority saw itself somewhere between the Old Orders on one side,
and the the Egly evangelicals and the Stuckey progressives on
the other.

An Amish Mennonite future

In 1878, Woodford County, Illinois, hosted the last Amish
Mennonite ministers' meetings. Since about 1870, the meetings
had given more time to sermons and less to church business
and controversy. If fewer heated debates remained after the
exit of the Old Orders, the Egly followers, and the Stuckey faction, the issue that became more important was the future and
implications of the annual meetings themselves. What was the
purpose of the *Diener-Versammlungen* now that permanent division, instead of unity, had been their result? Should the ministers' meetings be discontinued? Should they become a
deliberative body to govern Amish Mennonite churches? At
the final 1878 gathering, a committee charged with strength-
ening the work of the assemblies proposed a plan to organize
completely an Amish Mennonite denomination.[60]

Under the committee's provisions, congregations would
operate autonomously, but if ensnared in situations that elud-
ed peaceful resolution, they would be required to bring the
matter to a regional meeting of Amish Mennonite leaders.
Should that group prove unable to address the local problem

successfully, the matter would come before the annual meeting for North America—and decisions rendered by that body would be final. Such a rational, bureaucratic approach to church government was too much even for change-minded Amish Mennonites, open to innovative ideas popular in main-

Bishop Benjamin Eicher, leader of the progressive Amish Mennonites of Washington County, Iowa.

stream society. The three-tiered system of appeal and review seemed more like the polity practiced by denominationally-oriented Protestants.

The Amish Mennonites never tested the committee's idea before the annual *Diener-Versammlungen* mysteriously came to an end. Although the meetings did not close on a formal note, no one convened another such gathering after 1878. Historian Paton Yoder has suggested that the demise of the annual meetings perhaps stemmed from a personal falling-out between conference advocates bishop John K. Yoder of Wayne County, Ohio, and full deacon John P. King of Ohio's Logan County.[61] With the leadership of Yoder and King divided, the Amish Mennonites lacked an important piece of the vision that had sustained the yearly schedule.[62] But perhaps, too, the meetings ended because they no longer served a purpose. After all, the conferences were originally supposed to settle local disturbances and unify the church. The church had found unity—or rather unities—by dividing into several factions, each of which sought renewal through different means. As the ministers' meetings ended, the Amish church was more formally divided than either conservatives or progressives might have imagined 17 years earlier when all sides had gathered to find common ground.[63]

By 1878, not all the results of the great division were apparent. It took some years for churches and certain communities to sort out which path they would take. In the midst of mid-century social and cultural turbulence, each group had sought church renewal. Renewal came, but in multiple and not always compatible ways. The Old Order Amish looked for spiritual renewal through a restored commitment to discipleship guided by a common *Ordnung*. The Egly churches sought new life through a highly personal spirituality, while the Stuckey people found Christian strength and love through a measure of tolerance and broad-mindedness. The turbulent years of the *Diener-Versammlungen* produced several Amish churches—each fairly united, but not with one another. In the decades that followed, the gap between the groups only widened as the Old Order Amish continued to maintain a life and faith whose implications made them easily recognizable, while their progressive Amish Mennonite cousins moved toward the American mainstream.

8.
Merging Traditions: Amish Mennonites and Mennonites in North America and Europe, 1870-1937

> *"We are willing to join hand in hand."*
> — Mennonites and Amish Mennonites
> in Antrim County, Michigan, 1886

Committed to cooperation

"On Sunday Sept. 17th, we met at the house of Joel Detweiler, and organized a German Sabbath-school under the auspices of the Omish [sic] Mennonite Church. . . . By the grace of God we hope to derive such spiritual blessings therefrom, as will enable us to grow in grace."[1] This news from Knox County, Tennessee, came from a new Amish Mennonite settlement formed in 1871 under the leadership of deacon "Tennessee John" Stoltzfus. Almost immediately the group established a Sunday school program and announced its beginning in the Mennonite-published, English-language periodical *Herald of Truth.* It was hardly coincidental that Amish Sunday

Three generations of Amish Mennonite women, Wayne County, Ohio: Mary Conrad Smiley (1825-1912), Elizabeth Smiley Ramseyer (1853-1928), and Clara Ramseyer Miller (1885-1918), holding her son Lloyd (1907-1995). Note the progressive change in dress styles.

school news appeared in a Mennonite magazine. The article pointed both to the continued interest in and promotion of progressive ideas and programs such as Sunday schools among change-minded Amish Mennonites, as well as the growing connection between that group and the Mennonites.[2] Within a few years, Mifflin County, Pennsylvania, Amish Mennonite layman Jonathan K. Hartzler was supplying children's stories for the Mennonite paper, and Amish Mennonite obituaries were listed on its back pages. During the early twentieth century, most North American Amish Mennonites would give up their public Amish identity and merge with the Mennonites who published the *Herald.* The Sunday school article from Tennessee portended changes to come.

The number of Amish identifying with the Amish Mennonite wing of the church grew significantly after 1865. After the annual ministers' meetings ceased, the process of

sorting out church affiliation continued with more congregations choosing the Amish Mennonite path. Into the 1880s and
1890s in some areas—notably Ontario, parts of Pennsylvania,
and Iowa—many congregations had not decided whether they
would align with the Old Orders or the Amish Mennonites.[3]
Meanwhile, a small but noticeable number of change-minded
members in conservative Old Order fellowships quietly left
their congregations for neighboring Amish Mennonite ones.

Excommunication and shunning did not always follow such
a change in affiliation. In the late nineteenth century, there
seems to have been a measure of mutual recognition on the
part of both the Old Orders and their progressive cousins. Until
about 1896, for example, in southeastern Pennsylvania's
Conestoga Amish community, shunning was not practiced
against those who left the Old Order group for the more liberal church. Joining the Amish Mennonites was a frowned-upon,
but tolerated "release valve," for those Amish who found Old
Order discipline too confining, yet wanted to remain a part of
broader Amish community affairs.[4]

Some people chose the Amish Mennonite camp for familial
reasons. John Lais was a Roman Catholic immigrant from
Germany who worked as a hired hand on an Indiana Amish
farm. Attracted to his employers' faith and life, Lais wanted to
join the Old Order church, but his wife Susannah (Plank) Lais,
did not. Susannah was of Amish background herself and was
disenchanted by what she perceived to be Old Order legalism.
The Laises compromised and joined the Amish Mennonites,
eventually moving to northwestern Oregon's Amish
Mennonite community.[5]

By century's end, Amish Mennonite churches were spread
across the continent. Not only did the older Amish communities in Pennsylvania, Ohio, Ontario, and Indiana include some
progressive Amish Mennonites, but almost all of the Illinois
and many of the Iowa Amish were of the change-minded
stripe. Then, too, many younger Amish settlements in

Arkansas, Colorado, Kansas, Missouri, Nebraska, Oklahoma, Oregon, and Tennessee joined Amish Mennonite ranks.

The church was not only growing, but also changing. Naturally there was variation from place to place and from congregation to congregation, but several notable trends emerged among late nineteenth-century Amish Mennonites. Members were acculturating, attracted—sometimes slowly, sometime more quickly—to mainstream American ideals and habits. Less traditional clothing styles, the use of English instead of German in family conversations, and the taking up of popular pastimes were several measures of Amish Mennonite movement toward fuller ownership of the rights and privileges of the surrounding culture.

Mahala Yoder, a McLean County, Illinois, Amish Mennonite woman in her twenties, kept a diary for several years, filled with observations of life around her home community.[6] While her family affiliated with the decidedly progressive Joseph Stuckey congregation, some of Yoder's comments reflected attitudes common to Amish Mennonites elsewhere, especially of her generation. To Mahala, her Amish Mennonite parents still seemed too conservative. Her father bought "the very plainest wooden" chairs for their home when Mahala had hoped for fancy new cane-bottoms. And her stepmother gave "the girls so little liberty to visit their friends," Mahala felt sad for her sisters. Despite this traditional orientation, the Yoder household was raising a rather different second generation of Amish Mennonites.

The luxuries of an industrial society were becoming common for the Yoder young folks. For her twenty-first birthday Mahala received carpeting for her bedroom. Her room looked so much better, she thought. It needed "only a table and pictures" to be complete. Her sister Mary went to town some weeks later and—with the full knowledge of their stepmother—chose new spring hats. "She got white straw hats," Mahala observed, "trimmed with blue ribbons and a pretty red rose."

Recreation, too, was changing. The Yoder family now played

what Mahala called "a new game"—the card "game of Authors." And they read *Scribner's* magazine. Although Mahala was barred from traveling much because of a physical handicap, her siblings and friends went to town to see "Barnum's [Circus] Show" and an orchestra in Bloomington. Stepsister Magdalena even found a social outlet in political party politics. Around election day, 1876, she spent "all afternoon . . . doing up her white dress and making a cap and sash." The next day she was going to a Republican "mass meeting at Bloomington" as part of a delegation of "twenty-nine girls in uniform to represent the states of the Union."

Mahala was able to go to church, and her comments on its services also reveal evolving Amish Mennonite attitudes. Not much longer would congregations be satisfied with preachers who stumbled through traditional sermons or spoke extemporaneously. Mahala strongly approved when a visiting preacher addressed the Stuckey congregation using "pure, rich German . . . which did one's soul good to hear." Proper German or standard English were fine by Mahala, but not the "horrid 'Pennsylvania Dutch'" dialect that she so much detested. Ethnic dialects only detracted from worship. She believed that her "church-going" did her "more good because the sermon was delivered in simple, correct language." To Mahala's way of thinking, "The beautiful goes with the good and true, always, in God's method." Beyond proper sermons, Yoder also received theological insight from reading contemporary novels—one of which she found "as helpful and encouraging and suggestive as so many chapters of the Bible." She wondered why some Amish Mennonites were "ashamed to read a good novel." But her wonderment only betrayed how removed Mahala's generation was from traditional Amish understandings that viewed secular entertainment as frivolous, wasteful, and perhaps even dangerous.

Ripples of reservation

Central Illinois was not the only place where Amish Mennonites were becoming more heavily involved in the goings-on of larger society. Near Johnstown, Pennsylvania, Amish Mennonite Isaac Kaufman involved himself in financing toll roads, Johnstown's First National Bank, and various federal bond programs. As an important local financier, Kaufman's portrait hung in the lobby of the Johnstown bank. His heirs received $246,000 from their money-wise forebear.[7] And in eastern Pennsylvania, the Conestoga Amish Mennonite congregation had a bishop, John "Johnny P." Mast, who served as a local bank director and successful miller.[8]

While such commercially successful financial activity was remarkable even for Amish Mennonites, it illustrates the general acceptance of upward mobility among church members. In the early nineteenth century, a number of Amish had always engaged in business and politics, or had purchased the latest in household furnishings. But then there had been some resistance to doing so, and even an Old Order reaction against it. Since 1865, Amish Mennonite circles included fewer voices willing to speak words of caution. In 1889, the Oak Grove Amish Mennonite congregation in Ohio's Wayne County even granted seven lay members the privilege of formulating a new, more relaxed church discipline.[9]

In their later years, some of the older, first generation Amish Mennonite leaders became alarmed that so much change had come so quickly into their congregations. The rapid pace of innovation among the next generations of Amish Mennonites unnerved old *Diener-Versammlungen* promoters "Tennessee John" Stoltzfus and John P. King.[10] Early leaders like Stoltzfus and King had envisioned a church guided by moderate progressive philosophy, not a wholesale loss of Amish Mennonite values. Nevertheless, as the nineteenth century's last decades closed, Amish Mennonites were taking more hints from the larger society as they organized and operated their churches.

One reaction against the liberal "drift" of the Amish Mennonites came from a number of highly unusual Amish Mennonite lay members known as "sleeping preachers," who

Amish Mennonites Daniel Graber (1858-1930) and Fanny Conrad Graber (1871-1943) of Wayland, Iowa, about 1890. Daniel served as minister in the Sugar Creek Amish Mennonite Church for 37 years and preferred preaching in German.

addressed audiences while in a deep, sleep-like trance. Convinced that their unconscious sermons were messages from the Lord, these preachers and their adherents preferred to describe the phenomenon as "Spirit preaching." Typically the Spirit preacher would appear to fall asleep early in the evening, only to rise several hours later and begin to preach (in German or English) on the themes of repentance, spiritual renewal, or the return to simpler lifestyles.[11]

Two of the best-known Spirit preachers were Noah Troyer of Johnson County, Iowa, and John D. Kauffman of Elkhart County, Indiana.[12] Troyer began preaching in 1878 and Kauffman in 1880. Both men claimed to have no knowledge of what happened during their ecstatic states, who listened to them, or what they said. Other Amish Mennonites affirmed the Spirit preachers' messages with revelations of their own. Barbara (Hochstetler) Stutzman, for example, claimed to have received a deathbed revelation which confirmed the Spirit-preaching truth of Kauffman.[13] A member of Elkhart County's Clinton Frame Amish Mennonite Church, Stutzman was disturbed by her congregation's rapid pace of change.[14]

To be sure, the Spirit preachers were not Old Orders, and they did not ask their listeners to forsake the general change-minded agenda. Nor were their messages identical. Troyer, for example, focused more on the need for personal conviction and commitment on the part of Amish Mennonite faithful, while Kauffman's sermons centered on avoiding the temptations of "worldly" luxury and individual pride. In either case, Spirit preaching emerged and found an audience among people experiencing unsettling change and transition from traditional ways.[15]

For the true believers, Spirit preaching was nothing less than divine revelation. For the doubters, men like Troyer and Kauffman were either victims of self-induced hypnosis or charlatans. But Spirit preaching was a phenomenon in other groups during the period, too. In nineteenth-century Europe and

North America, Spirit preaching occurred among various Protestant denominations and even to a degree among Native Americans' so-called "Ghost Dancers." The Amish Mennonites were not alone in their experience.[16]

Most Amish Mennonites eventually discounted the Spirit preachers. In fact, local opposition to Kauffman forced him to move to Shelby County, Illinois, in 1907. There Kauffman and his followers formed their own congregation, nicknamed the "Sleeping Preacher Amish" or the "Kauffman Amish." The group later spread to other parts of the Midwest and remains active today, although the practice of Spirit preaching itself has long since ceased in the group. Though they now drive cars, members of the loose network of Kauffman churches maintain fairly plain dress and lifestyle traditions reminiscent of nineteenth-century Amish Mennonite custom.[17]

Progressives in institution-building

Remarkable as the "sleeping preachers" were, they represented few Amish Mennonite interests or intentions. Instead, many were caught up in the craze of creating, supporting, or endowing church institutions. Institution-building occupied the time and energy of a great many Americans during the late nineteenth century. States organized university systems. Banks and businesses formed dozens of new corporations, trusts, and holding companies. Charitable organizations created inner-city settlement houses. Special interest groups—from the National Geographic Society to the American Federation of Labor—formed during this period. Churches were not immune from the spirit of the age, forming national denominational offices, publications, schools, and programs at a rate until then unparalleled in American history.

The Amish Mennonites were institution-builders as well—even cooperating at times with fellow Mennonites who were also hard at work creating their own institutional world. News of these organizations and their often cooperative underpinnings

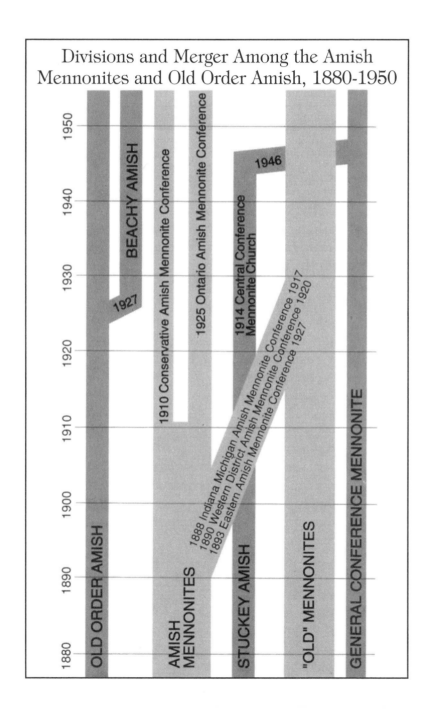

Divisions and Merger Among the Amish
Mennonites and Old Order Amish, 1880-1950

traveled through new churchly magazines subscribed to by both groups. In fact, so many Amish Mennonites read the Mennonite periodical *Herald of Truth* (and its German language companion *Herold der Wahrheit*) that for a time its editor listed the paper as the "Organ of 14 Mennonite and Amish Conferences," even though it never really held any such official status.[18]

The Amish Mennonite "conferences" to which the *Herald's* masthead referred were real Amish Mennonite creations, however. Consolidating congregations into denominational structures was one of the major Amish Mennonite tasks of the 1880s and 1890s. Absorbing the pulse and feel of larger society, the Amish Mennonites were quick to adopt apparatus and programs that clearly marked their divergence from the style and tenor of the Old Order. The demise of the *Diener-Versammlungen* had not brought Amish Mennonite conversation or connectedness to an end, and not long after 1878, new structures were taking the place of the old ministers' meetings.

Perhaps taking their cues from the regionally-organized Mennonites who reported their church activities in the *Herald*, the Amish Mennonites began holding conferences on a regional, rather than national, level. Three geographically-based Amish Mennonite groups were soon meeting on a frequent basis. In 1888, the Indiana-Michigan group formed itself into a fully constituted body known as the Indiana-Michigan Amish Mennonite Conference. Two years later, the Western District Amish Mennonite Conference followed, with members in Illinois, Iowa, Missouri, Arkansas, Kansas, Oklahoma, Nebraska, Colorado, and Oregon.[19] Including a few Pennsylvania congregations in its ranks, the Ohio Amish Mennonites in 1893 became the Eastern Amish Mennonite Conference. Ohio bishop John K. Yoder, so active in the workings of the earlier *Diener-Versammlungen*, played a role in the new Eastern Amish Mennonite organization and provided some continuity between the old ministers' meetings and the new Conference.

Each of the new groups met regularly, had elected moderators and secretaries, and acted as autonomous, self-governing
bodies. Often leaders from one of the other Amish Mennonite
conferences—or even from a Mennonite conference—attended
particular regional meetings, demonstrating the mutual regard
and companionship the conferences felt for one another. By
creating formal conference structures, the Amish Mennonites
were one step closer to being indistinguishable from the
Mennonites. Earlier, the Amish Mennonites had emphasized
the congregational autonomy that was a part of their Amish
heritage. Now, by adopting the Mennonite model of regional
conference authority and structure, the progressive Amish
built another bridge of connection with the Mennonites and
further distanced themselves from their own past.

Another field in which the Amish Mennonites joined in the
American penchant for institution-building was higher education. While most Amish had long supported local public elementary schools, and some Amish served as teachers or school
directors at the township level, higher education that cultivated critical thinking and upward social mobility was a different
matter. Not all Amish Mennonites immediately supported
efforts toward formal, advanced education, but a significant
number did. Schooling beyond the elementary level was
uncommon for all Americans before 1900 (in 1900 only 6.3
percent of all 17-year-old Americans graduated from high
school), but especially for the Amish, who often downplayed
the value of worldly knowledge.[20]

By the turn of the century, several signs pointed toward an
Amish Mennonite interest in formal education. When able,
more Amish Mennonite youth enrolled in high schools, teachers' colleges ("normal schools"), or universities. Wayne
County's sizable Oak Grove Amish Mennonite Church had a
significant number of young people attend Ada Normal School
(now Ohio Northern University) and the College of Wooster.[21]
Amish Mennonite leaders were also at the forefront of one of

the first Mennonite secondary schools in America. Elkhart Institute, a private high school opened in 1894 in Elkhart, Indiana, had a board of directors comprised of four Amish Mennonites and nine Mennonites. While some western Amish Mennonites initially had reservations about the school, by 1899 the Indiana-Michigan Amish Mennonite Conference was recommending attendance at Elkhart for its youth who aspired to continue their studies.[22] One of the Institute's instructors, C. Henry Smith, was an Amish Mennonite who had pursued advanced degrees.[23]

Common cause

As the twentieth century approached, Amish Mennonites increased their cooperation with the Mennonites. Men and women from both groups participated in joint Sunday school leaders' gatherings where they shared ideas and materials. At other times, neighboring Mennonite and Amish Mennonite ministers exchanged pulpits during Sunday services. In other cases, churches from both groups invited preaching teams composed of one Mennonite and one Amish Mennonite minister to hold a series of "protracted meetings"—revival services held several nights in a row. Mennonite bishop John F. Funk and Amish Mennonite bishop Daniel J. Johns were one of the first such teams. Amish Mennonite bishops Jonathan P. Smucker and Jonathan Kurtz also frequently participated in such arrangements, as did Mennonite John S. Coffman.[24]

Such teamwork was not without its hitches. Visiting preachers were supposed to encourage teens and young adults to join their families' congregations. In 1890 in the Logan County, Ohio, Amish Mennonite community, several youth responded to Johns's and Funk's invitation to follow Christ and join the church. However, the young men and women reported that they wished to join a Mennonite congregation, not the Amish Mennonite church of their parents. After much embarrassed deliberation, the visiting preachers suggested that local Amish

The family of Amish Mennonites Samuel J. Miller (1842-1924) and Barbara Yoder Miller (1842-1923), front row, McPherson County, Kansas. Of the couple's 10 children, five joined Mennonite churches, four chose the Church of the Brethren, and one did not affiliate with any group. Two sons-in-law are also pictured.

Mennonite leaders allow the young people to form a separate and officially Mennonite fellowship—which they did under the name Bethel Mennonite Church.[25]

The controversy in Logan County pointed up the fact that "Amish Mennonite" and "Mennonite" were still not completely interchangeable designations. In many places, the Amish Mennonites still dressed a bit more conservatively, their men wore beards, and many were still committed in principle to shunning—although the actual practice of shunning by Amish Mennonites quickly and quietly fell into disuse.[26] In some places, the Mennonites were perceived to be the more progressive group. Especially for those young people interested in institution-building, the larger resources—human and material—of the Mennonites were appealing. Mission interests among the Mennonites also ran strong (by 1899 they would have medical missionaries in India), and so those Amish Mennonites interested in international outreach felt a close kinship with the Mennonites.

For several decades, a few Amish Mennonites and Mennonites had been suggesting the merger of their two groups. Perhaps the first published appeal for such union had come in 1864 from the pen of Elkhart, Indiana, Amish Mennonite minister John Ringenberg. Then, at the 1866 *Diener-Versammlung,* there had been talk of bringing the Amish Mennonites and Mennonites "into a closer union," but nothing concrete resulted.[27] In 1874, the Indiana Mennonite Conference invited any "Amish brethren who are of one mind with us" to participate in Mennonite communion services.[28] Three years before, a Mennonite leader had written of his "Omish [sic] brethren," adding, "Now there may be some who think that we are out of place by calling the Omish, brethren." However, in his opinion his church "should not be too ready to censure [the Amish Mennonites]." In fact, "if there was more visiting done [between the two groups], there would be more union of thought," he was sure.[29] Indeed, since the 1860s, the traveling Illinois Amish Mennonite schoolteacher Christian Erismann had referred to his people simply as "Mennonites."

Some "union of thought" did develop on the local level as a few Mennonite and Amish Mennonite congregations quietly merged. In 1886, the *Herald of Truth* reported on a congregation in northern Michigan's Antrim County in which both Mennonites and Amish Mennonites had managed their own merger and formed a joint congregation. They were "willing to join hand in hand, and be united as one body in the Lord," the paper reported. Their traditional distinctions no longer seemed to matter.[30]

Sometimes local unity efforts were the result of the decline of one or another of the groups. "Tennessee John" Stoltzfus' Knox County, Tennessee, community languished and nearly died after the old leader's passing. The appearance of a Mennonite minister and several Virginia Mennonite families revived the group's health and changed its character; the whole group simply became Mennonite. And after 1900, when a few Ontario Amish families moved west to Saskatchewan and Alberta, they joined existing local Mennonite congregations rather than establishing new Amish Mennonite ones.[31] Whatever the reasons, congregations and families from both groups were growing closer together.

Amish Mennonite and "old" Mennonite unity

Increasing joint ventures and a growing sense of common spirit led more and more Amish Mennonites and Mennonites to consider formally uniting their two groups and to take serious steps in that direction. This merging of traditions followed several paths, but for the sizable majority of Amish Mennonites, the obvious partner in any such churchly integration were the so-called "old" Mennonites.[32] Not to be confused with "Old Order," the designation "old" described the largest and oldest existing Mennonite body in North America. Most of its members were of Swiss and south German descent—the very people with whom the Amish had originally divided in Europe. Over the years, for various reasons, both conservative and progressive minorities had split from the "old" Mennonites, so that by 1900, the "old" Mennonites represented a rather middle-of-the-road Mennonite church. Organized into about a dozen fairly autonomous regional conferences, the "old" Mennonites possessed a structure that allowed them to move toward merger with the Amish Mennonites in a way that respected local timing and regional pace.

After 1898, most of the "old" Mennonite regional conferences met together for biennial North American-wide gatherings, and Amish Mennonite leaders attended as invited and expected guests. These contacts only added to the many examples of local community cooperation and paved the way for the eventual uniting of the two groups in the first quarter of the twentieth century.[33]

In 1917, the Indiana-Michigan Amish Mennonite Conference merged with its "old" Mennonite counterpart. The new group's name—Indiana-Michigan Mennonite Conference— did not acknowledge the Amish heritage of half its members. But that designation was not necessarily the result of Mennonites trying to squash Amish identity. Apparently many of the new conference's former Amish Mennonite members were ready to forget their past. For example, Noah Long, trustee of the Clinton Frame Amish Mennonite Church in Elkhart County, Indiana, removed the word "Amish" from the meetinghouse sign only a day or two after his conference voted to merge with the Mennonites.[34] Long's congregation wasted no time in letting passers-by know that Clinton Frame was no longer Amish.

The Western District Amish Mennonite Conference was the next to dissolve itself into a new Mennonite family. In 1920, the Western District Amish Mennonites and "old" Mennonites living west of Indiana reshuffled their organizations and formed five new Mennonite conferences, each with joint Amish Mennonite and "old" Mennonite membership. The Amish Mennonites outnumbered the "old" Mennonites 4,400 to 2,800 in these new groups, so there was somewhat less drive to surrender Amish identity.[35] Several Amish Mennonite con- gregations continued to use their historic "Amish" name for a time, and for several years, one of the five new western groups, the Iowa-Nebraska Conference, used neither the word "Amish" nor "Mennonite" in its name so as not to offend either party.[36]

In 1927, the Eastern Amish Mennonite Conference brought Mennonite-Amish merger to Ohio and Pennsylvania. In that year, Amish Mennonites in those two states fused their confer- ence with the Ohio "old" Mennonite body. The new group judi- ciously acknowledged both halves of its constituency, using the name Ohio Mennonite and Eastern Amish Mennonite Joint

Conference. By mid-century, though, any Amish Mennonite identity was so far removed from most members that the conference simplified its title to Ohio and Eastern Mennonite Conference.[37]

The Canadian Amish Mennonites represented a fourth example of regional identification with the Mennonite tradition. The Ontario Amish Mennonite Conference did not immediately merge with the "old" Mennonite conference in its province, choosing instead to retain its distinct organization. But the group did work more closely with neighboring Mennonites as the century wore on, and by 1963 it had dropped the word "Amish" from its name, becoming known instead as the Western Ontario Mennonite Conference.[38]

Thus, in a few short years during the early 1900s, several thousand people knowingly or unknowingly lost their historic Amish faith identity. This was one of the most profound legacies of the merger of the two groups. As historian Paton Yoder, himself a child of an Amish Mennonite home, has lamented, the Amish Mennonites paid the price of a lost heritage and "covered their tracks" in the process of becoming Mennonites so quickly. Now Yoder "and all other Mennonites with Amish Mennonite roots, find it necessary to uncover these tracks" in order "to discover—or rediscover—[their] Amish and Amish Mennonite origins."[39]

But the unity of the Amish Mennonite conferences with the "old" Mennonites was also one of far-reaching impact for the Mennonites. The addition of 7,500 to 8,000 Amish Mennonites increased the size of the "old" Mennonites significantly. While the "old" Mennonites had been the largest Mennonite group in 1900, they had not been much bigger than the next largest body. With the absorption of the Amish Mennonites, however, the "old" Mennonites clearly became the largest North American Mennonite group. Had the Amish Mennonite congregations not augmented the "old" Mennonite church in the early 1900s, it is doubtful the "old" Mennonites would have had the resources necessary to engage in the various twentieth century activities they later did. Then, too, an often latent Amish predilection for congregational authority—buried though it had been in the change-minded Amish Mennonite conferences—continued in many local Amish Mennonite-turned-Mennonite congregations. The addition of this congregational impulse to "old" Mennonite life would have a significant impact on Mennonite polity and politics for years to come.

The Conservative Amish Mennonites

Some Amish Mennonites were hesitant to unite so quickly with the "old" Mennonites. They were progressive-minded to a degree, adopting meetinghouses, Sunday schools, and organized mission work, but often they retained German-language worship, conservative clothing standards, and other marks of traditional Amish church life. Typically, they were less certain

Lunch at a Conservative Amish Mennonite Conference Sunday school meeting, Grantsville, Maryland, in 1912.

that the benefits of higher education outweighed its unsettling influence on community, and in churchly affairs they wanted to retain more local congregational autonomy. These "conservative" Amish Mennonites were certainly not Old Order, but neither were they completely comfortable with the Amish Mennonite groups that seemed to emphasize immediate unity with the Mennonites.

In 1910, representatives of three such conservative-leaning Amish Mennonite congregations met in Pigeon, Michigan, and formed a loose fellowship under the banner Conservative Amish Mennonite Conference.[40] With leadership from Pigeon's bishop Solomon J. Swartzendruber, the Conservative Conference grew to include congregations throughout the Midwest and Mid-Atlantic regions. An important center of Conservative Amish Mennonite membership was Lewis County, New York. The sizable Amish community there had never associated closely with the *Diener-Versammlungen* or other Amish Mennonite groups.

Later, other congregations joined the new conference, and both tradition-minded Amish Mennonites and progressive-thinking Old Orders found a middle ground in the Conservative Conference. For a time, some churches in Ontario considered membership in the Conservative Conference, but then decided against it. Interestingly, the Canadian Amish Mennonites were a bit unsure of taking on the name "Conservative Conference" because they feared the title would link them with their nation's Conservative Party and its politics. Such were the difficulties of international church work: a common descriptive word in one society held powerful political connotations in another.

On one level, the Conservative Amish Mennonite Conference followed the larger Mennonite and Amish Mennonite pattern of church work and institution-building, but at a slower pace. In 1914, Conference churches opened a home for orphans, and an official mission board charged with sponsoring domestic and foreign mission activities followed four years later. In 1952, the Conference opened a Bible school near Berlin, Ohio (later moved to Irwin, Ohio, and now known as Rosedale Bible College).

By 1954, most members had decided that the word "Amish" in the Conference title held little meaning and shortened their name to Conservative Mennonite Conference. Unofficial connections and official cooperation with the "old" Mennonites took place in the decades that followed, but the Conservative Conference increasingly took on a denominational life of its own. In the early twenty-first century, some members of the Conservative Conference find identity primarily in conservative evangelical theology, while others seek to link those convictions to some measure of "nonconformity" to the world in dress, education, and entertainment choices.[41]

Amish links to the General Conference Mennonite Church

While the majority of Amish Mennonites who moved toward union with the Mennonites chose to merge or affiliate with the "old" Mennonites, some chose other paths. For the more progressive Stuckey Amish, and several independent Amish congregations in Ohio and Iowa, the road to cooperation led to the General Conference Mennonite Church.[42]

Organized in 1860 in West Point, Iowa, the General Conference (GC) was the fruit of progressive Pennsylvania and Midwest Mennonites to form a denomination strongly supportive of higher education and organized mission work, while allowing a great deal of congregational autonomy in matters of discipline and everyday life. By accenting congregational authority, the General Conference took a position in line with historic Amish understandings. Of course, among the Old Order Amish, congregational autonomy was checked by deference to the *Ordnung*; GC congregationalism, in contrast, promised relatively more freedom and individualism.

The Amish Mennonites
Merge with the Mennonites

1865 Egly Amish division.

1872 Joseph Stuckey Amish division.

1888 Indiana-Michigan Amish Mennonite Conference forms.

1890 Western Amish Mennonite Conference forms, including congregations in Illinois, Iowa, Missouri, Arkansas, Nebraska, Kansas, Oklahoma, Colorado, and Oregon.

1893 Eastern Amish Mennonite Conference forms, including congregations in Ohio and Pennsylvania.

1908 Egly Amish become Defenseless Mennonite Church.

1908 Stuckey Amish become Central Illinois Mennonite Conference.

1910 Conservative Amish Mennonite Conference forms.

1914 Central Illinois Mennonite Conference becomes Central Conference Mennonite Church.

1917 Indiana-Michigan Amish Mennonite Conference merges with the Indiana Mennonite Conference to form the Indiana-Michigan Mennonite Conference.

1920 Western Amish Mennonite Conference merges with several Mennonite conferences in Illinois, Iowa-Missouri, Kansas-Nebraska, and Oregon.

1925 Ontario Amish Mennonite Conference forms.

1927 Eastern Amish Mennonite Conference merges with the Ohio Mennonite Conference to form the Ohio Mennonite and Eastern Amish Mennonite Joint Conference.

1946 Central Conference Mennonite Church joins the General Conference Mennonite Church.

1948 Defenseless Mennonite Church becomes Evangelical Mennonite Church.

1954 Conservative Amish Mennonite Conference becomes Conservative Mennonite Conference.

1955 Ohio Mennonite and Eastern Amish Mennonite Joint Conference becomes Ohio and Eastern Mennonite Conference.

1963 Ontario Amish Mennonite Conference becomes Western Ontario Mennonite Conference.

Initially, the General Conference included members of Swiss and south German ethnic backgrounds, and it remained fairly small until 1874. Then the arrival of several thousand Russian Mennonite immigrants who joined the General Conference swelled GC ranks. This irenic-spirited, multiethnic, progressive Mennonite group attracted liberal Amish Mennonite congregations. By 1884, Butler County, Ohio, Amish leader Peter Schrock was attending General Conference Mennonite meetings, and members of his own Augspurger Amish congregation and the neighboring Hessian Amish church were subscribing to the GC periodical *Christlicher Bundesbote.* Several years later, the Butler County Amish adopted the GC hymnal.[43]

In 1892, the Hessian Amish congregation—renamed Apostolic Mennonite Church—relieved its three untrained Amish leaders of ministerial responsibilities and called Iowa-born Mennonite Henry J. Krehbiel as its new pastor. Krehbiel had just graduated from Evangelical Theological Seminary (now Eden Theological Seminary) in St. Louis, Missouri, and was one of the few seminary-trained Mennonites in North America. That same year, the Apostolic Mennonite Church joined the General Conference, and five years later the neighboring Augspurger Amish Mennonite congregation merged with it.[44]

Two independent Amish churches in Washington and Davis counties, Iowa, also affiliated with the General Conference Mennonites. Under the progressive leadership of bishop Benjamin Eicher and preacher Philip Roulet, these churches had become disenchanted with the Amish Mennonite ministers' meetings of 1862-1878, considering the gatherings too conservative. Eicher attended the 1874 *Diener-Versammlung* session held in his home county, but registered as an observer, not a participating leader. A newspaper reporter covering the gathering described Eicher as "a man of broad and liberal views," one "who has rebelled against the old custom."[45] By then, Eicher had been attending GC meetings and had become interested in world missions. In 1893, his Amish church, under the name Emmanuel Mennonite, joined the General Conference.[46]

Other independent Amish congregations were following suit. In 1888, Davis County Amish preacher Roulet had invited a General Conference itinerant evangelist to conduct eight days of special meetings with his Amish group. The response of the congregation was so positive that formal unity with the General Conference soon followed.[47] And before the nineteenth century ended, GC Mennonites had received additional churches of Amish Mennonite background.[48]

The Central Illinois Amish Mennonite Conference

A slower, more measured merger with Mennonitism took place among the collection of Amish congregations associated with bishop Joseph Stuckey, the beloved McLean County, Illinois, leader affectionately known as "Father Stuckey."[49] Despite his falling-out with Amish Mennonite leaders in 1872 over his leniency with Joseph Joder, Stuckey did not break all contact with fellow Amish Mennonites. While he never attended another ministers' meeting, he did occasionally preach in some of the very congregations whose leaders had expelled him. Some returned the favor. In 1889, at a service in Stuckey's own church (by then named North Danvers), visiting Wayne County, Ohio, bishop John K. Yoder preached to an audience that included Stuckey and Illinois Amish Mennonite leader Christian Ropp.[50] Just 17 years earlier, Ropp had asked Yoder to come and investigate Stuckey's handling of church affairs, an investigation that had led to Ropp's and Yoder's breaking fellowship with the North Danvers bishop.

Despite such signs of forgiveness and healed relationships, Stuckey and the several Illinois Amish congregations aligned with North Danvers never joined the larger Amish Mennonite conference movement represented by Yoder and Ropp. Instead, Stuckey was drawn to the activities of the General

Conference Mennonites.[51] His articles appeared more frequently in the pages of the GC periodical and less often in the
"old" Mennonite *Herald of Truth.* Traveling GC preachers often
filled Stuckey's pulpit. In 1890, Stuckey's North Danvers
church filed an annual report with the General Conference,
and eight years later North Danvers hosted a regional GC
meeting.[52]

The open stance of the General Conference on matters of
dress and church organization appealed to Stuckey and his
broad-minded friends. While the bishop himself retained his
beard and somewhat traditional Amish garb, members of his
congregation quickly adapted their styles and patterns to the
larger society. Within Stuckey's lifetime, female members of
his churches stopped wearing devotional prayer coverings, and
the dress of male members became indistinguishable from
their non-Amish neighbors.[53] Yet the Stuckey Amish maintained a clear sense of identity and connection to one another
that was rooted in their common history and regional cluster-
ing in central Illinois. So while they were eager to cooperate
with Mennonites, they resisted a formal union that might have
resulted in their being swallowed up by another conference.

Father Stuckey's death in 1902 did not stunt the group's
growth. Six years later the Stuckey fellowship had 12 congregations and adopted a formal constitution and new name:
Central Illinois Conference of Mennonites (later shortened to
Central Conference Mennonite Church).[54] The new Central
Conference embarked on an ambitious program of work and
witness. The Conference opened city missions in Chicago and
Peoria, and by 1912 its mission board was sending overseas
workers to the Belgian Congo (now Democratic Republic of
Congo) in cooperation with the Defenseless Mennonites.[55] A
similar partnership with the Defenseless Mennonites spawned
the Mennonite Hospital in Bloomington, Illinois.[56] Stuckey's
spiritual heirs also supported the General Conference
Mennonite college at Bluffton, Ohio.[57]

In time, Central Conference (Stuckey Amish) ties to the GC Mennonites grew stronger, and in 1946, the one-time Amish congregations of the Central Conference decided officially to join the General Conference Mennonites Church.[58]

From Egly Amish to
Fellowship of Evangelical Churches

Not all change-minded Amish merged with other Mennonite groups. The supporters of bishop Henry Egly, in fact, evolved their own expression of Mennonite faithfulness. The churches allied with Egly had always had a unique flavor stemming from their blend of revivalism, evangelical fervor, and Amish background.[59] Under Egly's leadership, the loose association of congregations known as the Egly Amish retained an informal sense of organization. Sunday schools gained gradual acceptance as did church buildings.

In some ways the Egly people remained close to their Amish roots. For example, Egly Amish meetinghouses often included a kitchen and dining area in which families remained after Sunday services to enjoy a common meal, continuing in a modified way the old Amish practice of eating a noon church meal together after worship. The Egly congregations also remained traditionally Amish in their attitude toward attire and worldly fashion. In 1883 an early conference of Egly-affiliated churches adopted strict standards of nonconformity. Male church members were not to neglect beards and women could not discard prayer coverings. As one historian observed, during "Egly's lifetime his people appear to have learned from revivalism without departing radically from Amish faith and practice."[60]

But after Egly died in 1890, the fellowship of churches he had shepherded changed rapidly. A series of annual business meetings convened after 1895, a church periodical *Zion's Call* began publication two years later, and the group took on an official name—Defenseless Mennonite Church—that did not

2003 when the denomination dropped its Mennonite label in favor of the name Fellowship of Evangelical Churches.[64] For many members, it seemed, any links to an Amish past had long disappeared.

The path of the European Amish

All the while North American Amish Mennonites were joining neighboring Mennonite groups, a somewhat similar pattern was taking shape in Europe. In the Old World, no Old Order Amish group ever developed; all the European Amish took the path of merger with the Mennonites. The European Mennonites (like most of their North American cousins) had always been more a part of the social mainstream than had the Amish. Thus, as the European Amish became more acculturated and gave up many of their distinctive dress and worship practices, they rather naturally identified with the Mennonites. The distinctive Amish practices of simple apparel, full beards for men, and hook-and-

C. Michel Richard (1829-1913) and Francoise Conrad Richard (1828-1906), members of the Montbéliard, France, Amish community.

George Guth (1836-1871) and Magdalena Oesch Guth (1844-1870) lived near Bitsche in the French Lorraine region and were members of the Ixheim Amish congregation. Both died of typhoid fever as a result of the Franco-Prussian War.

eye coats gradually fell into disuse among the spiritual heirs of Jakob Ammann. One practice that continued to distinguish Amish from Mennonites was the observance of footwashing as a part of communion. The European Mennonites did not hold a literal footwashing service, but the Amish always did.

Amish membership in Europe probably peaked in 1850, with some 5,000 members in Alsace and Lorraine alone.[65] Thereafter, numbers declined, and emigration played a key role in draining membership and leadership from many congregations.[66] Although steady emigration trailed off after 1860, throughout the late nineteenth century, scattered Amish individuals and families continued to leave for North America (where virtually all joined progressive Amish Mennonite congregations in the Midwestern United States).[67] In time, the drive to emigrate faded as European Amish increasingly felt at home as citizens and cultural participants. Young Amishman Christian M. Nafziger fled German conscription in 1883 and ended up in New York's Lewis County Amish Mennonite settlement, but many other European members of his church came to terms with military service.[68] Nor was the world of politics completely foreign. In the 1880s, fellow citizens elected Amish elder Peter Schlabbach to the Prussian legislature. Within a decade, Schlabbach's Hessian congregation had merged with the Mennonites.[69]

Indeed, few Amish were left in Hesse, once a territory with a high concentration of the church's members. The few hundred Amish remaining there during the second half of the nineteenth century, like Peter Schlabbach, gradually came to identify themselves with neighboring Mennonites, or else joined socially respectable Lutheran state churches. Many Hessian Amish congregations were quite conscious of their move toward Mennonitism. At a May 1867 Amish ministers' conference held in the Hessian town of Offenthal, 17 leaders from six Amish churches discussed ways to adapt church practices and unite with the Mennonites.[70]

Of the Offenthal Conference's 10-point agreement, four items were especially telling. Regarding footwashing, the conferees decided that "It shall be left to each congregation whether it is to be literally carried out" or not. As a symbol of servanthood, footwashing might be a fine idea, "But it shall not be the basis of a future division," the leaders decided. On the subject of military participation, the conference offered no clear word. "We leave to the careful consideration of each one," the delegates wrote, how "to do justice first to his own conscience and then also to the government." In a world of moral ambiguities and conflicting claims to loyalty, the church would leave such ponderous choices to individual young men. In two other decisions, the Offenthal gathering approved religiously-mixed marriages and rejected social shunning in favor of merely excluding the excommunicated from communion. Most of the congregations represented at Offenthal died out in a decade or two; the few that survived became Mennonite. By 1900, no Amish congregations existed in Hesse.

Likewise, the Bavarian Amish declined rapidly during the nineteenth century. By the mid-1800s, two of the kingdom's three congregations had nearly dissolved, due simply to heavy emigration to Illinois and Ontario. A third church, near Regensburg, was still 200 members strong in 1888, but was quickly losing its Amish distinctiveness. Regensburg member Josef Gingerich long remembered his turn-of-the-century boyhood when "a considerable number left the [Amish] church."[71] In 1908, Gingerich's congregation both ceased the observance of footwashing and formally joined the German Mennonite Conference.

A number of fairly small Amish congregations remained in the French Lorraine, Alsace, and Montbéliard regions, but they, too, found themselves working more closely with German Mennonites. Especially after 1871, when Alsace came under German rule and Lorraine remained French, church connections were divided politically. A new 1872 military conscription law drew little reaction from the Alsatian Amish. Excommunication became rare in the closing decades of the nineteenth century, and often the church implemented strict discipline only in cases of religiously-mixed marriages.[72]

In 1896, the originally-Amish congregations in Alsace, Lorraine, and Basel, Switzerland, created a regional conference. Formally constituted in 1907, the Alsatian-based conference considered itself Mennonite, despite its historic Amish background. Two other small Amish congregations remaining in Switzerland joined the Swiss Mennonite Conference. The two fellowships— Mennonite and Amish—were quietly reuniting after two centuries of separation, but the reunion was always on Mennonite terms.[73] Not every vestige of Amish heritage disappeared immediately. Often Mennonite churches of Amish background continued the Amish practice of footwashing as a part of the Lord's Supper. The Luxembourg Amish-turned-Mennonites, for example, observed footwashing as late as 1941.[74] Still, the connection to any Amish heritage was faint or foggy for most.

The last European Amish

The few Amish congregations that survived into the twentieth century soon dissolved or merged with surrounding Mennonite groups. The old Bitscherland Amish congregation in Bitsche, Alsace, dissolved after its elder Christian Schantz died in 1902.[75] Seven years later, another Amish fellowship, Hornbach-Zweibrücken, also ceased meeting after the death of its elder Christian Stalter. The deaths of preachers Christian Jordy and Johannes Guth also signaled the demise of the Frönsburg congregation in the Vosges Mountains on the French-German border; worship services ended there in 1929.[76] In many of these places, members who wanted to maintain some ties with an Amish fellowship traveled occasionally to worship with the Ixheim or Saar Amish. Then, in 1936, the Saar and Ixheim congregations themselves merged, having a combined membership of 134.[77] Ixheim now represented the lone Amish congregation in Europe since all others had affiliated with the Mennonite conferences in Alsace, Lorraine, or south Germany.

Meetinghouse, built about 1844, used by the Ixheim Amish until 1937 when the group united with local Mennonites.

Long one of the most traditional Amish congregations, the Ixheim church continued to ordain unsalaried, untrained leaders, and at least in theory held to the social shunning of excommunicated members. Until 1932, they still included a footwashing service as part of their communion observance, and some men wore

Jakob Schönbeck (1902-1981) of Ingweilerhof, Germany, was one of the last people baptized into the Ixheim Amish congregation before the group merged with neighboring Mennonites.

beards. But Ixheim, too, was considering giving up its independent Amish identity. Serious consideration began after 1929 when Ixheim member Ernst Guth married Mennonite Susanna Weiss. Weiss' Mennonite pastor Hugo Scheffler met with Amish elder Christian Guth to discuss the wedding, since the Ixheim Amish did not approve of mixed marriages. Rather surprisingly to Scheffler, the conversation resulted in Amish openness to officially recognizing and cooperating with the Mennonites.

On January 17, 1937, after several years of dialogue, the Ixheim Amish church and the nearby Ernstweiler Mennonite congregation united as a single fellowship, taking the name Zweibrücken Mennonite Church. One week later, during a special unity service, the two groups sang together, shared a common meal, listened to Mennonite brass instrumentalists, and watched a slide show about the previous year's Mennonite World Conference gathering. Amish elder Guth read a statement of unity, and Mennonite pastor Scheffler officially took over leadership of the new group. The Amish church in Europe lost any distinct existence.[78]

Sociologist John A. Hostetler once suggested that such a loss of European Amish identity was perhaps to be expected. Being primarily farm-renters, the Amish in Europe were not always able to live close to one another, existing instead on scattered farms and some distance apart. Most of their neighbors were members of other, established churches. The lack of close contact may have worked against the development of a strong church solidarity and left them more vulnerable to the influences of the surrounding culture and the state. The European Amish, like their North American Amish Mennonite cousins, embraced Western assumptions about the goodness of technological progress, educational advancement, and social mobility. Unable to develop a durable sense of community and peoplehood, the European Amish lost their reason for being a distinct church.[79]

Within the first few decades of the twentieth century, Amish Mennonites on both sides of the Atlantic had dropped their

C. Henry Smith, Ph.D.

One of the best known children of the Amish Mennonite church was C. Henry Smith—educator, banker, historian, and first Mennonite to earn a doctor of philosophy degree from an American university.

The son of Amish Mennonite bishop John and Magdalena (Schertz) Smith, Henry grew up in the Partridge Creek Amish Mennonite Church near Metamora, Illinois. He joined his parents' church at age 15 and remained a member for about a decade before affiliating with the Mennonites. He was married to Laura Ioder of Tiskilwa, Illinois.

Smith's educational journey began with high school studies—still rather unusual for Amish Mennonite youth at that time—and the encouragement of his father. Over the years, Smith was a student at several colleges and universities, and in 1907 completed doctoral studies at the University of Chicago. By that time he had already taught several years at the Elkhart (Indiana) Institute, a secondary school sponsored by a board of Mennonite and Amish Mennonite directors. Smith also taught at the school when it reorganized as Goshen (Indiana) College and came under direct Mennonite church administration. At Goshen, Smith taught history and served as academic dean.

In 1913, Smith moved to Bluffton, Ohio, and helped reorganize another Mennonite school, Bluffton College, where he served as professor of history until his death. He encouraged peace studies at both colleges and co-founded the Intercollegiate Peace Oratorical Association. A member of the General Conference Mennonite Church for much of his life, Smith served on its historical and publishing committees.

Smith's major contribution to his people's collective memory was his pioneering research of and prolific writing on Amish and Mennonite history. The author of a dozen books

Henry Smith at age 18.

and scores of articles, Smith produced influential historical narrative and interpretation. He also helped organize and edit the 3700-page *Mennonite Encyclopedia* (4 vols., 1955-1959).

In addition to his academic activities, Smith organized and directed two national banks, one of which he served as president for many years. He managed both institutions so scrupulously that they operated without restrictions throughout the Great Depression.

Smith was rather ambivalent about his Amish heritage. He prized the Amish tenets of religious liberty and peace. But while acknowledging that "the Amish Mennonites were decidedly religious as well as an industrious people," Smith nevertheless regarded them as too conservative and separatist. The Amish "developed a sense of aloofness . . . that doomed them to . . . spiritual and social isolation," he concluded. While he later wrote that his upbringing left him with "an inferiority complex . . . from which I never recovered," Smith's heritage also spurred him to pioneer research into its origins and development—and Smith's church is richer for his work.

See C. Henry Smith, *Mennonite Country Boy: The Early Years of C. Henry Smith* (Newton, Kans.: Faith and Life Press, 1962).

public *Amish* identity, signaling their distance from an Amish past. Certainly in giving up the practices of social shunning the Amish Mennonites surrendered one of the convictions that had set them apart for two centuries. In some quarters, they also quickly discontinued the practice of footwashing in conjunction with communion observance and surrendered most of their distinctive dress and symbolic separation from the world.

Amish-turned-Mennonites did continue to stress simple, ethical living as a response to God's grace. A commitment to congregational authority, the church as the body of Christ in the world, and Jesus' teaching of peace and forgiveness also marked erstwhile Amish churches in the twentieth century. However, the Amish Mennonite emphases that such tenets received often expressed themselves through institutions and language that sounded more broadly North American or European than distinctively Amish. The continuance of historic Amish principles in a way that did not easily adopt society's values and idioms fell to the Old Order Amish and related churches.

9.
Preservation and Perseverance: The Old Order Amish, 1865-1900

> *"We are minded, and promise to strive for simplicity and uniformity in all things."*
> — an Iowa Old Order Amish congregation, 1891

Choosing the Old Order

The tradition-minded churches that came to be known as the Old Order Amish were a small group during the last decades of the nineteenth century. In the aftermath of the annual ministers' meetings, about two-thirds of local church districts had chosen the progressive Amish Mennonite path. By the close of the 1800s, the Old Orders who continued to worship in private homes, maintain traditionally simple clothing patterns, and rigorous church discipline numbered only about 5,000.[1] Yet the Old Order church proved remarkably healthy for a body that had undergone a series of wrenching schisms and turbulent unrest.

Even while the debates of the *Diener-Versammlungen* were closing the door to compromise and sealing the reality of a fractured Amish church, conservatives who would make up the Old Order fellowship were establishing new settlements. In 1866, as progressive Amish Mennonites met for that year's ministers' meeting in McLean County, Illinois, tradition-minded families were also heading to the state. The Amish moving to Moultrie County, Illinois, though, were not attending the change-minded church gathering, but rather forming a new

A poster advertising land for sale in Michigan noted the presence of "Colonies of Amish and Mennonites" in the state.

Old Order district. During the two previous years, families from Somerset County, Pennsylvania, had settled in Moultrie near the small town of Arthur. Before long, Indiana, Ohio, and Iowa households relocated there as well, and Arthur, Illinois, grew into a sizable Old Order community. Founded during the years of Amish controversy and division, Arthur represented the conservatives' ability to continue and thrive, even as the majority of their church moved toward broader social acculturation.[2]

Nor did the great schism among the Amish affect the local relationships that might lead non-Amish individuals to join the conservative wing of the church. Around 1863, for example, Lutheran Jacob Lambright joined the Old Order church in northern Indiana. Within a decade, the Bawell, Barkman, Flaud, and Whetstone surnames (among others) became part of Old Order Amish communities in various states, as people bearing those names joined the tradition-minded Amish church.[3] Apparently Old Order Amish life and faith appealed to some Americans, even as it drove other Amish Mennonites away.

As the Old Order church slowly grew, important new settlements started in Daviess County, Indiana (1868); Reno County, Kansas (1883); and Geauga (1886) and Madison counties (1896), Ohio. In the late 1800s, new districts formed in a dozen other states, but troubled church affairs or the economic difficulties of homesteading caused these settlements to dissolve.[4]

A congregationally organized church spread across North America and without a national bureaucracy might easily have fragmented. Nevertheless, the Old Orders remained remarkably close-knit considering their many settlements and relatively small numbers. One way in which Amish people kept in contact with one another was through correspondence newspapers such as *The Belleville* (Pennsylvania) *Times* and *The Sugarcreek* (Ohio) *Budget*. Originally published as local papers, journals such as *The Budget* regularly printed news items from

Others Who Rejected Modernity or Chose the Way of Tradition

The Old Order Amish were not the only religious group that spurned the progressive spirit of nineteenth-century, North-American life. Primitive Baptists, for example, rejected Sunday schools, church bureaucracy, salaried clergy, and innovations in traditional Calvinist doctrine. Some members of the Churches of Christ also rejected progressive institution-building and the professional pastorate. During the last quarter of the nineteenth century, an influential Protestant movement known as dispensationalism also dissented from the optimistic tenor of the times. Dispensationalists did not assume that North American society was improving, but rather that the world was become more corrupt as the second coming of Christ neared.

Among the Religious Society of Friends (Quakers), a conservative wing emerged from 1845 to 1904. Known as the Wilburites, these traditional Friends preserved early Quaker worship practices and theology. Members also stressed the importance of wearing plain attire and maintained traditional Quaker speech patterns.

The Old Order groups that emerged among Amish, Mennonite, and German Baptist Brethren perhaps rejected most strikingly the spirit of progressive nineteenth-century American society. Several distinct Old Order Mennonite groups formed between 1845 and 1901 in Pennsylvania, Indiana, Ohio, Ontario, and Virginia. These tradition-minded Mennonites were concerned that the larger body of Mennonites was moving too quickly down the path of worldliness and cultural compromise. The Old Order Mennonites, for example, rejected Sunday school, church bureaucracy, and other formal institutions. In most cases, they also retained German-language church services.

In contrast to the Older Order Amish, the Older Order

Mennonites met in simple church meetinghouses (rather than members' homes) and did not practice shunning. Old Order Mennonite men were clean-shaven, and, while their dress was plain, it was somewhat different from the Amish. In the twentieth and twenty-first centuries, Old Order Mennonites (like the Old Order Amish) avoided higher education and continued the use of horse-drawn transportation.

During the 1800s, Old Order groups also formed in other Anabaptist-related churches. During the first half of the nineteenth century, the River Brethren divided into Old Order River Brethren and progressive Brethren in Christ camps. Among the German Baptist Brethren ("Dunkers"), an Old Order wing formed after 1881, taking the name Old German Baptist Brethren. The progressive wings of this group became the Church of the Brethren and the Brethren Church. In each case, the Old Order churches among the Brethren have retained plain dress, simple lifestyles, and traditional worship patterns and church structures. Only a very small fraction drive buggies, however, and all use English as their first language.

In the 1900s, Old Order Amish, Mennonites, and Brethren often found themselves on the same side of controversies with the state regarding matters of compulsory education. Members of various Old Order churches often feel a fraternal bond with one another, despite the important differences that exist between them. Many Old Order Mennonites, for example, subscribe and contribute articles to the Old Order Amish magazine *Family Life.*

For more on other Old Order groups, see Donald B. Kraybill and Carl F. Bowman, *On the Backroad to Heaven: Old Order Hutterites, Mennonites, Amish, and Brethren* (Baltimore: Johns Hopkins University Press, 2001); Stephen Scott, *An Introduction to Old Order and Conservative Mennonite Groups* (Intercourse, Pa.: Good Books, 1996), 11-104; and Beulah Stauffer Hostetler, "The Formation of the Old Orders," *Mennonite Quarterly Review* 66 (January 1992): 5-25. For discussion of a wider cultural context, see T. J. Jackson Lears, *No Place for Grace: Antimodernism and the Transformation of American Culture, 1880-1920* (New York: Pantheon Books, 1981).

Amish communities far and wide. Thus, an Indiana *Budget* subscriber could read news not only of the publisher's Tuscarawas
County, Ohio, area, but also reports from settlements in Iowa,
North Dakota, Nebraska, Maryland, and elsewhere. Originally
The Budget was primarily an Amish Mennonite newspaper, but
it also functioned within Old Order circles as that fellowship
grew and spread.[5]

Old Order Amish communities also remained connected
through personal contacts and visiting. Amish young people
frequently traveled by rail to other settlements. The autograph
books of these teens and young adults record the names of
friends and acquaintances from across the country.[6] At times
young people—most often young men—would take jobs in
other Amish communities for a season or a few years. The
youth learned to know other areas and families, and their correspondence with relatives at home offered insights even to
those who never traveled. The brothers Isaac and Andrew
Ebersol, for example, were among those who left their parents'
eastern Pennsylvania farm and lived elsewhere for a time. The
Ebersols took jobs with their uncle in Arthur, Illinois. During
their time in Arthur, each wrote to their cousin Sarah E. Lapp,
who had remained in Lancaster, Pennsylvania.[7] The boys
described life in Illinois, Midwestern commodity prices,
Moultrie County weather, church affairs, and the Arthur young
people's social life.

In January 1897, Sarah Lapp received another letter from a
traveling Amish youth, one Isaac Zook, a Lancaster boy who
had gone to work in Mifflin County, Pennsylvania. Zook
described Mifflin's "Big Valley," and then told about a minor
accident in which he had been involved. He also listed the
names of young Amish couples whose wedding engagements
the local bishop had recently "published" (announced to the
rest of the church). Zook continued: "If that is the go, I guess I
must tell them to have me published while I am here too—"
then added, "O excuse me, it takes two Don't it? Well then I'll

waite [sic] a while yet I guess."⁸ He did wait and returned to Lancaster. Later that year, Isaac and Sarah married.

Weddings and special occasions were certainly times of celebration among the Old Order Amish. Although most Old Orders avoided extravagance, some exchanged holiday greeting cards and, in a few cases, even decorated a tree for the holidays. Two days before Christmas 1888, a young Sallie J. Fisher wrote to her cousin, wishing that the other girl could "see our ever green," because the Old Order Amish Fisher family intended "to make it white with popcorn and candy."⁹

Of course everyday life also included hard work. One evening, quite tired, Lancaster County teen Bettsy Speicher

Late nineteenth-century observers considered the Old Order Amish superior farmers. The Amish in Lancaster, Pennsylvania, and elsewhere, continue to be known for their agricultural skill, even though today a declining percentage makes its living tilling the soil.

reported that her family was finally finished with cornhusking and making 100 crocks of apple butter, but still had "the whole house left to clean." Speicher also said that her family kept three cows and "a hundred chickens more or less." The animals provided some income, as selling cream earned the family a few dollars.[10] Several years later, Bettsy's friend Rebecca S. Smucker described her full day of washing and ironing, noting that her mother had been patching clothes, her father caring for the livestock, and her brothers working in the "smith shop" and repairing shoes.[11] Old Order Amish life was like that of other rural Americans—family, fun, and strenuous labor combined to challenge the elements of weather and economic unpredictability.

In general, Amish farmers adopted new agricultural technologies—mechanical hay loaders, grain binders, and grain threshing machines—as they became available, but used these tools toward certain ends. In Johnson County, Iowa, at least, Steven Reschly found that Old Order farmers in the late 1800s maintained a distinctive balance of "livestock, meadows, innovative technology, family labor, and production for the marketplace" in a way that supported mixed agriculture and resisted the sort of intensive cash grain or specialized livestock farming that was becoming common among their non-Amish neighbors. While some observers noted that the Amish often put stock in almanac folklore that Americans increasingly considered outdated and unscientific, popular opinion and the national press were already celebrating the Amish as accomplished farmers.[12]

Tradition and change

Although similar in many ways to their rural neighbors, the Amish also stood apart in often easily identifiable ways. Old Order church districts worked diligently to preserve family and community life and stood against pride and wastefulness. The Old Order Amish in the Midwest, for example, continued to

drive open carriages throughout the nineteenth century, considering closed-top buggies an unnecessary luxury.[13] They also
maintained traditional grooming styles. The plain clothing of
Old Order Amish men and women demonstrated humility and
pointed to separateness. Men continued the use of hook-and-
eye fasteners instead of buttons on their coats (and in some
communities, shirts), as well as wearing untrimmed beards.
Amish women wore devotional head coverings as a sign of biblical obedience.[14] During the late 1800s, a number of North
American denominations (and especially churches in the
Holiness and Adventist traditions) encouraged or required
members to dress simply and conservatively, but Old Order
Amish appearance was noticeably plain, even by the standards
of the time. In the opinion of one observer of Old Orders in
eastern Pennsylvania, the men wore "remarkably wide
brimmed hats" and coats "plainer than those of the plainest
Quakers."[15] Church custom, grounded in biblical principle and
supported by the community, shaped everyday life as faith
informed even how one got dressed in the morning.

Important as tradition and community were, they were not
rigid, and a fair amount of local variation and flexibility seasoned Old Order life. The Old Order notion of *Ordnung*, after
all, was one that prized local custom, so exact uniformity
across the continent was never the ideal. Even within a local
church district, the peculiar circumstances of a particular person might justify a degree of latitude in tampering with tradition. Old Order prescriptions were flexible in handling special
needs.[16]

Nor were tradition and community stifling forces that
smothered creative thinking. Those who chose the Old Order
path were not uninformed people who retained conservative
values because they knew no better. One important Amish lay
leader who remained with the Old Order wing of the church
for most of his life was the educated and articulate Samuel D.
Guengerich.[17] Born in Somerset County, Pennsylvania, Guen-

gerich moved with his family to Ohio and then to Iowa. As a young man he taught in local schools and decided to return to Pennsylvania to receive formal training in education. In 1864, he received a teaching certificate from Millersville State Normal School (now Millersville University), and then taught several terms in Somerset County before going back to Iowa.

"A good education and well-cultivated mind may be regarded as almost indispensable in many respects," Guengerich wrote at one point in his studies.[18] He cultivated his own mind with visits to such places as Washington, D.C., where in 1889 he saw the Botanical Garden, the Smithsonian Institute, the

S.D. Guengerich, late in life, at his Iowa home.

headquarters of the Federal Fish Commission, and the Capitol. At age 28 he had purchased a "telescope and a mikeroscope [sic] and a box of drawing instruments" with which to explore his world.[19] Always reading and learning, Guengerich also established a private publishing business and issued a German periodical and German youth publication.

Near the end of Guengerich's life, his congregation affiliated with the change-minded Amish Mennonites, but Guengerich himself seems to have been satisfied with his life as an Old Order and did not view his studies as incompatible with his church membership. Although Guengerich's foray into the classroom was unusual, other Old Orders accepted him both as a student and teacher. His diaries record his regular interaction and full church fellowship with the Old Order Amish of Lancaster County, Pennsylvania, while he studied at the local normal school.

Nor was Guengerich the only trained school teacher among the Old Orders. Isaac Huyard, a Millersville student of a generation after Guengerich, joined the Amish. Huyard came from a Lutheran family, and from 1886 to 1888 attended the Normal School at Millersville. In 1892, he converted to the Old Order Amish faith and remained a committed member the rest of his life. His wife, Mary Zook, had been raised in an Amish home, and Isaac himself had boarded with a Lancaster County Amish family during some of his growing-up years.[20]

Even in areas of church life and religious ritual, Old Orders were not a uniform lot. The Somerset County, Pennsylvania, Kalona, Iowa, and Arthur, Illinois, Old Order settlements, for example, replaced the old Anabaptist hymnal, the *Ausbund*, with a newer collection. First published in 1860, *Eine Unparteiische Lieder-Sammlung* (called the "Baer book" because it was printed by Johan Baer of Lancaster, Pa.) included *Ausbund* material with other songs. Likewise, the Daviess County, Indiana, Old Orders switched to the 1892 *Unparteiische Liedersammlung* (called the "Guengerich book"), a more recent hymn compilation that also included much *Ausbund* material.[21]

Some Old Orders even initiated innovative ways to practice mutual aid. In the mid-1870s, for example, the Lancaster County church created a special fund to assist families in the event of fire or storm loss. While the purpose was as old as the church itself, the methods were somewhat novel. Instead of church deacons receiving anonymous donations of alms for those hurt by the elements of nature, Amish Aid Society directors now assessed member families and charged them fixed rates. The whole program was far from bureaucratic and never completely replaced the work of the deacons who continued to collect money for the needy, but Amish Aid did represent a modest move in the direction of increased formality for a growing church.[22]

Perhaps most unusual were the Somerset County, Pennsylvania, Old Orders who built four church meetinghouses. In 1881, they erected two structures in Pennsylvania and two across the border in Garrett County, Maryland. The appearance of a meetinghouse in an Amish community had always signaled its decided move toward progressive Amish Mennonitism, but the Somerset group built physical church structures and remained Old Order.[23]

Not all communities were so successful in balancing tradition and selective change. In 1891, the Old Order Amish in Johnson County, Iowa, also built meetinghouses with the intent of remaining conservative. Members even signed a statement which promised, "This church house shall and dare not be a means of granting us more freedom toward worldliness . . . ." In fact, the statement continued, "we are minded, and promise to strive for simplicity and uniformity in all things, and to remain true to the fundamentals of our faith."[24] Such statements summed up Old Order purposes nicely. Yet the two congregations involved proved less than successful; within three decades they had moved into the progressive Amish Mennonite camp, notwithstanding their earlier intentions.

The ability to make selected changes but not be swept away by social acculturation and accommodation became a sort of Old Order art. Sensing the implicit dangers of some cultural trends, the Amish reacted in ways that seem today to have had deep sociological insight. But even Old Orders disagreed on how much change was threatening to Christian community and healthy family life. By 1881, some Mifflin County, Pennsylvania, Amish were feeling that their own tradition-minded people were becoming caught up in material pursuits. Newer clothing styles, grooming habits, and technological innovation were being slowly accepted even in some conserv-

The so-called "Nebraska" Amish are among the most conservative of all Old Orders. Clothing styles, for example, reflect early traditions: men and boys wear white shirts with no suspenders and notably wide-brimmed hats. Nebraska Amish drive simple buggies with white cloth enclosures, a practice that has given them the nickname the "white top people" (Weiss-Wegli Leit). Today there are some 13 Nebraska Amish church districts in Pennsylvania (mostly in Mifflin County) and one in Ohio.

Modern Assumptions
and the Old Order World View

Many moderns find Old Order life perplexing and perhaps even misguided. Much of this puzzlement stems from
the disconnect between the fundamental assumptions of
modern people—assumptions about self and society—and
the assumptions of Old Order people. More than simply a
collection of distinctive clothes and technological prohibitions, Old Order life is an expression of a distinct worldview
and cluster of values.

Historian Theron Schlabach has suggested that North
Americans wanting to understand Old Order life need temporarily to set aside modern assumptions and mental habits.
This does not mean, Schlabach notes, that "one must roman-
ticize Old Order groups or finally accept the Old Order out-
look and critique of modern life. It is only to step outside the
prison of mental habits long enough to understand a different view." Moderns trying to understand Old Orders must
not assume:

"That ideas expressed and tested in words are brighter
and truer than ideas which take their form in personal community life.

"That people who accept the ideas of the eighteenth century's so-called Age of Reason are the 'enlightened' ones of
the world.

"That change is usually good, and usually brings
'progress.' (The Old Order-minded accepted this change or
that—a new tool, perhaps, or rail travel. But they were not
progressi*vists*.)

"That the individual is the supreme unit, individual rights
are the most sacred rights, and human life richest when individuals are most autonomous.

"That the really important human events are those con-
trolled in Washington, New York, Boston, London, Paris, and
other centers of power—rather than events around hearths
or at barn raisings or in meetings at Weaverland
[Pennsylvania] or Plain City [Ohio] or Yellow Creek [Indiana]
or Kalona [Iowa].

"That vigor of programs, institutions, activity (including
Protestant-style missions) are a test of a Christian group's
validity and faithfulness.

"That large organizations, organizational unity, and
denominational and interdenominational tolerance are better measures of Christian success than is close-knit congregational life.

"That people who imbibe some alcohol or use tobacco
have deeply compromised their Christianity.

"Similarly, that people are poor Christians if their sons
and daughters wait until adulthood to put off youthful rowdiness and become sober-minded Christians.

"That a structure of rules and explicit expectations (some
moral, others mainly just practical for group cohesion) is
always legalistic and at odds with the Christian idea of grace.

"That *salvation* refers almost entirely to the individual's
original transaction and covenant with God at the time of
personal conversion.

"That in church history, words such as *reform* or *renewal*
apply only to movements which share the progressivist faith
and apply new methods and new activities; and that leaders
who look to the past, or who think faithfulness may come
by strict discipline, are simply reactionary and formalistic."

Quotations from Theron F. Schlabach, *Peace, Faith, Nation: Mennonites and
Amish in Nineteenth-Century America* (Scottdale, Pa: Herald Press, 1988),
201-203.

ative families. Because the concerned group of ultra-conservatives was comprised only of lay members and a deacon, they wrote to bishop Yost H. Yoder of Gosper County, Nebraska, and asked him to help organize their fellowship. Only the year before he had helped found the Gosper settlement.[25]

Yoder traveled to Pennsylvania to help the new ultra-conservative fellowship get started, and his role in the group's beginnings earned them the nickname "Nebraska Amish," despite their Appalachian home. The Nebraska (also called "Old School") Amish maintained especially traditional church and family life. The group retained some clothing standards typical of colonial American dress, and adopted remarkably few technological innovations in farming practices and technology, earning a reputation as the most conservative of all Old Orders. After 1904, their numbers increased somewhat as Yoder's Gosper County settlement dissolved and several of its families moved to Pennsylvania and joined the group bearing their old state's name.[26] Within the Old Order circle, then, there was some diversity. From the ultra-traditional "Nebraskans" to Somerset County Old Orders who met in meetinghouses and used new hymnals, the spectrum—though not terribly wide— was broader than many observers realized.

What Old Orders held in common, though, was a commitment to connecting spiritual experience and the very ordinary activity of daily life—and to do so in a church community of mutual accountability. More than anyone in the later nineteenth century, Holmes County, Ohio, bishop David A. Troyer articulated these understandings in his essays and poems, most of which he penned for his children. In 1870, at age 43, Troyer became ill and feared he would not live to see his offspring to maturity. During the next 15 years or so, he put his convictions on paper as a living legacy to his family. Troyer stressed the power of prayer and the goodness of God in offering salvation to stubborn and ungrateful humanity. He also warned against the popular religious sentiment of the day which argued that "the outward has no significance, if only the heart is right." "Oh my beloved," the Old Order father cried, "do not be led astray by this destructive spirit of liberty." If personal freedom was the crown jewel of American political and popular culture, it pointed for Troyer only to self-destruction.

In "a short admonition and instruction relating to the so-called traditional lifestyle," the bishop explored the logic of Old Order living. He began by asserting that every church or social group has some markers of acceptable or expected behavior—some set of boundaries—whether explicit or implicit. The only question is whether those habits and practices support Christian faithfulness or not. Here Troyer could be both critical of and sympathetic toward his Old Order community. Tradition by itself was not the key. Do "not build on an *alte Ordnung* [just] because it is an old lifestyle, but rather because it is based on God's Word," he cautioned. If the orientation of other churches betrayed more of an interest in self-fulfillment than discipleship, "neither is ours praiseworthy in every respect," he admitted. Troyer especially bemoaned the presence of sexual immorality in some Amish families and feared the influence of popular politics and nationalistic patriotism on Christians whose primary loyalty was to be the church. "[Y]ou precious children," he concluded one of his pamphlets, "my sincere admonition to you is: Stay with what you have promised and accepted on bended knee before God and many witnesses, and remain steadfast and faithful and always increase in the work of the Lord."[27]

Debating boundaries

It was significant that David Troyer connected faithfulness and baptismal vows to God and the church. The sort of discernment he advocated required a churchly context. The other side of that commitment was the accountability that sometimes worked itself out in church discipline if members flaunted their individual right to choose their own path. Both pieces

The children of Moses and Magdalena Hartz in 1934: David (1860-1959), Mennonite; Rebecca (1854-1946), Amish Mennonite; Jacob (1857-1936), Amish Mennonite; and Moses, Jr. (1864-1946), one-time Mennonite, but by 1934 a member of the Religious Society of Friends (Quakers). In the 1890s, controversy over church discipline had swirled around Moses, Jr., and his parents.

were central to Old Order identity, and, during the 1890s, Old Orders engaged in debates over the place and meaning of church boundaries. The immediate issue often involved the practice of shunning, but the underlying significance was broader. To which community was a Christian accountable, and how easily could the individual abandon one group and pick a more convenient one? Most specifically, did Old Orders break their baptismal promise to give and receive counsel in the church if they turned their backs on that church and affiliated with the Amish Mennonites?

During and after the *Diener-Versammlungen*, as the Amish sorted themselves into tradition-minded and change-minded camps, the two groups had maintained an uneasy, but cordial relationship. Those who left Old Order ranks as members in good standing and joined the Amish Mennonites were not

excommunicated or shunned by the conservative group.²⁸ For
their part, the Amish Mennonites did not meddle in Old Order
church discipline. If someone left the Old Order Amish on bad
terms, the Amish Mennonites would not accept that person as
a member until the errant party had made peace with his or
her former church district. In short, those quietly leaving the
Old Order church found a welcome among the Amish
Mennonites, but the progressive church would not accept
those who left the Old Orders in anger or in disobedience.

An incident involving Old Order preacher Moses Hartz, Sr.,
and his wife Magdalena (Nafziger) Hartz, challenged the two
groups' delicate balance.²⁹ Hartz had been a German orphan
who found work and a home in the Conestoga Amish community of Lancaster and Berks counties, Pennsylvania.³⁰ Joining
the church as a young man, Hartz was eventually ordained and
served faithfully for many years, remaining with the conservative side during the division of the 1870s.³¹ After 1894, trouble
erupted in the Hartz home when their son Moses, Jr., took a
job as a traveling mechanic for a millwork company and began
to miss Sunday morning worship and wear clothing that did
not comport with church understandings of appropriately
modest and simple dress. When the church counseled Hartz to
find another job, he left the church. But he had trouble finding
another church home. The more progressive Amish
Mennonites denied him membership because of the angry
terms on which he had severed his former ties, and so Hartz
joined a Mennonite congregation that accepted him, despite his
irregular participation in their congregational life.

Unlike joining the Amish Mennonites, taking membership
with Mennonites was a considered a breaking of one's baptismal vows. The younger Hartz's action excommunicated him
from the Old Order church and called for his shunning by that
group. But preacher Moses, Sr., and Magdalena announced
that they would not shun their son. Now two generations of
Hartzes were being disobedient as the parents refused to prac-

tice a key church teaching because of family favoritism. The elder Hartz's congregation silenced him from preaching. Wanting to maintain ties with their son and with their Old Order family and friends, the Hartzes devised a way around their situation. They would simply apply for membership in the nearby Amish Mennonite church. By quietly joining the Amish Mennonites they could leave the Old Order church without being excommunicated themselves, and once they were Amish Mennonites, they would not need to shun Moses, Jr., since Amish Mennonites had abandoned the practice of social avoidance.

The Old Orders now faced a dilemma: should they discipline the elder Hartzes? Some argued that so long as the couple were joining another nonresistant, somewhat plain, Amish-related church, the ban and avoidance were unnecessary. Another party stood for what became known as *streng Meidung* ("strict shunning"). Advocates of "strict shunning" felt that excommunication and avoidance were required in any case where Old Order members broke their baptismal vows and left the tradition-minded group.

A series of Amish Mennonite and Old Order negotiations, including mediators from Ohio, failed to settle the matter. Under the assumption that the Old Orders would not object to the Hartzes becoming Amish Mennonites, the progressive church accepted them as members. A year later in 1897 at a special gathering of conservative Amish leaders, the Old Order church decided it was necessary to excommunicate the Hartzes for joining the Amish Mennonites under the conditions that they had. Thereafter, no one else would slip into the Amish Mennonite meetinghouse from an Old Order church district without also facing excommunication. The embrace of "strict shunning" marked another break between the Old Orders and the Amish Mennonites.

Not all Amish communities chose the path of "strict shunning," especially in the Midwest, and a situation in the Arthur,

Illinois, church concluded differently. There in the mid-1890s, Joni F. and Anna (Yutzy) Helmuth began attending a new Amish Mennonite church after they were excommunicated from the Old Order church.[32] When the new Amish Mennonite church received the Helmuths as members, some Old Order Amish suggested that their excommunication be lifted and the shunning ended. After all, the couple were now members in good standing of another Amish-related congregation, even if it was not Old Order. But some in the community felt that the ban should remain in place. In their minds, the Helmuths had made solemn baptismal vows before God that they would give and receive church discipline. Now they had broken that promise, their excommunication could not be forgotten until they confessed their wrong. In the end, both groups got their way, and the Arthur community compromised. Those who felt that the ban should be lifted acted as though it was. Other Old Orders who wished to continue practicing shunning did as they saw fit.

The "strict shunning" question did not go away entirely. Into the twentieth century it lingered in some areas, demonstrating the seriousness with which many Amish regarded baptismal vows and the sin of disobedience, two centuries after Jacob Ammann and Hans Reist had first debated the issues.

Depression politics

Old Order life certainly was not limited to church affairs. Although intent on remaining symbolically—and often substantially—apart from worldy society, the Old Order Amish were never unaware of or unaffected by current events that shaped the surrounding culture. In the 1890s, for example, many Amish faced the same harsh economic realities that their non-Amish neighbors did. The depression of 1893-1897 was the worst the United States had experienced in 60 years. During 1893 alone, 500 banks failed and 16,000 businesses closed their doors for good. Probably 20 percent of the work force was unemployed for some part of those bleak years.[33]

The Budget

For more than a century, Amish community news has circulated on the pages of a weekly newspaper called *The Budget*. Published in Sugarcreek, Ohio, *The Budget* contains brief reports in the form of correspondents' letters from Old Order Amish, Beachy Amish, and Old Order Mennonite communities throughout North and South Americas. Correspondents (known as "scribes") write about newsworthy local events, including births, deaths, weddings, illnesses, the weather, and (in the case of the Old Order Amish) which family hosted church services. Scribes mail their handwritten columns to Sugarcreek, where each week editors typeset the material and publish another issue of their unusual publication.

First printed in 1890, *The Budget* initially was a biweekly local paper for the Sugarcreek community. During its first year, however, the paper included news items from communities as far away as Arkansas. Those who sent news from other states or areas within Ohio generally had relatives living around Sugarcreek and used the paper as a means of staying in contact with them. The paper still catered to Sugarcreek readers and kept its subscription price at 50 cents a year, but in 1891 it became a weekly and took on a more national flavor. By 1899, each issue of *The Budget* contained about 30 letters from correspondents who lived in other areas.

The paper's owner and second editor was Sugarcreek resident John C. Miller, a progressive Amish Mennonite who had been raised in an Old Order home. Miller's paper included reports from both Amish groups, though in 1900 probably less than a third of the correspondents were Old Order. *The Budget* was primarily an Amish Mennonite paper, and progressive institutions such as the Mennonites' Goshen (Indiana) College placed school news, announcements, and advertisements in the paper's pages.

After about 1920, the subscriber list began to change. The Amish Mennonite and Mennonite merger had prompted many Amish Mennonite readers to purchase official Mennonite periodicals, and circulation of *The Budget* dropped as Amish Mennonites allowed their subscriptions to expire. The Amish Mennonite family that owned the paper even sold the business to Samuel A. Smith, a local Lutheran who had warm friends among the Old Orders. Under the editorship of Smith and his son George R. Smith, *The Budget* took on more and more Old Order Amish scribes and readers.

Known as *The Sugarcreek Budget* during its first years, the paper has gone by its shorter name since 1930. Yet the publication has not forgotten its home community, and since 1946 it has appeared each week in both a Local Edition and a National Edition. The local run is much like other small-town newspapers and includes news of Sugarcreek's non-Amish community. The National Edition offers only the scribes' reports. By providing a forum for the exchange of family and church news, *The Budget* has helped link Amish settlements in important ways.

Over the years, two other papers have also offered Amish community news. *The Belleville Times* (published from 1894 to 1973 in Mifflin County, Pennsylvania) and *Die Botschaft* (published since 1975, today from Lancaster, Pennsylvania) includes correspondents from across the continent. *Die Botschaft* began when readers in certain communities wanted a paper with somewhat stricter policies on editorial and advertising content than those observed by *The Budget*. Nevertheless, *The Budget* and *Die Botschaft* are quite similar, and some scribes write columns for both.

See David Luthy, "A History of The Budget," *Family Life* (June 1978): 19-22; (July 1978): 15-18; Elmer S. Yoder, *I Saw It in* The Budget (Hartville, Ohio: Diakonia Ministries, 1990); and Harvey Yoder, "The Budget of Sugarcreek, Ohio, 1890-1920," *Mennonite Quarterly Review* 40 (January 1966): 27-47.

The farm economy was particularly hard hit, especially in the Midwestern and Plains states, where drought conditions in some areas added to the problems. Commodity prices dropped sharply and land values plummeted, while anti-inflationary monetary policies made loans harder to repay. Despite lower land costs, many productive farms were still out of reach for young families setting up business on their own, and hard-pressed farmers moved in search of cheaper acres. The Amish were a part of these migration patterns, as well. Old Orders formed at least 11 new settlements during the depression years. The new communities were scattered in Illinois, Indiana, Kansas, Michigan, Minnesota, Mississippi, North Dakota, and Ohio. Not all of the new settlements survived; often the depression that gave them birth eventually forced them to dissolve.[34]

One of these new settlements was located in southern Indiana's Brown County. In October 1896, families from northern Indiana's Elkhart County were scouting for affordable acres there and took the train south. Stopping in Indianapolis, Daniel M. Hochstetler, Eli J. Miller, S. J. Slaubaugh, David Hochstetler, Joseph Schrock, and Jacob Troyer were surprised by the "immence [sic] crowd of people" on the streets and in the yard of the State house. Soon the men realized that presidential candidate and popular orator William Jennings Bryan "was to arrive and talk on the money question." Evidently the Amish travelers witnessed the parade that escorted Bryan to his hotel, but they "did not hear his speech" because their train was scheduled to leave for Brown County before Bryan began.[35]

Nationally, the 1896 election generated more interest than any since before the Civil War, and the Old Order Amish were aware of its significance. That year's bid for the White House pitted Ohio's Republican Governor William McKinley against Bryan, the 36-year-old spellbinding speaker and Nebraskan Democrat. The depression colored the debates as McKinley stood for strict monetary policies and gold-backed currency, while Bryan countered with demands for lower interest rates, government regulation or purchase of utilities and railroads, and other seemingly radical economic measures. Even the candidates' personalities were a study in contrast. While McKinley calmly campaigned for office from his home in Columbus, Bryan canvassed the country, making hundreds of speeches and meeting thousands, like those in Indianapolis.[36]

Studying the Amish response to the 1896 election, Old Order Amish historian David Luthy concluded that likely many Amish sympathized with Bryan.[37] "Amish people, generally not involved in political affairs, were caught up in the debate and suspense of this election," Luthy discovered as he read *Budget* letters. Bryan "had great sympathy for the farmers and the working-class people," Luthy noted. "He appealed to the common man and thus to the Amish." Bryan was well-known as a sincere and theologically conservative Christian, which also may have increased his standing in Amish circles. In communities where some Old Orders may have voted, Bryan was the clear winner. In Holmes County, Ohio, for example, he logged a 2,300-vote majority.

Nevertheless, Bryan lost the election. The new President McKinley took office and promised that public confidence would bring back prosperity. When conditions in rural America only worsened, many farmers became angry and resentful. McKinley seemed to be a friend of big business and the urban rich, and farmers felt abandoned. Old Order Amish writers in *The Budget* shared the sentiments of other rural folks. An Indiana Amish farmer noticed a *Budget* piece in which the writer had applauded McKinley's victory. The Indiana man replied, "That hurrahing [for McKinley] was rather out of place for this part of the globe, because corn has dropped 3c a bu[shel] since the election." A Nebraskan Amishman agreed, adding sarcastically, "Prosperity is here and corn has advanced from 10c to 9c. If it keeps on it will soon go up to 5c a bu[shel]. Hurrah for McKinley." Other Amish writers were equally bitter.

After 1897, the economic picture began to brighten, and by 1900, farmers who had made it through the depression years were pulling their operations together and looking toward turning a profit. The election of 1900 brought little reaction from Amish *Budget* scribes. Bryan once again challenged McKinley, and once again lost. If the Amish had involved themselves in the politics of the 1890s, in the years that followed 1900, the nation itself would increasingly draw the Amish into political, military, and economic affairs, whether the Amish wanted to be involved or not.

As 1899 drew to a close, Old Orders found themselves in circumstances far different from those that had begun the century. A new wave of immigration in the early 1800s had dramatically increased the Amish population, as well as settled the church more firmly in the Midwest and Ontario. By mid-century, deep differences within the church had led some leaders to propose a series of unity meetings—which ended in permanent division. As the majority (Amish Mennonites) slowly moved toward merger with the Mennonites, the smaller (Old Order Amish) branch of the church struggled to define and maintain itself in a world obsessed with scientific progress and material change. The Old Order response had not been to reject anything and everything that was new. But they did aim to be selective and careful in what they adopted into their homes and communities. While the pace of change seemed rapid enough during the last quarter of the 1800s, it only increased after the new century began.

10.
Challenges in a New Century, 1900-1945

> *"If the world should stand another century, who can tell what it might bring forth?"* — a Missouri Amishman, 1900

Finding a place in modern America

In 1908, the Amish took center stage as characters in a novel by Ohio social-reform advocate Cora Gottschalk Welty. If larger society had long ignored the Amish or considered them irrelevant, the dawning of the twentieth century brought the prospect of new relationships between modernity and a people who stood apart from its promises and goals. Welty's book pointed to some of these possibilities and problems, as the novel was one of the first to use the Amish for popular affect. On the surface, the book's plot was innocent enough. The main character in *The Masquerading of Margaret,* a young woman from New York, went to live on an Amish farm and dressed in Amish clothes, a turn of events that concealed her true identity and complicated the romantic situation that developed between her and the book's male hero.[1]

But clearly the novel was more than a romantic comedy. Author Cora Welty was a political Progressive committed to redeeming society, restoring lost virtues, and building a brighter national future.[2] *The Masquerading of Margaret* used the example of the Amish to condemn gambling, political corruption, and

A picture postcard produced about 1910 showing an Amish family on the streets of Ephrata, Pennsylvania.

unscrupulous monopolies. Readers also learned Welty favored expansion of public welfare and the freedom of investigative news reporters. In Welty's telling, the Amish became upstanding models for Americans compromised by the quest for individual gain—though she was decidedly vague about how or why the Amish maintained the values she praised. As a political Progressive, she endorsed government intervention and cultural management to shape society as a whole, efforts that actually afforded little room for dissenting religious minorities like the Amish to be different.

Without intending to, Welty's novel suggested themes that would take on importance for Amish people in the century to follow. Among other things, the book illustrated an emerging fascination with the Amish on the part of Americans at large. Romance writer Helen Reimensnyder Martin had published an Amish-theme novel about the same time as Welty, and by 1915 a Lancaster, Pennsylvania, tobacco shop owner was selling Amish picture postcards.[3] The development of mass tourism was still decades away, but Amish resistance to modernity already attracted Americans wistful for quieter, simpler days they believed were behind them.

The progressive impulse behind *The Masquerading of Margaret* also foreshadowed conflict with the state that would mark much of the Amish experience after 1900. Reforming society along progressive lines would involve pressing citizens into a common mold, socialized through public high school curricula, integrated through the programs of the welfare state, and given a patriotic sense of identity through participation in global war. If Welty thought her vision of the future was compatible with Amish sensibilities, time would prove otherwise.

The Amish, of course, were hardly oblivious to the claims of social progress and turn-of-the-century technological change. "Many wonderful inventions were made during the past century," a Missouri *Budget* scribe wrote in 1900, "and if the world should stand another century who can tell what it might bring forth?"[4] Phonographs, telephones, electric lights, and other household gadgets were becoming more common in American homes, soon to be joined by automobiles and "aeroplane" travel. Just two years before, the United States had defeated Spain in a quick, calculated war to establish itself as a new imperial power with colonial holdings in the Caribbean and the Pacific. Whether such changes and developments implied moral improvement, as progressives believed, remained to be seen, especially as improved communication and intriguing inventions failed to banish war or economic depression in the years that followed.

Technology, *Ordnung*, and identity

Welty's progressive optimism was widespread, in part because of the apparent promise of a brighter economic future, even among rural residents hit hard by the 1890s depression. Now farm profits increased almost annually, and the years 1910-1914 were financially the best in American farm history. As a decidedly rural people, the Amish shared in this turnaround. They remained concentrated in the Midwest and Pennsylvania, though the early twentieth century also saw the beginning of new settlements in Kansas, Ohio, Michigan, Iowa, and Oklahoma. Amish families also moved to Kent County, Delaware, in 1915, taking their church to that state for the first time.[5]

Some of the boost in agricultural output and profitability resulted from the general strength of the larger economy in those years, but changes in technology and farm efficiency also contributed. Yet that new technology brought a variety of social changes in its wake, changes involving automation and the transformation of some community "work frolics" into single-operator tasks that made neighborly cooperation and the value of family labor less important. Until then, Old Order identity had not been tethered to technological taboos, but, as the new century opened, the response of the Amish to mechanization and the individualism it spawned sparked a reappraisal.

For example, the automobile, another convenience of the twentieth century's first decades, promised what its name suggested: automatic mobility. For a people who valued community and accountability in their daily activity and choices, cars symbolized the worst of worldly modern culture. Autonomous mobility weakened interdependent family ties and encroached on time spent at home. Moreover, the expense of vehicles and the way in which car models quickly became recognized status symbols made them incompatible with Christian stewardship and humility, the Amish believed. The particularly troubling elements of status and individual choice were linked most closely to car *ownership*, which the Amish forbad, even as they acknowledged that in some cases automobile travel might be beneficial or necessary. The Amish would ride in cars or even hire a driver if circumstances demanded, though they might disagree among themselves on just what those necessary circumstances were. In any case, the advent of American automobile culture was gradual enough that most Old Orders were able to respond to it in a constructive way.[6]

In some cases, however, technological change and its accompanying social implications were sudden enough to create church conflict. During the fall and winter of 1909-1910 in Lancaster County, Pennsylvania, for example, about a fifth of the Old Order church withdrew from their larger fellowship and reorganized under the leadership of a sympathetic Mifflin County bishop. Nicknamed the "Peachey Church," the seceders were still upset about the Moses Hartz incident and wanted to do away with "strict shunning."[7] But the disagreement over excommunication was only part of the story. In addition to favoring a more lenient church discipline, the new group sanctioned in-home telephones and alternating current electricity in houses, barns, and shops. The quick adoption of such things on the part of the breakaway group pushed the larger Old Order church in Pennsylvania to oppose more firmly such an innovation as dangerous to community stability. Before 1910, Old Orders had not arrived at complete consensus on the use and abuse of new gadgetry, but the eager embrace of change by the Peachey faction helped incorporate technological cautions and prohibitions more decidedly within the Old Order church's *Ordnung.*[8]

During the early 1900s, telephones had come into limited use among the Lancaster Amish. Only after serious community problems erupted from gossip spread over the lines did the church take a stand. By 1910, the Old Orders prohibited convenient in-home telephone ownership as a dangerous temptation—though phone *use* itself was never forbidden. Modern means of communication might prove necessary in an emergency, but easy access to private conversation would only lead to trouble, the church was sure. The breakdown of face-to-face conversation and community, which rode on the coattails of in-home phones, would not be tolerated in a church that placed the quality of human relationships above individual convenience. Amish families who had purchased phones then removed them, and the *Ordnung* barred future in-home installation. The simultaneous "Peachey Church" adoption of the phone only galvanized Old Order opposition. The withdrawal of a minority group of Lancaster progressives helped to unite the majority along more definitely conservative lines.[9]

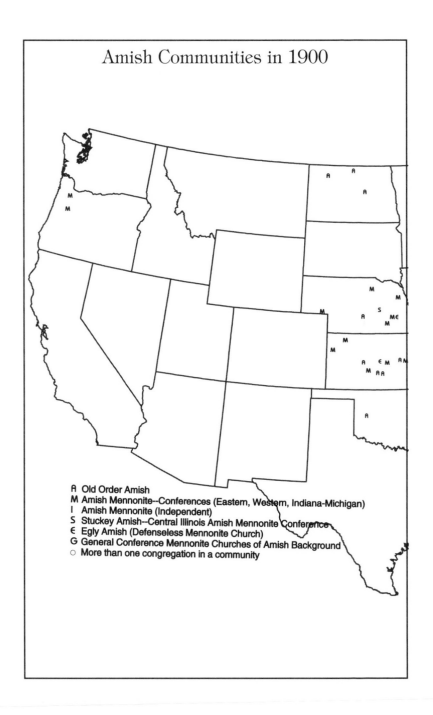

Amish Communities in 1900

ᴚ Old Order Amish
M Amish Mennonite--Conferences (Eastern, Western, Indiana-Michigan)
I   Amish Mennonite (Independent)
S Stuckey Amish--Central Illinois Amish Mennonite Conference
ᘓ Egly Amish (Defenseless Mennonite Church)
G General Conference Mennonite Churches of Amish Background
○ More than one congregation in a community

Change and reaction did not follow a uniform pattern, however, and change-minded members were not the only ones to secede into identifiable subgroups. In Washington and Johnson counties, Iowa, it was the more conservative-leaning members who separated from the larger church in order to maintain congregational, farm, and family life as they understood it. The Upper and Lower Deer Creek districts there had begun a process of slow but steady change, erecting meetinghouses in 1890 and abandoning the *Ausbund* in favor of a new hymn collection that included fewer Reformation-era songs.[10] Some households were displeased with what they saw as the church's progressive "drift," and, in 1914, seven traditionalist families left and moved north to Buchanan County, Iowa. Although they had worshiped in a meetinghouse for nearly a quarter century in their old community, after moving to Buchanan the new group reverted to gathering in homes on Sunday mornings. (The withdrawal of the conservative families may have hastened Lower Deer Creek's pace of change. In 1917 that congregation approved in-home telephones, severed ties with other Old Orders, and soon affiliated with a Mennonite conference.)

The new Buchanan County settlement gained a reputation as a notably conservative and tradition-minded community, even by

Patriotic neighbors vandalized the Metamora, Illinois, Amish Mennonite Church during World War I.

Old Order standards. Yet rather than hindering growth, this orientation attracted Amish families from Kansas, Wisconsin, Indiana, and elsewhere who were disappointed with the level of innovation they saw in their home districts. The distinctive mix of Old Orders eager to maintain a strict *Ordnung* and unusually suspicious of the promises of progress gave the Buchanan County church a special flavor—almost a conservative conscience within the larger Old Order world.[11]

About the same time the Buchanan group formed, another markedly conservative-minded movement emerged within the Wayne County, Ohio, settlement. The precise issues that sparked the separation are no longer clear, but, after 1913, an ultra-traditional Amish group took shape around Apple Creek bishop Samuel E. Yoder. Nicknamed "Swartzentruber Amish" after a later leader, they became a distinct sub-group within the eastern Ohio Old Order community. In subsequent decades, as most Amish in the area adapted some of the century's new technologies for farm and home in limited and selective ways, the Swartzentrubers did not. For example, Swartzentrubers rejected pressure naphtha lamps and indoor bathrooms, virtually all changes in clothing patterns and carriage styles, and nonelectrical appliances such as natural gas refrigerators. Nor did belt power from tractor engines find a place on Swartzentruber farms. While many Swartzentrubers remained in the Wayne and Holmes counties area, by the early twenty-first century there were some 64 Swartzentruber districts in 12 states.[12]

The Buchanan County and Swartzentruber Amish signaled a growing variety within Old Order circles—variety not unrelated to the issues that had divided the Amish in the 1800s, but now stemming more from different visions of how to apply *Ordnung* in an increasingly technologically-driven and -determined world. These ultra-conservatives, along with the older "Nebraska" group in Mifflin County, Pennsylvania, resisted in remarkable ways pressures to accept change as inevitable. Most church districts, though, combined serious reservations about the benefits of progress with a limited willingness to make practical concessions to modernity. They would impose taboos on things that undermined family and community ties—automobiles, public utility electricity, in-home telephones—but adapt belt power from stationary steam engines to operate threshing machines and other small equipment. In the early 1900s, some began using tractor engines to provide a similar source of belt power, while resisting the use of tractors to do field work. While all Old Orders remained purposefully out of step with larger society, some—like the "Nebraska," Swartzentruber, and Buchanan County Amish— were more disciplined than the rest. Soon, the coming of World War I tested the discipline and commitment of Amish throughout North America.

War fever

Church members in Ontario faced the prospect of war in 1914, although Canada did not begin drafting men until late summer 1917. At first, officials freely gave agricultural releases to the Amish, but easy deferment did not last, and the next spring Ottawa suddenly canceled all draft exemptions. After April 1918, no one could claim conscientious objector (CO) status in Canada. Instead, Amish men were to join the army and then wait for a government directive asking their commanding officer quietly to issue them indefinite leaves of absence. Most Amish did, in fact, receive this second-hand military deferment, but the situation was not satisfactory to the Amish, since it meant they were officially registered soldiers, even if they returned home. But before anything could be done to change the arrangement, the war ended.[13] The First World War experience of the Canadian Amish was hardly ideal, but it turned out to be better than what happened south of the border.

America's spring 1917 entry into World War I came as a surprise to many Americans. While Europe had been at war, politicians had preached noninvolvement, insisting that the United States had no interest in the fighting. America would remain

Amish conscientious objectors at Camp Funston, Kansas, during the First World War.

"neutral in fact as well as in name . . . impartial in thought as well as in action," President Woodrow Wilson had assured the country.[14] So, when the country suddenly entered the fray, the federal government mounted a swift and massive public propaganda campaign to rally national support. Although at first many Americans were skeptical of the war effort—still sure that the affair was none of their business—the posters, rallies, war-bond sales, and organization of patriotic citizen groups soon engendered broad sympathy. The government also systematically used churches and church periodicals to stir up war fever.[15] The Amish, however, would not be stirred.

The first test for many young Amish men came with the military draft.[16] Because of early public opposition to conscription, no draft law immediately followed the declaration of war. By late spring, however, Congress had instituted national conscription with an act that included only vague provision for religious conscientious objectors. Still, the possible promise of conscientious objection was enough to prompt some draftees to try and gain exemption from military training. In Mifflin County,

Pennsylvania, active Amish layman John S. Peachey worked tire-
lessly as a draft counselor for Amish youth in his area. Peachey
kept abreast of changes in conscription regulations, learned how
to fill out government forms properly and met with Mennonite
leaders to discuss questions of draft exemption or deferment.
Occasionally Peachey was successful, yet even when young men
did receive formal recognition as conscientious objectors from
local draft boards, they typically had to report to an army camp
anyway.[17]

Once COs arrived at their assigned military posts, no specific
guidelines detailed what they were supposed to do, nor what the
military was to do with them. The army had planned to send all
men to training camps and sort out the CO question there. Once
COs were in the camps and part of the military routine, the War
Department hoped the men might forget their scruples and join
the regular forces. Peer pressure and separation from their parents and church leaders would weaken young conviction, the
government hoped.[18]

In some cases, the military strategy worked. Of the dozens of
young Amish men drafted and sent to camps, a few did join the
fighting corps. The pressure to stand alone in a martial environment was too great for these young men facing a threatening
army establishment. Amishman Enos Stutzman, of Bucklin,
Kansas, gave in to pressure, but took a noncombatant role as a
bugler.[19] Some accepted regular infantry positions. Although
Secretary of War Newton D. Baker had told a Mennonite leader,
"Don't worry. We'll take care of your boys," the army's policy
became one of intimidation and threats to coerce drafted COs
into taking up rifles.[20]

But army tactics did not always produce Amish soldiers.
Drafted in October 1918, Holmes County farmer Rudy Yoder
reported to Camp Jefferson, Jefferson City, Missouri. Scared and
tired, he tried to explain that he was a CO, but under intense
pressure he agreed to don a uniform, march with the other men,
and wait for word on his status from the commander. After sev-

eral weeks it became obvious that no directive would appear, and he was about to begin rifle training. Yoder decided that he would stop wearing his uniform and withdraw from the routine camp activities in which he slowly had become involved. The decision was momentous and could have brought a court martial trial. Officers took him outside the camp to what looked like three fresh graves. Menacingly brandishing pistols, the officers told Yoder his would be the fourth grave if he did not put on his uniform the next morning. After a sleepless night, Yoder reported for breakfast in civilian clothes. Although other abuse continued, the officers never carried out their death threat.[21]

Unlike Yoder, most Amish men refused to participate in the army from the moment they reported to camp. Despite threats and pressure, Amish draftees remained unwilling to fight, wear military uniforms, or perform jobs they felt aided the army's war-making ability. At times the military kept COs separate from each other in an attempt to wear down their resolve, while, in other camps, COs were herded together and dealt with as a group. Either way, many Amish conscientious objectors—along with other objectors—received verbal abuse, beatings, and wire-brush scrubbings. In addition, soldiers sometimes forcibly shaved Amishmen's beards. COs might be ordered to stand for long periods of time in the sun without refreshment, and those who refused to wear military uniforms were at times left in cold, damp cells with no clothing at all. In some cases, officers "baptized" Amish objectors in camp latrines in mockery of their Anabaptist beliefs. Many COs remained in abusive camp situations from the time of their induction until well after the war was over and demobilization began. For the Amish who endured World War I draft experiences, the memories remained powerful and deeply emotional.[22]

Pro-Germanism?

Young men in military camps were not the only ones to feel the pressures of patriotic war fever; in some communities

"I Make This Humble Plea"

Old Order Amish woman Rosa (Bender) Bontrager wrote the following letter to Secretary of War Newton D. Baker a month and a half after her husband Gideon J. Bontrager was drafted and went as a conscientious objector to Camp Taylor, Louisville, Kentucky.

> Shipshewana, Indiana
> August 12, 1918

To the Hon. Secretary of War, Baker
Washington, D.C.

I am informed that the administration does not favor the practice of taking registrants for military service whose wives have no means of support other than their own labor. I therefore take the liberty to present my case to you and humbly plead that you consider it.

I am a child of an orphan's home. I have no money of any kind and have no inheritance to expect.

I was married on January 25, 1917 at the age of 21 to Gideon J. Bontrager. He was called to camp on July 2, 1918, leaving me alone without any means of support other than my own labor. We have no home of our own and I am compelled to work

onlookers and officials labeled the Amish German sympathizers. After all, they spoke a German dialect, would not join the United States Army, and in most cases refused to buy war bonds. The conclusion seemed inescapable: the Amish (and members of other ethnically-German peace churches such as the Mennonites and Hutterites) wanted Germany to win the war. To those promoting the war effort, the possibility of such sentiment was intolerable. Citizens' groups regularly hounded Amish and Mennonites who would not buy bonds or otherwise financially support the national campaign. Patriotic neighbors torched two out[side of the home] for my living. We failed to state all these facts fully when my husband filled out his questionnaire.

I may further state that my husband is a so-called conscientious objector and cannot because of conscientious scruples render any service under the military establishment, and must therefore also refuse to accept any pay from the government, and neither can I as his wife accept any money from the government for my support.

Because of these facts I make this humble plea to you, trusting that you may consider it and give instructions to the effect that my husband be returned to me.

Yours truly,
Mrs. Gideon Bontrager

Tragically, Rosa received her wish. In October 1918 she became ill with Spanish influenza and Gideon obtained a leave of absence to visit her from October 16 to 27. On the 25th, Rosa died. Gideon had to report back to Camp Taylor the day of her funeral. One month later he was given the farm furlough his wife had requested.

The complete story is found in Nicholas Stoltzfus, comp. *Nonresistance Put to Test* (Salem, Ind.: Nicholas Stoltzfus, 1981), 25-27.

Mennonite meetinghouses, while community civic groups vandalized several Amish Mennonite meetinghouses or posted American flags in front of them.[23] Not having church buildings, the Old Order Amish escaped such attacks, but they were the subjects of official government observation.

Throughout the conflict, the War Department's Military Intelligence Division kept Mennonites and Amish under surveillance. A lengthy Division memorandum (prepared in final form after the war was over) detailed the domestic spying. Apparently most of the government's research information came from arti-

The Smoketown, Pennsylvania, consolidate public school, built 1937 and razed 1993. Local Amish opposed the new building.

cles in the 1911 *Encyclopedia Britannica,* but the document also included original espionage material that the Division had collected. Names, addresses, and information on church leaders suddenly appeared in War Department files, though the decentralized Old Orders were something of a frustration to the Division. Amish congregationalism left no single leader or denominational office to target. About the Old Orders, Military Intelligence could only note: "No organization. Services generally held in German."[24] Nevertheless, Washington officials were watching the Amish.

When Old Order bishop Manasses E. Bontrager of Ford County, Kansas, wrote a lengthy letter for publication in *The Budget,* federal officials caught wind of the content. In the letter, Bontrager urged Amish not to buy federal war bonds. He chided those who had voted in the elections that brought the current administration into office, but he also praised the young men who remained steadfast in their refusal to join the armed forces, even to the point of spending time in army prisons. "What would become of our nonresistant faith," Bontrager asked rhetorically, "if our young brethren in camp would yield? From the letters I receive from brethren in camp, I believe they would be willing to die for Jesus rather than betray Him." The bishop urged his readers to muster the same resolve: "Let us profit by their example they have set us so far, and pray that God may strengthen them in the future."[25]

Two-and-a-half months later Bontrager was arrested on grounds that his *Budget* piece was "inciting and attempting to incite insubordination, disloyalty and refusal of duty in the military and naval forces of the United States."[26] Bontrager appeared for trial in Cleveland, Ohio, the jurisdiction of the paper's home state. He and *Budget* editor Samuel H. Miller were convicted and fined $500 each. The freedom to express religious conviction, it seemed, was one of the war's casualties.

Scuffles over schools

Conflicts with state authority did not end on Armistice Day in 1918. The return to post-war "normalcy" brought its own share of difficulties, including Old Order relations to new public-school legislation. Born of Progressive optimism about social engineering, and recent war-time anxiety over the place of unassimilated ethnic groups, the drive to reform public education was grounded in a belief that schools would produce forward-thinking, patriotic citizens. Exposure to new ideas through a centrally managed curriculum would strip away old values, customs, and traditions and provide the rising generation with a common culture.[27] New state guidelines mandated additional subjects and textbooks, longer school terms, and attendance often through age 16 in an effort to make the social ideal more quickly a reality.

While the Amish had never opposed education as such, and had participated in the locally managed nineteenth-century public school system, many Old Orders were wary of the tone and approach of early twentieth-century secondary schools. Parents believed that learning under such circumstances was of little practical value, and even posed a threat to their way of life. Troubling, too, was the "worldly wisdom" of competition and individual self-improvement that seemed to lie at the heart of the high school curricula championed by public-school reformers.

Formal education should remain basic, the Amish believed, in harmony with the church and the home, and be one part of a broader education that included developing work and vocational skills on the farm or in family businesses. Learning how to live with one's family, church, and community were skills missing from the expanded public school studies, yet with longer school-years and increased attendance requirements, children had even less time to be at home.[28]

In 1921, Indiana mandated school attendance through age 16 and set a new high school curriculum. Amish parents resisted sending their teens beyond eighth grade, objecting to certain high school classes, immodest physical education uniforms, and the general tone of the high school program. Controversy brewed for several years and resulted in the arrest, fining, and in some cases imprisonment of as many as two dozen fathers in the Elkhart and LaGrange counties settlement before the state backed down.[29]

An Amish parochial school in Elkhart County, Indiana, in 2002.

Next door in Ohio, the 1921 Bing Act made school attendance compulsory through age 18, though it allowed some children to receive work permits and leave school at age 16. Considered a major reform bill in Columbus, the Bing Act was no favorite of the Holmes and Wayne counties Amish who kept their teens at home and objected to content in high school social studies and hygiene texts. In January 1922, officials arrested five fathers on charges of neglecting their children's welfare. Authorities declared most of the men's school-age children wards of the court, sent them to an orphanage, and would not allow them to wear their Amish clothes. Distressed parents decided that keeping their families together was more important than opposing the Bing Act, and promised to comply with the law. Amish teens would apply for work permits at 16 and hope the state would be generous.[30]

For some Amish, these school difficulties on the heels of World War I draft difficulties were enough to start them thinking about leaving the United States. When word arrived in Wayne County of inexpensive, productive land in northern Mexico, some Amish decided to move south of the border.[31] In the fall of 1923, 10 Amishmen signed a contract for 5,000 acres in Paradise Valley (now Sacodell Valley), Nuevo Leon. Eventually, 11 households—most from Ohio, but some from Missouri—moved there. Traveling by rail, they took their household goods and animals with them. The land in Mexico was fertile and with some irrigation proved quite productive. The Amish built mud-brick homes and traveled the 60 miles to town to buy and sell. Free from restrictive Ohio school laws, they organized their own school without state interference.

Although the settlement had the potential for economic growth, it did not last long. A promised railroad connecting Paradise Valley with other communities never materialized. Then too, the smoldering guerilla war in northern Mexico caught Amish families in troop-pillaging. Perhaps most importantly, no Amish church ever developed there. No church leader moved to

Mexico, and no ordinations ever took place there. Without the formation of a more stable spiritual base, the community found life discouraging. By 1929, all the Amish had left Mexico, returning either to Ohio or to a new settlement in North Carolina.[32]

A legal battle in Pennsylvania

School controversy erupted in eastern Pennsylvania more than a decade after it did in the Midwest. Since 1925, Pennsylvania law required school attendance until age 14, but often school boards—some of which had included elected Amish members—gave work permits to Amish youth who left the classroom before that age. Instead, the confrontation that developed in the mid-1930s had to do with the consolidation of local schools. Lancaster County districts began closing rural one-room schools and busing children out of their immediate communities to larger buildings. By 1937, school centralization came to involve the area in central Lancaster County in which many Amish lived. The resulting public protest on the part of the Amish, while perhaps not unprecedented, drew more media attention and cast a higher profile than any previous event involving Old Orders.[33]

That year, East Lampeter Township announced plans to close 10 local schools and replace them with a consolidated institution in central Smoketown. Breaking with tradition, some Amish and a few non-Amish friends hired Philadelphia lawyers and received a court order halting construction of the school. A higher court overturned the injunction and the building went up, but the Amish had shown their resolve to keep education locally-oriented and managed.[34] Amish leaders disapproved of members' resorting to lawsuits, seeing the action as a violation of the church's nonresistant faith, but apparently a majority of lay members were set against the new school, and many would not send their children to it.[35]

Added to the mix was new legislation passed in the summer of 1937 that raised to 15 the age at which students were eligible to leave school on work permits. Now even church leaders thought

George W. Beiler (1884-1959) and Susie Kauffman Beiler (1887-1953) with their four daughters, Hilda, Lillian, Mary, and Katie, going to church in their 1929 Chevrolet. In 1927, George had been ordained minister in the "John A. Stoltzfus Church" in Lancaster County, Pennsylvania, one of the congregations that formed the nucleus of the emerging Beachy Amish fellowship.

it was time to petition the legislature. A 130-foot-long letter containing 3,000 signatures (including Old Order and conservative Mennonites) went to Harrisburg, asking the state to rescind the new requirement.[36] An Amish committee known as the "Delegation for Common Sense Schooling" worked with legislators to reach a compromise. The Delegation reported that it did "not wish to withdraw from the common public schools," but "at the same time we cannot hand our children over to where they will be led away from us."[37]

As matters grew tense during the 1937-1938 school year, the Amish began to consider withdrawing from the public system altogether. The following November, two private elementary schools opened in Lancaster County, marking the beginning of a new era in Amish parochial education.[38] Meanwhile, new petitions arrived at the capitol asking relief from the age 15 requirement. By the end of that school year, the legislature had rolled back the compulsory attendance age to 14, though some children might have to attend consolidated public high schools until their fourteenth birthday if they completed eighth grade before that age. Fearful that the agreement would not last, some families made plans to leave Pennsylvania. Beginning in 1940, several households moved to Saint Mary's County, Maryland, where the state seemed more ready to work with the church.[39]

The Beachy Amish

During the 1920s and 1930s, the Amish adjusted not only to changes in state law, but also to shifting loyalties within their own ranks. After 1927, an important new Amish group emerged—the so-called Beachy Amish (also called, at times, the

---

The Beachy Amish Fellowship of Churches— A Brief Chronology

1909-1910	Thirty-five families, collectively nicknamed the "Peachey Church," withdraw from the Lancaster County Old Order church, objecting to "strict shunning."
1926	John A. Stoltzfus becomes bishop of one branch of the "Peachey Church."
1927	The Somerset County, Pennsylvania, Amish community divides. Moses Beachy and the progressives reject "strict shunning." Moses Yoder leads the Old Orders.
1928	(October) Lancaster County Stoltzfus Church permits automobile ownership; (December) Somerset Beachy Church permits automobile ownership.
1929	Leaders from the Beachy Church and Stoltzfus Church begin fraternal exchanges.

1930	Lancaster group begins holding worship in the Weavertown Meetinghouse.
1930s-1940s	Moses Beachy helps organize congregations in other states, forming a loose network of "Beachy Amish" congregations.
1940	Nappanee, Indiana, bishop David O. Borkholder leaves the Old Order Amish, forming a church eventually aligned with the Beachy fellowship.
1950-1955	Old Order Amish (not Beachy Amish) interested in mission work hold a series of "Amish Mission Conferences," begin publishing *Witnessing* newsletter, and organize Mission Interests Committee, which sponsors work in Mississippi, Minnesota, and Arkansas.
1955	Beachy Amish organize Amish Mennonite Aid, a relief and service organization.
1960s	Amish who had been involved in the 1950s' mission movement leave Old Order circles; some join Mennonite congregations, but many affiliate with the Beachy Amish. The influx of new members with an interest in evangelism changes the tone and tenor of the Beachy fellowship.
1970	Beachy Amish begin sponsoring Calvary Bible School, Calico Rock, Arkansas.
1970	Beachy Amish begin a monthly church periodical, *Calvary Messenger.*
2002	There are 153 Beachy Amish churches in 22 U.S. states, Belize, Canada, Costa Rica, El Salvador, Ireland, Kenya, Nicaragua, Paraguay, Romania, and Ukraine.

Beachy Amish Mennonites). The Beachy movement had roots in the 1890s "strict shunning" controversies. In 1895, the settlement that spanned the border between Somerset County, Pennsylvania, and Garrett County, Maryland, had divided into two groups—the Old Orders to the north and a Conservative Amish Mennonite congregation in Maryland—but numerous friendly and family connections continued between the two groups. How would the Old Order church respond to those who wished to transfer their memberships to the progressive group?[40]

For two decades, the traditional leanings of Somerset bishop Moses D. Yoder muted the controversy. Yoder supported "strict shunning" and insisted on socially avoiding those who switched their allegiance to the Garrett County church. After 1916, however, the dynamics changed when Moses M. Beachy was ordained bishop to assist the aging Yoder, and Beachy let it be known that he would not excommunicate or shun Old Orders who became Amish Mennonites. Mediation efforts failed, and in June 1927, in the last summer of his life, old Moses Yoder and those who wished to maintain a discipline that included "strict shunning" quietly separated from the rest of the Amish and began holding their own worship and communion services. The majority of the Somerset church followed Beachy's leadership.[41]

But the issue of shunning soon moved into the background. From the Old Order's point of view, the Beachy church's loose application of avoidance symbolized a more significant reorientation. Indeed, Beachy's congregation soon adopted progressive Sunday schools and some members wired their homes for alternating current electricity. Within a year and a half, the group decided to tolerate automobile ownership, and somewhat less traditional dress standards followed. Whereas Beachy and his supporters saw their openness to change as selective and in the service of church renewal, their Old Order neighbors were more apt to find a fairly thoughtless chasing after the world's goods. Regardless of the interpretation, the Beachy Amish use of motor vehicles and other innovations clearly set them apart from the

Old Order Amish and marked them as a distinct body and not simply an Old Order subgroup.[42]

Beachy's change-minded congregation slowly formed a network of like-minded Amish in other parts of North America. The first connection was with heirs of the progressive "Peachey Church," who had withdrawn from the Lancaster Old Orders back in 1909. Under the leadership of John A. Stoltzfus, a portion of that Peachey group had adopted automobiles in 1927 and soon began meeting in a church building, further distinguishing itself from its Old Order neighbors.[43] During the 1930s and 1940s, bishops Beachy and Stoltzfus—sometimes together, sometimes separately—helped organize similarly minded congregations in central Pennsylvania, Ohio, Ontario, and Indiana, further expanding the Beachy fellowship.[44] As the Beachy circle grew, it remained loosely structured, in line with traditional Amish congregationalism. This orientation was one way the Beachy churches represented a continuation of Amish tradition despite notable departures. Later, in the 1960s and 1970s, the Beachy church would experience an influx of former Old Orders who had a deep interest in mission work and who would change the character and tenor of the Beachy fellowship significantly. At mid-century, however, the Beachy Amish probably still represented equal measures of innovation and tradition.

Depression days

While the Beachy division initially affected only a few Amish settlements, the financial squeeze of the Great Depression troubled virtually all communities. America's farm and small-town families felt the effects of the October 1929 stock-market crash as much as did the nation's city-dwellers. One notable effect of the Depression on the Amish was a near halt to the establishment of new settlements. Of the few settlements begun during the Depression years, none survived long. Economic hardship and the lure of cheap land did lead some families to new ventures in Arkansas, Indiana, North Dakota, Oklahoma, and

Jonathan Fisher: Traveling Amishman

Jonathan B. Fisher of Bareville, Pennsylvania, was perhaps the most adventuresome Amishman of all time. As a
farmer, cheesemaker, and farmers' market merchant, Fisher
led a typical Old Order life. But Jonathan Fisher also har-
bored an intense desire to explore the world and, as a young
man, visited many places in the United States, Canada, and
Mexico.

Fisher also took several longer trips and wrote two books
about his adventures. In 1908 he sailed for Europe to learn
about European methods of cheese production. He visited
England, France, Switzerland, Germany, Denmark, and the
Netherlands; rode to the top to the Eiffel Tower; and went
on an Alpine-mountain climbing expedition. Returning
home, he published *A Trip to Europe and Facts Gleaned on the
Way*, a 346-page book detailing his excursion. The cover
promised that the contents were "interesting reading matter
for both young and old; teachers or pupils; country and city
folks."

In 1934 Fisher set off again—this time on an around-the-
world tour during which he hoped "to take a peep into foreign
lands, to note the customs of their natives, the beauty of their
sceneries; [and] also, to glean about facts one may learn on the
way." By the time he left on this second voyage Fisher was
married, but according to contemporary newspaper accounts
his wife Sarah (Farmwald) Fisher "elected to stay at home."

Fisher sailed from New York City, down the east coast to
Cuba, then through the Panama Canal and north to Portland,
Oregon. Next he headed for Japan, then China, Singapore, and
Indonesia. After visiting Sri Lanka and India, he traveled
through the Red Sea and the Suez Canal to Egypt. Fisher
remained in the Holy Lands for six months of touring biblical
sites. Eventually he turned home, but not without stops in

Italy, Spain, Portugal, Morocco, and England. In each place his ship docked, Fisher observed people and customs, asked questions, and wrote in his diary.

Fisher kept two thick autograph books while on this world tour, and people from many countries signed their names or penned short sayings in their native languages and scripts. Fisher described this second journey in *Around the World by Water and Facts Gleaned on the Way.* He described local history and architecture, as well as his impressions of other cultures and ethnic groups. For example, the tea produced in Indonesia was superb, he thought, and the traveler in Japan was safer than in many parts of the United States.

Even at age 74, Fisher could not be kept at home. In 1952, he went to Europe again, this time under the auspices of the relief organization Church World Service. Fisher oversaw a ship-load of livestock the group was sending to the Continent. While in Europe, Fisher attended the Mennonite World Conference held that year in Basel, Switzerland. He was the only member of the Amish church to attend.

Jonathan and Sarah had three daughters and a foster son. Though interested in learning about other people, he also shared his own convictions and "carried religious pamphlets, which he gave to everyone he met." While on his global trip, he visited the U.S. Navy base in San Diego and engaged officers in a discussion of peace and conscientious objection to war.

A remarkable figure, Jonathan Fisher enjoyed people and learning about other cultures. Sharing his experiences through books, Fisher widened the worlds of many Amish readers, as well.

See Jonathan B. Fisher, *A Trip to Europe and Facts Gleaned on the Way* (New Holland, Pa.: Jonathan B. Fisher, 1911); Jonathan B. Fisher, *Around the World by Water and Facts Gleaned on the Way* ([Bareville, Pa.]: Jonathan B. Fisher, 1937). Both of these books also appeared as serials in *The Budget.* See also H. Harold Hartzler, *Amishman Travels Around the World: The Life of Jonathan B. Fisher* (Elverson, Pa.: Mennonite Family History, 1991).

Pennsylvania, but the same harsh realities that brought the new communities into existence also caused most to fail rather quickly.[45] Some younger men could not afford farms anywhere, and in northern Indiana a handful took factory jobs, beginning a shift toward non-agricultural employment that decades later would become common among Amish in that region.[46]

Some Amish interpreted the tough times as a challenge to deepen spiritual roots. "The Depression years were such times when we all needed to look to a Higher Power," one Amish minister later thought. He was impressed with "how some people could have patience with each other, the creditor with the debtor."[47] Other members believe fewer controversies and debates surfaced during those years as church districts pulled together in the face of uncertain financial futures. Mutual aid and sharing scarce resources took more frequent and concrete forms.[48]

In 1931, one anonymous Amishman's diagnosis of the country's economic ills found its way onto the front page of the Lancaster, Pennsylvania, *Intelligencer Journal*. Under the title, "Adoption of Too Many Labor Saving Devices Blamed for Depression," the author argued that "Extremity Is Cause of Many Ills Today." Mechanized farming practices, which increased agricultural production faster than population growth, were the root of Depression problems, he was sure. If only farmers and other business leaders had been satisfied with less, they would have avoided the troubles brought on by too much borrowing and debt, he claimed. The use of so-called labor-saving machinery simply threw hard-working people out of jobs. "They made a profit before they used labor-saving devices," the Amishman charged, but greed had led business down the road of bankruptcy.[49]

When U.S. Department of Agriculture agents visited the Lancaster settlement, however, they found fewer people reflecting philosophically on the Depression's causes and most digging in to the daily task of surviving hard times. The USDA was especially taken with the contribution of Amish women to their family's financial well-being, noting that many put in cash-crop potatoes, raised poultry, and sold eggs to make ends meet. Surveys showed that, on average, farm wives processed the equivalent of $422 worth of food, thanks in large part to their annually canning of 345 quarts of vegetables and fruit per household. Coupled with limited consumer consumption—Amish women also did much of their families' sewing, for example—this productivity led agents to conclude that "women's labor was central to successful family farming."[50]

Families still struggled, despite a commitment to hard work. By 1933, United States farm income had fallen on average more than 60 percent, and the federal government took drastic steps to stabilize the rural economy.[51] The most famous measure was President Franklin D. Roosevelt's Agricultural Adjustment Administration (AAA). One facet of the AAA that drew response from the Amish was the provision paying farmers to reduce the acres they planted. An attempt to boost prices by reducing supply, the tactic seemed wrongheaded to most Amish, especially when they heard stories of starvation in America's cities. Said one Amishman, "We felt this was a cruel way to get money into circulation again, being so many people were going hungry."[52] While some Amish farmers did reduce their planting in line with AAA guidelines, virtually all refused government reimbursement.[53] "I don't think it's right to take money that isn't earned," one Amish farmer told a *Philadelphia Inquirer* reporter. "That means, if you come down to it," he continued, "that a farmer is being paid to not work. Then there's farmers that don't tell the truth about their acreage [to get a greater subsidy]. That isn't right. That's just not right."[54]

The Amish also took no part in the 1935 Social Security program, known then as Old Age and Survivors Insurance. The public pension plan was optional for those who were self-employed—a category that included virtually all Amish—and the Amish opted out. Taking care of orphans, the poor, and the

An Old Order Amishman discusses the World War II military draft with Major General Lewis B. Hershey, Director of Selective Service, as three Mennonites look on.

elderly was the duty of the church, they believed, and they refused to surrender those responsibilities to the secular state.[55] The pressure to take part in government farm and social welfare programs would grow after 1935, but the Amish had already begun to resist.

Coincidentally, the Depression era saw the beginning of an important new Amish publication, which would prove popular in subsequent years. In 1929 Baltic, Ohio, bookstore owner and Amish deacon John A. Raber announced his intent to issue an annual publication, *Der Neue Amerikanische Calender* (since 1970 also issued in English as *The New American Almanac*). Appearing the next year, the almanac quickly became a yearly Amish favorite, not least because it included a directory listing all Amish church districts and leaders' names and addresses. In time, son

Ben J. Raber took over publication of his father's almanac and ably continued the Raber tradition, annually supplying a key source of Amish community connectedness across North America.[56]

A world at war

As the economic depression began to fade, trouble surfaced on another horizon, as rumbles of war in Europe and the Pacific grew louder. Beginning in 1939, Canada became involved in the Second World War, and two years later the United States entered the global conflict. Already during the 1930s, North American leaders of the Religious Society of Friends, Brethren, and Mennonites had been at work on both sides of the border in an effort to avoid repeating the disastrous experiences of World War I COs, should war erupt again.[57] In the United States, 22 Old Order Amish bishops from Indiana, Kansas, Michigan, and Pennsylvania signed a letter in 1939, declaring their support of a Mennonite statement entitled "Peace, War, and Military Service." In offering their approval, the bishops wrote that they were expressing not only their personal convictions and beliefs, but also "that of the entire membership" of their church.[58]

The statement to which the bishops affixed their names explained Christian nonresistance and denounced military involvement. It did, however, offer Washington their willingness "at all times to aid in the relief of those who are in need, distress or suffering, regardless of the danger in which we may be placed in bringing such relief," suggesting an openness to alternative service.[59]

The draft alternatives the governments offered COs were significantly different from those of World War I, especially in the United States. The programs that emerged in 1940 typically put Amish and Mennonites in state-regulated, often geographically isolated work camps, instead of sending them to military camps or jail. Ottawa and Washington established systems in which COs provided free labor for government projects or agencies.

The Canadian Alternative Service Work (ASW) and American Civilian Public Service (CPS) enrolled the efforts of thousands of conscientious objectors. ASW men worked in Canadian national parks as ground crews and forest firefighters. Others staffed psychiatric hospitals and cleared land for the Trans-Canada Highway. Additionally, some Canadian Mennonite and many Amish COs received farm furloughs and worked at home.[60]

In the United States, the CPS program provided similar jobs for its participants. In addition to receiving forestry and hospital assignments, some COs worked in social work programs or agricultural experimentation stations. Thus, while the Amish had refused farm subsidies and social security payments during the Depression, they later helped to subsidize the government itself by providing free labor for various state and federal projects. While the CPS program was an arm of the government, its participants worked under civilian direction, and the sponsoring peace churches managed and funded the program. And although men in CPS camps occasionally felt local hostility towards their peace stance, they were not subject to the physical abuse that had plagued COs in World War I.[61]

An unknown number of Old Order Amish men received farm or other deferments from local draft boards during the Second World War, but at least 772 men were drafted. Twenty-three enlisted in regular army service, 27 chose noncombatant military assignments, and 722 declared themselves conscientious objectors, the vast majority working in service assignments under CPS auspices.[62] CPS thrust many participants —Amish and non-Amish—into challenging experiences that stirred new interests and widened parochial horizons. Most Amish COs served in Mennonite-sponsored camps, but the Amish did operate one camp of their own: an experimental farming station near Hagerstown, Maryland. Amish churches purchased the farm in 1942 and managed it under U.S. Soil Conservation Service supervision. The camp had only about 35 COs at any one time, but it received strong support from Amish districts. The camp newsletter, *The Sun Beam,* had an extensive circulation to Amish homes.[63]

Life in Mennonite CPS camps was alternately comfortable, eye-opening, and troubling for young Amish men. On the one hand, the Amish were among fellow COs in an environment sympathetic to their historic views and peace teaching. At the same time, being in a Mennonite-run camp could be challenging, since many Mennonites were unfamiliar with specific Amish customs and convictions, and some looked down on the Amish as "backward" and uneducated. Rubbing shoulders so closely with Mennonites convinced some Amish that their religious cousins were alarmingly worldly and individualistic, while others found Mennonite-sponsored religious activities and worship services refreshingly innovative. When a few Amish decided while in camp to leave their church and join the Mennonites, relations were strained on all sides.[64] Nevertheless, most Amish memories of CPS were positive, and COs felt the support of friends and family who wrote regularly or even visited the camps. For his part, the remarkable LaGrange County, Indiana bishop Eli J. Bontreger made an effort to visit every Amish CPS man. Crisscrossing the country, mostly by rail, Bontreger once traveled more than 16,000 miles in five months, all the while earning the deep appreciation of Amish draftees.[65]

Some of those relatives and friends experienced problems of their own on the home front. In an especially troublesome situation in Reno County, Kansas, five Amish families lost their farms to the U.S. Navy Department. The Amish-owned acres were part of a four square-mile tract taken over by the government to establish a navy pilots' training base.[66]

The wartime economy produced other problems, as many Amish refused to use the ration stamps distributed by the government for the purchase of food and other necessities. The stamps bore the images of tanks, cannons, air corps planes, navy ships, and torpedoes, which some Amish could not use in good conscience. For others, the very idea of state-regulated commerce was troubling. Amish families that decided not to participate in the ration program provided their own food or simply did without other scarce material goods.[67] Their wartime thriftiness became their trademark, and in a 1942 *New York Times* article, one reporter called the Amish "models for the nation's consumers."[68] By declaring themselves conscientious objectors and refusing to use war-glorifying ration stamps, the Amish had ironically become models for American patriots. But in a world turned upside down by depressions, dictators, and atomic bombs, irony no longer seemed out of place.

When the war ended, some young Amish men signed on for extended voluntary service as "Sea-Going Cowboys." The Allied relief and reconstruction work in Europe involved sending hundreds of horses, cattle, and donkeys to the Continent, and the U.S. merchant marine needed people with experience in animal handling to care for the livestock during the Atlantic passage. After a successful voyage and unloading of the animals, these adventuresome Amish youth often were able to take in a few tourist sites before returning home.[69]

European sightseeing was certainly a different way for Amish teens to spend part of a summer. But after 1945, the Amish were living in a very different world. The turbulent first four-and-a-half decades of the twentieth century had left western society reeling. Despite their efforts to remain aloof from the chaos that surrounded them, the Amish were caught up in many of the events of those troubled years. The pressures of a changing economy, a growing welfare state, military conscription, and encroaching urbanization would continue to challenge Amish peoplehood in the decades to follow.

11.
Peoplehood in a Changing World: Amish Life Since 1945

> *"The Amish people feel that their mission is to lead an humble life that needs no publicity."*
> — an Amish farmer, 1978

Popularity and peril in post-war society

With the end of the Second World War, the thoughts of Americans turned homeward. Reunited families took vacations again, and states and cities scrambled to capture a share of America's growing leisure time and tourist dollars. The Pennsylvania Department of Commerce issued an advertisement encouraging would-be visitors to take a "post-war vacation." The ad included a picture of an Amish buggy with the caption, "Pennsylvania's Plain People." While the piece did not specifically mention the Amish by name, the picture clearly implied that Old Order folks should be a part of every family's excursion fun.[1]

For the Amish, however, life after 1945 was no vacation. The post-war years were shaped by serious conflicts with the state over military conscription and public schooling, as well as by internal theological debate that divided Amish communities in

Amish farmers near Yoder, Kansas, use tractors instead of horses for field-work because of the climate and summer heat. The Yoder settlement is one of a handful of Old Order Amish communities that permit tractor farming while continuing to use horse-drawn transportation on the road.

ways that had not happened in a hundred years. Then, in the last decades of the twentieth century and the opening years of the twenty-first, Amish life was marked by three more notable developments: an occupational shift from farming to non-farm employment, rising interest in the Amish on the part of outsiders, and the dynamics of continued Amish population growth and migration. If popular notions of the Amish associate them with changeless and time-bound lives, events since 1945 have demonstrated the flexible and adaptive qualities of persistent peoplehood in the midst of modernity.

Surrounding social change seemed especially sharp in the late 1940s as the country began a long, steady period of economic growth and an accompanying baby boom. Prosperous middle class families entered a golden age of consumerism. In the four years from 1946 to 1950, for example, the number of households owning television sets skyrocketed from a mere 8,000 to nearly four million. Soon the new interstate highway system, sprawling suburbs, and shopping malls encouraged American mobility and changed spending habits. People lived farther from their jobs and spent more time each day on the road. And as household income continued to rise, so did the opportunities to spend it on the latest gadgets promising to revolutionize life.[2]

The Amish remained conspicuously aloof from this hurried buying, selling, suburbanizing, and expanding—and that disturbed some officials. In the spring of 1946, federal agents publicly urged Amish farmers to give up horse-farming and use tractors to help boost American agricultural exports. "By hitching them [tractors] to the plow and harrow they will be serving not only the needs of their owners, but will help to sustain life among the hungry nations in Europe," the federal officials stated in their appeal. The Amish were outdated and unscientific, the Department of Agriculture argued; if they did not mechanize, surely they would not survive.[3]

A few Amish settlements did adopt tractor-farming in the 1940s, but the vast majority continued to use horse-drawn equipment and reserved tractor engines for stationary belt power. Fully automated farming destroyed the need for working together, and the Amish valued group cooperation. After the Second World War, non-Amish "neighbors went for bigger tractors and combines and more modern ways of farming," one Amishman remembered, "until no one seemed to have any use for his neighbors anymore."[4] Horse-based farming kept operations small and labor-intensive. As well, tractors were too much like cars, and groups that approved tractor use in fields might soon be driving automobiles on the road.

In some communities, the pressures of life in post-war America were too great. In 1952, the long shadow of the atomic mushroom cloud fell across a newly established Amish settlement in Pike County, Ohio. That year, the federal government announced intentions to build a nuclear power plant in the area. Plans suggested a tripling in the county's population, with associated increases in real estate prices. While the project was a boon to some land-owning locals, it marked the demise of the young Old Order community. The area's winding roads would become too crowded for buggy travel, land quickly became too expensive to buy, and observers guessed the area would become a highly secret military district. Within a year, the Amish began moving away—most immigrating to Ontario. One of the reasons the families chose Canada was because that country had no military draft, and conscription was again an issue in the United States.[5]

Troubling alternative service

Only in 1947 had the U.S. demobilized the last World War II conscripts, and, nearly as soon as the old Selective Service system completed its business, a new draft took its place. The escalating Cold War between the United States and the Soviet Union persuaded Congress in 1948 to establish a large peacetime standing army for home defense and the ongoing occupation of West Germany and Japan. Amazingly, the new law granted conscientious objectors complete and total exemption. Such deferment lasted only a few years, though, as the outbreak of the Korean War in 1950 turned public opinion against COs, and the government demanded some type of alternative service. Beginning in the summer of 1952, objectors were to complete two-year assignments in a work program commonly known by its Selective Service code "I-W."[6]

The I-W program employed COs in city hospitals or nonprofit organizations. Most of the hospital assignees worked as orderlies, cooks, and maintenance personnel, and many public institutions benefited from the inexpensive labor I-W men supplied. The men needed to work outside their home communities, but few other restrictions applied, and the work was civilian-directed. COs often lived on their own in private apart-

Conservative Amish Mennonite Conference women chat with a Mennonite delegate from the Netherlands during the 1948 Mennonite World Conference, Goshen, Indiana.

ments, had charge of their off-duty hours, and even received modest pay. While at first glance such conditions seemed ideal compared with those of World War I, or even World War II, the Amish church was uneasy with the arrangement. The wages, unmonitored free time, and relative isolation of many I-Ws troubled parents.[7]

Some Amish I-Ws had difficulty adjusting to their surroundings. Working in large, impersonal institutions, with no family and few friends, they became lonely and in some cases depressed. Raised in strong extended families and church communities, Old Order youth were often shocked by attitudes and lifestyles of coworkers and superiors. Others reacted by escaping into the surrounding culture. Frequenting popular city nightspots, dating non-Amish hospital employees, and discarding traditional garb, Amish I-W assignees could lose themselves in urban society. Some never returned to their home communities; others came back emotionally distant from their families and disconnected from the church. They had felt out of place in their I-W assignments, but after two years in the city many no longer were comfortable at home, either.

In time, some draftees refused to work in I-W settings, and, in 1955, three Indiana Amish received five-year prison terms and $2,000 fines for resisting induction.[8] Incarcerated in Mill Point, West Virginia, the men could not wear their Amish clothes and refused to put on prison uniforms. Officials would not admit them to the dining hall, but after four weeks of malnutrition, the warden adapted clothing requirements to suit both the state and the men.[9] The government soon brought others to trial, including Joni L. Petersheim of Hazelton, Iowa, who in 1957 received a two-month jail-term and $5,000 fine.[10] In a Cold War context of popular patriotism, draft resistance by the likes of Holmes County native Aden A. Miller (sentenced to three years in federal work camp prison for rejecting I-W employment), made headlines across the country.[11]

Other media notoriety was much more problematic. At times, local police would arrest rowdy Amish teens for disturbing the peace or underage drinking. In the wake of such news stories, public outcry often demanded that older Amish young men liable for the draft not receive conscientious-objector status. After police arrested three LaGrange County, Indiana, Amish young people for public intoxication, the county's draft board president declared, "If they can do things like that . . . I don't see how they can refuse to carry a gun in defense of their country."[12]

While such charges ignored the question of how representative the unruly young people were, the stories were troubling to parents and church leaders alike. Embarrassed Amish adults worked harder to keep teens' behavior in line, yet the Amish were in some ways limited by their own theology. Parents needed to give children the choice between church membership or a life of worldliness. After all, an Anabaptist under-standing of believers' baptism included the real possibility that not everyone would take the way of discipleship. Some chil-dren would not live as their parents might hope, but that did not invalidate the convictions of those Amish who did.

Tragedy and a Christian response

While draft controversy put the Amish in the national lime-light, the church also drew press attention as it applied the principles of peace and nonresistance in a different situation. On a summer 1957 evening, two non-Amish young men recently released from prison rendezvoused in Holmes County, Ohio, to celebrate their freedom. Randomly targeting the Mount Hope home of Old Orders Paul M. and Dora J. (Yoder) Coblentz, the youths robbed the couple and killed Paul. The Amish apparently offered no resistance, and their 19-month-old daughter was unharmed.

Using a stolen car, the two assailants fled to Illinois where they shot a sheriff's deputy before surrendering to arrest. Returned to Ohio, they stood trial for the Coblentz murder, and one of them, Cleo Eugene Peters, was eventually convicted and sentenced to death by electrocution.[13] Shocked and grieving, the Amish community found itself in an uncommon situation. Since the days of the Anabaptist leader Menno Simons, Mennonites and Amish had taken a decided stand against cap-ital punishment. Human life was too valuable and the chance for repentance too real for Christians to approve of executions, they believed. But rarely had the issue been so immediate for the Amish. How would they respond?

God's forgiveness must be extended to all, they reasoned, and letters offering forgiveness and promising prayer arrived at Peters' cell from settlements in many states. Even the young victim and widow wrote to him. Amish families invited Peters' parents into their homes for meals, and church leaders visited him in prison. In addition, the Amish called for a stay of execution. Wrote one Ontario Amishman, "Will we as Amish be left blameless in the matter if we do not present a written request to the authorities, asking that his life be spared"?[14] Individual letters and petitions arrived at the office of Governor C. William O'Neill until the November 7, 1958, execution date. Seven hours before the scheduled electrocution, the governor commuted Peters' sentence.

The whole event had a marked impact on the Holmes County Amish. "God has been speaking to many of us Amish people through this act," several church leaders wrote to Peters. "We believe that God allowed this, especially to call us back to Him in the work of winning souls to His kingdom."[15] In the midst of conflict over military conscription, the Coblentz tragedy cut through that debate to bring into focus the deeper issues of forgiveness and peace in a broken world.

Crisis of conscience

Meanwhile, as the I-W program moved into its second decade, problems and anxieties remained. Some Amish continued to refuse work in alienating urban environments and received fines or prison terms, even as others considered the program worthwhile. "I have worked in a hospital as an orderly for two years and I have not lost my Amish faith," one I-W wrote to *The Budget.* There certainly were "temptations in these hospitals," he acknowledged, but that did not mean that everyone who went to the city would leave the church.[16] Yet, by the mid-1960s, some Amish leaders reported that only about half of their drafted men returned home to the church. Old Order and Beachy Amish leaders asked what might be done to change these realities.

The Beachy Amish launched a two-part strategy: draftee orientation, coordinated by minister Daniel N. King, and the creation of church-related institutions in which drafted men could fulfill their service obligations. King divided the country into six districts, each with a "counseler" who worked to keep connections strong between conscripted men and their churches, and to help I-W participants see their assignments as a type of church service. Beachy churches also created their own service positions, that were then designated by Selective Service as approved I-W assignments. These jobs included Beachy-managed homes for the aged and the international relief agency Amish Mennonite Aid, which employed I-W men in maintenance and clerical tasks.[17]

The Old Order Amish were less eager to construct organizational or bureaucratic apparatus, but they, too, considered how to improve the I-W experience. One response was to launch a modest monthly periodical, *Ambassador of Peace.* Beginning in 1966, each Amish CO received the *Ambassador*, which contained stories by I-W participants, as well as devotional articles and church news.[18] The magazine was the brainchild of Sarah M. Weaver, an Ohio woman living with muscular dystrophy.[19] Weaver spent a good deal of time thinking about and praying for the I-W men, and suggested an Amish periodical might encourage her church's COs.[20]

But by that time, other Old Order leaders were beginning to discuss the formation of a completely new alternative to military conscription. In November 1966, 18 Amishmen gathered in Washington, D.C. to discuss proposed changes in the country's draft law. The group appointed a three-member National Amish Steering Committee to represent them in negotiations with the government. Three months later, at a Holmes County meeting of more than 100 leaders from nine states, the Steering Committee received broad support from the wider church.[21] For Old Orders, forming the Steering Committee was a new step, indeed. Decidedly congregational, the church had never had a national hierarchy or single spokesperson. Committee officers were laymen, which helped ensure their authority was limited to Committee work and would not spill over into matters of church practice or doctrine—decisions that would remain in the hands of local church districts.

Almost immediately, Steering Committee chair Andrew S. Kinsinger of Lancaster County met with officials from Selective Service and began negotiating a compromise agreement—finalized in 1969—whereby young men could perform farm labor in lieu of their military service. Under its terms, the church leased privately owned Amish farms for 26-month periods and hired each farm's owner as farm "manager." Drafted Amishmen then worked on such farms for two years. During the last few years of conscription, many Amish chose such work, although some still took city hospital jobs. Even after the draft ended, the National Steering Committee continued meeting and serving as an intermediary in other church-state conflicts.[22]

More school entanglements

Another source of contention with the state continued to be the proper education of Amish children. The Amish refusal to send their children to large, consolidated elementary schools, or to high schools of any variety, resulting in repeated run-ins with the law.[23] During the late 1950s and 1960s, the pace of public-school consolidation increased in rural areas, and more private Amish schools opened their doors. Throughout the period, Amish parents from Kansas to Pennsylvania found themselves before local magistrates, paying fines and even serving jail terms.

Local officials in some places quietly reached compromise agreements that allowed the Amish to operate private schools without interference, or tailored special rural public schools to meet Amish needs. And in a few cases, Amish children took correspondence courses in an effort to meet state education requirements without attending modern high schools. In 1955, Pennsylvania introduced a "vocational school" plan, later copied by several other states. Under this system, Amish youth who completed eighth grade were free to work at home, but reported to a special "vocational school" one morning per week until they reached the age of 15. Here they continued practicing academic

Amish fathers being released from Lancaster County, Pennsylvania, prison in the early 1950s. The men had been jailed for violating compulsory school attendance laws.

skills and turned in weekly work journals. In 1967, Ontario's government also granted the Amish the right to establish and manage their own schools apart from provincial regulations.[24]

In other places, however, working agreements were elusive, and some communities suffered repeated conflicts. One of the most widely publicized cases occurred near the Buchanan County, Iowa, town of Hazelton.[25] After the 1947 school consolidation around Hazelton, local Old Orders withdrew from public school participation. Instead, they retained two abandoned one-room public schools, hired teachers, and maintained the facilities themselves. Fourteen years later, residents of Hazelton and a neighboring town voted to combine their already consolidated school systems. Some Hazelton citizens were upset by the merger and resented their high school moving to the next county, but because the Amish believed that the new combined district would allow them to continue their schools, a number of Amish had voted for the merger. In the end, the Amish votes may have been decisive, and local Hazelton citizens angry about the combining of the schools resented the Amish voting for a joint district in which Old Order children presumably would not participate.

In any case, the new school district conglomerate had no intention of allowing the Amish free reign to manage their own schools. Officials visited the one-room schools and declared them too primitive for long-term use. The Amish could use the structures for two more years, and then only through sixth grade; older students would need to attend the public junior high school.

The Amish balked, and in the fall of 1962 reopened their buildings with their own uncertified Amish teachers. Locals promised to take action against the schools for failing to meet state instructional standards. Yet the schools were not unusual. Amish private schools like those condemned in Buchanan County routinely received state approval to operate in other parts of Iowa. Nor was the use of uncertified teachers particu-

"Let's skip the Viet Cong for a moment—what are we gonna do about the Amish school kids in Iowa?"

larly uncommon; at the time, half of all Iowa's public secondary schools employed some uncertified teachers. What was unique in Buchanan County was the civic emotion that forestalled all compromise.

The controversy smoldered until the fall of 1965 when authorities moved to close the Amish schools, citing their uncertified teachers as the basis for their action. On the morning of November 19, officials arrived at one of the schoolhouses, intent on loading the students onto a bus and transporting them to Hazelton Elementary. The children began walking toward the bus in an orderly way when an Amish adult shouted "Run!" (in German), and the students dashed for the surrounding fields. The resulting mayhem left only a handful of children in police hands and the rest scurrying for home. Press photographers captured images of fleeing children and angry officials, and the day's events appeared in newspapers around the country.

The next week, public education administrators and local police arrived at the second Amish school, only to repeat the chaos of the Friday before. Instead of running, the children here sang "Jesus Loves Me" at the tops of their voices, while mothers cried and stern-faced fathers stood in protest by the doorway. Governor Harold E. Hughes declared a three-week suspension on interfering with the Amish, and national sympathy began to coalesce around them. Private contributions poured in to pay for Amish fines and penalties, and Governor Hughes asked the state legislature to address the situation. By 1967, the General Assembly had agreed to exempt from certain public-school requirements any Amish who had been in the state for at least a decade. The Buchanan County Amish could now manage their own schools with their own teachers, just as the Amish did in other parts of Iowa.

Supreme Court resolution

The Buchanan County incident attracted attention, and one person who took special interest was Iowa native Rev. William

C. Lindholm, who in 1965 was pastor of Grace Lutheran Church in East Tawas, Michigan.[26] Lindholm saw the situation in terms of religious liberty and, with the encouragement of the National Council of Churches, decided to get involved. He attended a University of Chicago conference on the regulation of non-public schools and called on those interested in Amish civil rights to organize. The resulting National Committee for Amish Religious Freedom (NCARF) included lawyers, academics, and Christian and Jewish religious leaders, and it bore

Amishmen ascending the steps of the U.S. Supreme Court. In 1972, the Court ruled in favor of the Amish request to end formal education with eighth grade.

Supreme Court of the United States: State of Wisconsin, Petitioner, v. Jonas Yoder, Adin Yutzy, and Wallace Miller. On *Writ of Certiorari* to the Supreme Court of Wisconsin. [May 15, 1972], No. 70-110.

Excerpts from the 1972 United States Supreme Court case *Wisconsin v. Yoder, et al.* The court unanimously sided with the Amish defendants. Chief Justice Warren Burger wrote the majority opinion. (Justice William Douglass dissented in part from Warren's opinion, but agreed in the main. Several other justices wrote concurring opinions.)

"Amish objection to formal education beyond the eighth grade is firmly grounded in . . . central religious concepts. They object to high school and higher education generally because the values it teaches are in marked variance with Amish values and the Amish way of life. . . . The high school tends to emphasize intellectual and scientific accomplishments, self-determination, competitiveness, worldly success, and social life with other students. Amish society emphasizes learning-through-doing, a life of 'goodness' rather than technical knowledge, community welfare rather than competition, and separation rather than integration with worldly society.

"As the record so strongly shows, the values and programs of the modern secondary school are in sharp conflict with the fundamental mode of life mandated by the Amish religion; modern laws requiring compulsory secondary education have accordingly engendered great concern and conflict. The conclusion is inescapable that secondary schooling, by exposing Amish children to worldly influences in terms of attitudes, goals and values contrary to beliefs, and by substantially interfering with the religious development of the Amish child and his integration into the way of life of the Amish faith community at the crucial adolescent state of development, contra-venes the basic religious tenets and practices of the Amish faith, both as to the parent and child . . . . The State's require-ment of compulsory formal education after the eighth grade would gravely endanger if not destroy the free exercise of respondents' religious beliefs.

"The State attacks respondents' position as one fostering 'ignorance' from which the child must be protected by the State. No one can question the State's duty to protect children from ignorance but this argument does not square with the facts disclosed in the record. Whatever their idiosyncrasies as seen by the majority, this record strongly shows that the Amish community has been a highly successful social unit within our society even if apart from the conventional 'main-stream.' . . .

"It is neither fair nor correct to suggest that the Amish are opposed to education beyond the eighth grade level. What this record shows is that they are opposed to conventional formal education of the type provided by a certified high school because it comes at the child's crucial adolescent period of religious development. . . .

"We must not forget that in the Middle Ages important val-ues of the civilization of the western world were preserved by members of religious orders who isolated themselves from all worldly influences against great obstacles. There can be no assumption that today's majority is 'right' and the Amish and others like them are 'wrong.' A way of life that is odd or even erratic but interferes with no rights or interests of others is not to be condemned because it is different. . . ."

By the Court: Chief Justice Warren E. Burger, Justices Harry A. Blackmun, William J. Brennan, Jr., William O. Douglas, Thurgood Marshall, Potter Stewart, and Byron R. White. (Justices Lewis F. Powell, Jr. and William H. Rehnquist took no part in the consideration or decision of the case.)

much of the moral urgency of interest-group advocacy that flowered in those years.

By the time NCARF formed, the Iowa conflict had calmed considerably, but new problems were surfacing in Kansas, where Hutchinson Amish resident LeRoy Garber had been convicted of not sending his daughter to the local high school, and Kansas rejected the Pennsylvania-style "vocational school" compromise. NCARF discussed the situation but could do nothing without the chance to argue a federal appeal, and the U.S. Supreme Court had refused to review the case.[27]

For their part, the Garbers and some other Old Orders decided to leave Kansas. Migration always had been an option for Amish facing inflexible state laws. The Adin Yutzy family had left Buchanan County, Iowa, during the height of that controversy and moved to a settlement in Green County, Wisconsin, that since 1964 had attracted Amish from around the Midwest.[28] Then in the fall of 1968, Wisconsin authorities arrested three Green County fathers for not sending their children to high school. Ironically, one of the men was Adin Yutzy, who had faced the same situation in Iowa. Hearing of the arrests, Lindholm contacted Harrisburg, Pennsylvania, attorney William Bentley Ball, who began to prepare a legal defense. In the spring of 1969, NCARF lost its case in Green County Court.[29] Although the court acknowledged that the government had violated Amish religious liberty, the decision held that a "compelling state interest" overshadowed religious rights. On appeal, the Wisconsin Supreme Court decided in favor of the church and parents. No such "compelling right" existed in this incident, the justices said, and the church posed no significant threat to society by choosing an eighth-grade education.[30]

The case was not exhausted, however, as Wisconsin appealed its state's high court verdict to the U.S. Supreme Court. In December 1971, attorney Ball argued persuasively in

The rise of Old Order Amish schools, 1925-2002

Many Old Order schoolteachers, directors, and parents subscribe to *Blackboard Bulletin,* an Amish-published magazine devoted to the interests of Old Order grade schools. *Blackboard Bulletin* includes features and columns about teaching, classroom management, and lesson ideas, as well as letters and editorials. The publisher maintains a school directory, which includes information on school origins that demonstrate the growth of such schools.

Number of current Old Order Amish Schools founded during each decade

1920s	1
1930s	2
1940s	12
1950s	50
1960s	153
1970s	171
1980s	212
1990s	363
2000-2002	156

An additional 126 schools listed did not report a founding date.

During the 2002-2003 school year there were 1,246 schools, with 1,778 teachers and 34,194 pupils, plus 71 special education classrooms that enrolled 209 students with 83 teachers.

Washington, D.C. The following spring, the Supreme Court handed down its decision in *Wisconsin v. Yoder, et al,* ruling that the government did not have reason to deny the Amish their right to practice their faith and teach their children—even if such teaching included no certified high school work.[31] Lack of formal secondary education has not made the Amish a social or economic "burden" to American society, Chief Justice Warren E. Burger reasoned in his majority opinion.

While legal conservatives such as Robert Bork criticized the decision as another example of special privilege for undeserving minorities, *Wisconsin v. Yoder* has become a key religious freedom case cited in hundreds of later rulings. Ball saw it as more than a victory for the Amish. "The results of the decision not only helped the Amish people everywhere," he later commented, "but the terrific emphasis on religious liberty and parental rights is just golden."[32]

Since *Wisconsin v. Yoder,* the Old Order Amish (and similar or related groups, such as Old Order Mennonites and Beachy Amish) have had the legal right to establish and operate their own schools or withdraw from public institutions after completing eighth grade.[33] In some places—notably in the older Ohio and Indiana settlements—a significant minority of parents has continued to send their children to public elementary schools, but *Yoder* settled most conflicts surrounding exemption from high school. Only in Nebraska did difficulties for the Amish persist. Not interested in additional court cases, the Amish finally left that state in 1982.[34]

Church life at mid-century: mission interests, conservative dissent, and the "New Order"

If conflicts with military and educational establishments were the most public parts of post-war Amish life, they were far from the only events to mark those years. Less well known to outsiders were the churchly discussions and debates of the 1950s and 1960s that resulted in renewal and division. Like the controversy of the 1860s that birthed Old Order and Amish Mennonite groups, the mid-twentieth century mix of ideas and activities is not always easy to simplify or categorize. There were more than two sides to most issues, and when division came it was typically a sorting-out process over several years, rather than a single or decisive break. Nor was the religious dissension of these years unconnected to the conflicts with the state that were occurring simultaneously. Many of the church-ly arguments involved the role of parents and teens, as well as interaction with the larger society—all issues that seemed more acute when Selective Service, public school officials, and media reporters were scrutinizing Amish young-adult and family life.

Starting in the late 1940s, a small but vigorous concern for mission work emerged among some Old Orders, especially in the Midwest.[35] The impulse had several roots, but was fanned into flame by Russell Maniaci, a convert to Mennonitism who took a keen interest in encouraging scattered Amish interest in evangelism.[36] In 1950, Maniaci organized an Amish mission conference in Iowa that drew about 150 people and signaled the beginning of an identifiable movement. Although Amish participants soon tried to distance themselves from the often brash Maniaci himself, they clearly were intent on cooperative church work that spanned various settlements and worked out-side traditional church structures. In 1952, they organized a Mission Interests Committee (MIC), and the next year launched a modest newsletter entitled *Witnessing*.

Eventually, the MIC sponsored Amish mission-workers in Mississippi, Ontario, and Arkansas, but another aim of these mission-minded folks was moral reform within Old Order cir-cles. Troubled especially by the rowdiness of some Amish teens, mission-movement advocates stressed tighter parental control and church-supervised youth activities. Such concerns may have had fairly broad sympathy, but when coupled with other mission-movement ideas, they failed to win Old Order endorsement. By the mid-1950s, when some younger mission advocates began saying that cars might be necessary for effective church work, and then enrolled in college courses to equip themselves for ministry, even once-supportive Old Orders expressed dismay.

Added to the mix was the remarkable preaching of David A. Miller, a Thomas, Oklahoma, Amish minister who, during the 1950s, became something of a traveling Amish evangelist. Preaching to sizable groups wherever and whenever he could command a hearing, Miller addressed Amish audiences in the Midwest and Pennsylvania, everywhere provoking a decidedly mixed response.[37] Although not formally connected to the mission movement, Miller combined sermons on temperance and courtship chastity with a highly innovative and emotional style, so that the medium often cast a shadow on the message.

The Amish in Latin America

As conflict with the state and pressure on rural communities seemed to increase in the 1950s and 1960s, some Amish floated the idea of leaving North America behind. As early as 1951, Samuel Hertzler of Saint Mary's County, Maryland, visited Honduras, exploring its suitability for settlement. Although he reported "it might be an ideal place for Amish to get away from the turmoil of our modern country including [the military] draft, unreasonable school laws, and high land prices," his family did not pursue his Central American dream.

In 1967, another family with a similar idea—Peter and Anna (Wagler) Stoll, of Aylmer, Ontario—scouted land opportunities in Honduras, and along with several other households moved to farms near Guaimaca the next year. Soon, 16 families from Ontario, Indiana, and Pennsylvania were part of the new community. The soil was productive, and the Amish adjusted to the climate and new crops while trying to master Spanish. A new issue they faced was the presence of poverty. In North America, they had lived simpler lives than their neighbors, but in Honduras the Amish were considered wealthy—they owned land, horses, and homes. "We have been challenged," wrote one Amishman from the Honduran community, "to live less luxuriously as we have come face to face with the poor and hungry." Several families adopted Honduran orphans, and, in 1974, the Guaimaca Amish built a small cement-block school for the neighboring children.

Tension within the Honduran church proved to be the group's major difficulty. From its beginning, the settlement included those with both New Order and Old Order leanings, and that mix proved problematic—especially as lifestyle and technological innovation seemed to increase. By 1977, some families returned to North America. The next year, almost all of the Old Orders resettled in Aylmer, Ontario, while several of the New Order-oriented members moved to eastern Ohio. Those who remained in Honduras eventually affiliated with the Beachy Amish.

While the Honduran experiment was taking shape, other North American families were packing their bags for Paraguay. In 1967, seven families from Orange County, Indiana, moved to Paraguay's Chaco region, already home to a sizable group of conservative Mennonites, and settled near these spiritual cousins. When more families arrived, the community seemed off to a good start. Bishop Noah J. Coblentz of Lakeside, Ontario, despite his advanced age, traveled twice by ship to Paraguay and helped organize the church and ordain resident leaders.

The Paraguayan farms prospered, but the Amish there never formed a stable congregation, and, in 1978, nearly all the settlers returned to the United States. A few tried to keep church life going, but with the departure of most of the members and all of the leaders, the remnant was hard pressed to continue. The few who remain in Paraguay use no motor vehicles, worship in Spanish and English, and have built a meetinghouse. They have no formal connection to any other Amish.

One participant in the Latin American settlements later reflected on his own disappointment in their demise. He always believed that "our way of life" actually was better suited for an agrarian Latin American context "than a rich and mechanized country such as Canada or the United States," and that "our churches should thrive better spiritually" among the poor. Yet the communities failed. "Perhaps," he speculated, it was "because the immigrants to Latin America have been the more adventuresome type, less stable and less conservative than the ones that do not go."

Sources: Joseph Stoll, *Sunshine and Shadow: Our Seven Years in Honduras* (Aylmer, Ont.: J. Stoll, 1996) and "The Amish Settlement at Guaimaca, Honduras," *The Diary* (October 1972): 200, 196-99; Enos Hertzler, *Time Out for Paraguay* (Gordonville, Pa.: Gordonville Print Shop, 1985); J. Winfield Fretz, "The Amish in Paraguay" [n.d.] and "Witnessing a Community's Death" [1978], unpublished papers, Heritage Historical Library; and *The Amish Moving to Maryland* (Gordonville, Pa.: A. S. Kinsinger, 1965).

Few Old Orders were surprised in 1957 when Miller and his church joined the car-driving Beachy Amish.[38] By then, many mission supporters were making similar choices, leaving their Old Order churches and joining nearby Mennonite or Beachy Amish fellowships. In several Amish church districts, mission-movement support had been nearly unanimous, and the entire district simply evolved into a Beachy congregation without schism.

The emergence and dispersal of the mid-century mission movement had several important results. For Old Orders, it confirmed a suspicion that agitating for reform in one aspect of church life probably was linked to a wholesale embrace of modernity. Even the innocent interests of mission-movement supporters quickly produced automobile ownership and higher education. As a result, many Old Orders became more wary of outside religious influences that promised to solve Amish problems with new spiritual insights. Longstanding Amish subscriptions to Mennonite periodicals, for example, began to wane. Significantly, the Old Orders' growing sense of churchly separation after 1960 coincided with their increasing economic integration into surrounding agricultural and business economies. But the demise of the Old Order mission movement may have had an even greater impact on the Beachy Amish, as it injected a sizable group of energetic new members and congregations into Beachy ranks and brought the MIC and its assortment of projects under Beachy auspices. If the Beachy Amish had once been most easily distinguished from Old Orders in technological terms, after about 1960 their outward evangelistic focus would be central to their identity.[39]

But not all reform currents flowed in the same direction. During the 1950s, a few Old Orders who shared some of the mission advocates' moral concerns took those convictions in decidedly different directions. Troubled by teenage antics and opposed to tobacco use, these Amish combined strict moral standards for young people with a principled desire to avoid technological change, maintain a rural way of life, and uphold the practice of "strict shunning." Launching new settlements in places such as Kenton, Ohio, and Paoli, Indiana, they formed a loose network of especially conservative-minded Amish who saw rigorous commitment to a traditional *Ordnung* as the key to spiritual renewal.[40]

A similar dynamic in 1952 sparked the formation in Holmes County, Ohio, of a new and significant Old Order affiliation under the leadership of bishop Andrew J. Weaver. The group sought to stand by the practice of strict shunning and to stave off creeping technological change and worldliness. But the "Andy Weaver Amish" were also concerned about young peo-

ple's activities and moved to restrict some of the liberty traditionally given to unbaptized Amish teens. For example, the
Weaver group disciplined church-member parents who
allowed their sons to purchase cars and then continue to live at
home. Parents could no longer turn a blind eye to the wild
antics associated with teenage car ownership.[41]

In the 1960s, yet a third impulse combining a desire for
church renewal and the interests of youth emerged in Amish
circles. After 1959 in Holmes County, certain ministers
expressed a burden for the spiritual state of their young people.
When some teens requested special "youth meetings" for Bible
study, these leaders gladly obliged.[42] Like the earlier mission-
movement advocates, these organizers stressed strict courtship
practices and nonuse of alcohol and tobacco. But they pressed
their case in terms of the local church and did not link these
causes with distant mission activism or highly emotional
preaching appeals. Proponents stressed their desire to remain
Old Order, though they did not share the highly traditional sentiments of the Andy Weaver folks.

For a time, supporters and skeptics agreed to allow the youth
meetings to run their course, but soon the gatherings became
entangled in a debate over the doctrine of "assurance of salvation," as detractors charged the meetings promoted such teaching. Citing Jesus' words in Mark 13:13 that "he who endures to
the end will be saved," the Amish traditionally had taught that
eternal life was God's gift to those who persevered in a lifelong
reliance upon God's grace.[43] To be sure, in this life Christians
had a living hope of salvation, but announcing that one was
absolutely certain of one's future smacked both of spiritual
pride and human arrogance. After all, the apostle Peter had
warned the early church that anyone could be "led away with
the error of the wicked" and "fall from . . . steadfastness"
(2 Peter 3:17). For their part, youth-meeting leaders insisted
they were misunderstood. In stressing the spiritual basis for
upright living, they claimed only that Christians entered a

knowable relationship with God, and that one could rely on God's sustaining grace. Soon, the youth meetings themselves became a symbol for a cluster of potentially divisive issues.

Low-grade tension simmered in Ohio until late 1966, when a district split over the youth meetings and related issues. In short order, a number of other such separations took place, ultimately dividing those who stood by the youth meetings from those who saw them as another religiously-coated cover for people unwilling to submit to the *Ordnung*. The youth meeting Amish received the nickname "New Order Amish," and, while they preferred the designation "Amish Brotherhood," they reluctantly accepted the New Order label. They were most uncomfortable with the word "new," since they saw themselves standing squarely in the Anabaptist and Amish traditions.[44]

At almost exactly the same time as the New Order church was emerging in Ohio, a similar movement took shape in the Lancaster, Pennsylvania, settlement. There, however, the calls for spiritual renewal were from the beginning tied up with agitation for in-house telephones and tractor-farming, which gave the New Order story there a different feel.[45]

Unlike the earlier mission-movement advocates, the New Order Amish self-consciously retained horse-and-buggy culture and biweekly German language worship, almost always in private homes. Indeed—confusing as the terminology is—the New Order Amish are probably best understood as a sub-group of the Old Order Amish, and they typically are included in tabulations of Old Order communities.[46] Nevertheless, the tone of New Order spirituality is different from most Old Orders. In the words of two leaders, "Many New Orders looked at the Old Order system as having many values, but saw a need for more spiritual convictions to make it effective."[47] Similarly, New Orders have produced a number of articulate tracts and booklets outlining, in a systematic way most Old Orders would be slow to do, their beliefs and practices.[48] Although the two groups remain distinct, today a more amiable relationship exists between them, and New Orders concede that many Old Order parents and leaders care deeply about their young people's welfare.

In 2000, there were some 60 New Order Amish church districts in 13 states, with the majority located in Ohio. All New Orders forbid things like tobacco and "disapprove of the idea that young people need to sow some wild oats before marriage." They also have Sunday schools and church-supervised activities for youth. But New Order churches differ among themselves on questions of appropriate technology, with some forbidding public-utility electricity and tractor-farming, and others accepting them. Dress standards also vary somewhat. In addition, since 1986 in Holmes County, there has been a small breakaway group known as the New Order Fellowship, which accepts a much wider range of technology and a more subjective religious experience.[49]

Life in the welfare state

Regardless of religious conviction, Amish life in modern America was also being shaped by the rise of the welfare state, one of the most far-reaching social developments of the twentieth century. In broad terms, welfare-state philosophy called for deliberate government involvement in economic and social policy to create a better life for all citizens. Rooted in turn-of-the-century Progressive thought, the welfare state took identifiable shape during President Franklin D. Roosevelt's response to the stark economic realities of the Great Depression. Public action on behalf of the unemployed, the poor, the aged, and the disabled were becoming standard public fare by the 1950s and 1960s. In the decades which followed, welfare-state activities grew to include such diverse programs as farm-commodity subsidies, tuition loans for college students, federal funding of airport construction, and pollution-control laws. From "the cradle to the grave," Americans now encountered a host of pro-

Amishmen wait outside the office of the Internal Revenue Service. Social Security taxes have been a point of tension between the Amish and the government.

grams, institutions, and activities designed to better their lives.[50]

For the Amish, the welfare state caused concern for two reasons. First, the "better life" toward which the system strove was not necessarily the Amish ideal. Based on middle-class professional values, most programs encouraged individual achievement and ignored the importance of other minority concerns. Then, too, the welfare state could undercut community-based mutual aid. Church-centered care and extended-family responsibility might become irrelevant in the face of public intervention. Beginning in the mid-1950s, Amish confrontation with the welfare state was frequent. The fact that the church ultimately was rather successful in limiting the state's encroaching power and influence cannot hide the fact that the Amish privilege to care for themselves was not easily gained.

One of the first conflicts erupted in 1955 when Congress extended the Social Security program to include self-employed farmers.[51] Self-employed Amish had never taken part in the 20-year-old program, and, now that participation was mandatory, many refused voluntarily to pay. Internal Revenue Service (IRS) agents began collecting through Amish bank accounts, but a few Amish closed their accounts, making it difficult for the state to tap their resources. In 1958, the government foreclosed on several farms to recover lost Social Security funds. During the next two years, the IRS forcibly collected from 130 other Amish households.[52] Such action, though, did not stop Amish opposition to involvement in a system they saw as misdirected and wrong.

The spring of 1961 saw the most dramatic encounter between the Amish and the IRS. Two years before, the federal government had placed a lien on the workhorses of Valentine Y. Byler, a New Wilmington, Pennsylvania, farmer who had not paid Social Security. The next summer, authorities arrested Byler after he failed to appear in court. The judge immediate-

Old Order Amish and Old Order Mennonites appear in an Ontario courtroom for a hearing on provincial education laws in July 1968.

ly released him, but the following April, agents arrived at Byler's farm while he was involved in spring plowing. Meeting Byler in the middle of the field, they unhitched three of his horses and led them away as confiscated property. The IRS then sold the animals to recover Byler's unpaid Social Security. While officials also seized horses from other Amish, Byler's case became the celebrated incident.[53]

Since the government's method of recovering funds deprived the Byler family of its livelihood, Byler sued Washington for damages. Church leaders forced him to withdraw the case, rejecting as un-Christian the use of the court system for revenge, but public outcry led to an IRS moratorium on collecting Social Security from the Amish.[54] In the summer of 1965, Congress addressed the problem with the nation's new Medicare bill. A subsection of that measure exempted self-employed Amish from both Medicare and Social Security.[55] But Amish employers and employees were still liable for all Social Security taxes. In 1982, the Supreme Court upheld the necessity of such payment, but six years later Congress sided with the church and passed another exemption. Since 1988, if Amish employees work for Amish employers, neither party must pay Social Security payroll taxes.[56] The IRS still requires Amish employees of non-Amish employers to contribute fully to Social Security, even though most refuse to draw benefits from the system.

After 1970, Amish men employed in construction rejected the hard-hats stipulations in the new Occupational Safety and Health Act, preferring their own felt or straw hats or knit caps. In 1972, federal authorities granted Amish workers a headgear exemption. Workers Compensation, farm-commodity subsidies, Medicare, Department of Agriculture dairy-herd reduction plans, and other welfare-state activity all have raised special problems. Much publicity resulted from the opposition of a few ultra-conservative Amish to the bright orange slow-moving vehicle signs required on Amish carriages. Often the National Amish Steering Committee has been involved in finding negotiated settlements agreeable to all sides, but sometimes the state resorts to litigation.[57]

In Canada, too, welfare-state policies resulted in conflict with the church. Ironically, in 1953, American Amish had begun migrating to Ontario, in part because they perceived Canada to have relatively fewer welfare-state entanglements.[58] Whether or not the Amish rightly judged the situation on that score, the rapid rise and spread of Canadian social programs was soon apparent, and Old Orders confronted their new home's National Pension Plan. By 1967, Revenue Canada was invading Amish bank accounts and garnering wages to collect unpaid Pension Plan taxes. Finally, in 1974, self-employed Amish received exemption from the system, but the situation for Amish employees and employers remains problematic. Some businesses have become multi-member partnerships so that each employee is a self-employed part owner. Canadian Amish also accepted Social Insurance numbers, but those numbers are digitized so that they cannot be used to receive benefits. Milk-marketing regulations have also proven difficult for the Amish, so that since 1977, the number of Amish-owned dairy operations in Canada has declined. Many Old Orders have moved to other types of farming or non-farming work, or returned to the United States.[59]

Occupational diversity and social change

During the last decades of the twentieth century, non-farming jobs became more common among Old Orders throughout North America. Along with the rise in popular tourism and the demographic growth of the Amish church itself, the shift away from farming as an economic and social base has been one of three significant developments marking recent Amish history.

As early as the 1930s and 1940s, a few Amish men in communities such as Nappanee, Indiana, had taken employment in area industry.[60] But after 1970, the shift to non-farm labor became much more pronounced, and by 2003 was a reality in

In recent decades, Amish employment has shifted away from agriculture. In most settlements, a growing number of men hold non-farm jobs in businesses such as this furniture shop in Holmes County, Ohio.

virtually every Amish settlement. In 1973, only 31 percent of Old Order household heads in the Geauga County, Ohio, settlement were farming. Two decades later, that percentage had dropped to 17 percent. By 2002 in the Elkhart-LaGrange, Indiana, settlement, less than 20 percent of the men under age 65 were farming. And even in the Lancaster, Pennsylvania, settlement where farmers had still been a majority in 1986, by 2000 the share had slipped to 44 percent.[61] Even in newer settlements begun by Amish exiting densely populated areas for cheaper land and more rural elbow room, farming often is a minority occupation.

The drift away from farming is rooted in long-term demographic and economic changes. Large families produced steady Amish-population growth that began to outstrip available farmland, and in certain communities—such as those near Lancaster, Pennsylvania; Cleveland, Ohio; or Fort Wayne, Indiana—suburbanization and rising land prices compounded the problem. Also, many Old Orders preferred small-scale, low-mechanized farming, which became less viable in the 1970s as corporate agriculture consolidated business, and government subsidies tilted the playing field in favor of big producers. As well, new cooling standards in milk-marketing added extra costs, and in some cases conflicted with the *Ordnung* of more conservative church districts, forcing them to settle for grade B production. Some Amish have tried to stay in farming by employing new approaches to raising livestock or switching to organic produce markets, with mixed success.[62]

Farming remains an esteemed and ideal way of life, and the basis on which many Amish cultural traditions originally rested. The abandonment of the farm by an increasing number of families carries with it the possibility of significant change, though it has by no means meant the end of Amish society. Indeed, a variety of studies have shown that children of Amish farmers are no more likely to abandon the church than children of Amish carpenters or factory workers.[63] The implications of occupational change hinge in part on the type of work Amish choose to take up after laying down their plows. Small businesses, industrial employment, and carpentry work crews constitute three broad categories of Amish employment.

Small businesses—from metal fabrication shops to dry-goods stores—are often at-home and family-centered. Like farming, they engage several generations and produce busy schedules that leave little time for leisure. But because they are home-based, they also offer the possibility of introducing change into the center of family life itself. And if the lack of high school and college credentials keep Old Orders from professional pursuits, Amish entrepreneurs have proven remarkably successful and, in some cases, quite wealthy. Many such small businesses are owned and operated by Amish women, which adds a new dimension to Amish gender traditions.[64]

Factory employment has been the most common occupation among Amish men in northern Indiana and Geauga County,

Ohio, for several decades. In Nappanee, Indiana, for example, in 2001, some 72 percent of Amish men age 35 and younger worked in factories. Most spent their days on assembly lines building recreational vehicles and mobile homes or in related plants supplying component parts for line assembly.[65] Industrial work introduces a somewhat different set of dynamics from that of at-home entrepreneurship. The 40-hour industrial workweek offers steady paychecks with plenty of free time. It also separates home and work environments, leaving children with fewer ways to contribute to the family's welfare.

Carpentry or other mobile work crews related to the construction trades has been a third popular option among Amish men who are unable to farm or are uninterested in farming. Such work is tied to a recognized Amish tradition of craftsmanship. It is also attractive to Amish who adhere to a more traditional *Ordnung* that bans most newer technology from the home or at-home shop. By working for a non-Amish employer or customer, these Amish carpenters are free to use power tools and other devices in the service of others, which they would not use on their own turf. The drawbacks of such arrangements, from the Amish perspective, include men's traveling (in a rented vehicle) sometimes great distances to work, and the consequent absence of fathers from home for especially long workdays. Nevertheless, mobile-work crews provide employment for sizable majorities of Amish household-heads in some communities.

Attracting attention

A second significant development in recent years has been a growing fascination on the part of larger society with the Amish. From the rise of Amish tourism and the popularity of Amish-built furniture, to the easy way politicians and comedians can make allusions to the Amish and safely assume their audiences know whom they are talking about, it is clear that a remarkable transformation has taken place. Without any public relations campaign, promotional budget, or celebrity spokesperson, a small and self-effacing group has become exceedingly well known, even as North American interest in other denominational differences and distinctions otherwise declines.

The 1930s Pennsylvania public school controversy brought the first extended media attention to the Old Orders, as *Time, Literary Digest,* and *The New York Times* featured the conflict.[66] Later, in the 1950s, articles on the Amish and military conscription also found their way into newspapers around the country, as did stories of other confrontations between the Amish and the state. The complex roots of Amish-related tourism included the effects of such public notoriety, along with the post-war penchant for travel and vacation and

Old Order Amish settlements with 14 or more church districts, 2002

Location	Church districts
Holmes-Wayne/adjacent counties, Ohio	197
Lancaster County, Pennsylvania	142
Elkhart-LaGrange counties, Indiana	115
Geauga-Trumbull counties, Ohio	78
Berne, Indiana	36
Nappanee, Indiana	33
Arthur, Illinois	25
Daviess County, Indiana	20
Mifflin/adjacent counties, Pennsylvania	19
Allen County, Indiana	15
Indiana County, Pennsylvania	14
New Wilmington, Pennsylvania	14

Source: *New American Almanac* [Raber's], 2003.

American anxiety about the modern society they were creating. Amish dissent from that set of national priorities was both intriguing and troubling for those who wondered if the Amish were simply relics from the past or sources of wisdom who knew something everyone else was fast forgetting.

Given its proximity to east coast population centers, Lancaster County, Pennsylvania, became a destination of middle-class vacationers eager to catch a glimpse of Amish life. In 1946, a major Lancaster City hotel offered bus trips through Amish farm country, and, by 1950, a New York City-based tour company boasted regular excursions to Lancaster's Amish community. An explosion of picture books and knickknacks satisfied the desires of those eager to consume the commercialized simple life. In 1955, a non-Amish entrepreneur opened The Amish Farm and House for tours, probably the first paid-admission Amish-theme attraction.[67] Two years later, as the number of annual visitors to Lancaster County approached a million, the local Chamber of Commerce launched the Pennsylvania Dutch Visitors Bureau to handle lodging arrangements and generally promote tourism in the region.[68] While Amish-related tourism in the Midwest got off to a slower start, by 1960, organized tours were bringing visitors to see the Holmes County, Ohio, Amish settlement, and a June 1967 article in *Travel* suggested visiting northern Indiana's Old Order community. Amish-theme restaurants and attractions soon opened in both states.[69]

Meanwhile, Amish characters were popping up in popular culture. Young children learned about the Amish through Marguerite de Angeli's 1944 story *Yonie Wondernose,* which received a wide audience after winning the American Library Association's Caldecott Honor for its illustrations.[70] Books for teens and adults—including a Nancy Drew mystery, *The Witch Tree Symbol*—further popularized Amish images, settings, and plots.[71] In 1955, Twentieth Century Fox released an Ernest Borgnine film, "Violent Saturday," in which criminals hid on an

Amish farm. Earlier that year, the Mark Hellinger Theatre in New York City opened "Plain and Fancy," a wildly popular Broadway musical that celebrated Amish rural life even as it subtly criticized the tradition and practice of Amish church discipline that underlay that life.[72]

Occasionally, offended Amish leaders have voiced protest against their people's portrayal in such secular formats. When the 1984 filming of Paramount Pictures' "Witness" disturbed the Lancaster Amish community, they addressed their concerns to the Pennsylvania government. ("Witness" portrayed the Lancaster Old Orders innocently entangled in a web of big-city drug crime.) A delegation of Amish leaders, including three bishops, traveled to the state capitol to register their complaint. As a result, Harrisburg promised not to encourage any future filming of motion-picture or television scripts involving Amish themes.[73]

Nevertheless, popular interest—measured in tourist numbers or pop-culture allusions or the commercialization of the word *Amish* by outsiders—only grew in the two decades that followed. The Amish themselves are often uneasy about their sudden popularity, fearing it provides a spiritual temptation to pride rather than an authentic witness. In 1998, when several Amish-reared men did become involved in a drug ring more bizarre than even "Witness" had portrayed, the publicity was enormous. Some Amish and other onlookers believed that society's earlier adulation only encouraged the resulting charges of Amish hypocrisy.[74]

Historian David Weaver-Zercher has looked at popular interest in the Amish and helpfully explained how it combines highly romanticized and deeply critical elements. Modern observers are intrigued by people who demonstrate the possibility of countercultural choices and show that life can be different. But, Weaver-Zercher found, moderns also desperately want to believe that such dissenters are deeply flawed, thereby reassuring themselves of modernity's superiority. In the end, pop culture actually encourages North Americans to admire, but then dismiss, the Amish way.[75]

If popular attention to the Amish reveals much about modern Americans' hopes and fears, it also has an impact on how the Amish think about themselves. Despite tourism's pressures, sociologist Donald B. Kraybill has suggested that visitation fortifies Amish life as it "galvanizes the cultural gap between the two worlds and helps define Amish identity." In fact, growing public interest in the Amish may bolster public sympathy for them and discourage government infringement on Amish rights that would force them to move away.[76]

The presence of tourism has other, more immediate results. In some communities, the press of popularity produces overcrowded roads and curious mobs clicking cameras and posing persistent questions.[77] While a few Amish have chosen to move away from such areas, most remain. Some take jobs in businesses that cater to the tourist trade, and a few operate full-scale retail shops that rely on visitor dollars. Amish women may supplement family income by selling quilts or other craft items from their homes or roadside stands. If modern Americans are ambivalent about their response to the Amish, the Amish have mixed feelings about tourism. Some find it a complete nuisance, while others profit from it. Yet most believe that tourists typically are sincere seekers, genuinely interested in learning about others.

Growth in the midst of modernity

Both the shift toward non-farm employment and the increasing public recognition of the Amish are related to a third feature of recent Amish history: persistent population growth. In the midst of modernity and assorted pressures from the welfare and warfare state, the Amish have remained remarkably resilient. Despite mid-twentieth-century predictions that they would not long survive the currents of assimilation or resist the inevitable logic of individual fulfillment in the liberal state, the

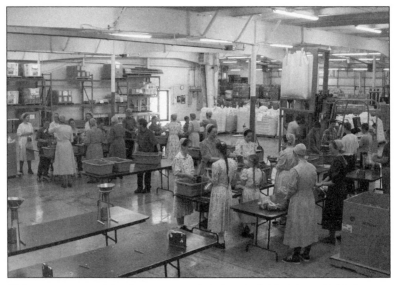

Volunteers prepacking beans at a Christian Aid Ministries (CAM) warehouse in 2003. CAM receives strong support from Beachy Amish churches, as well as from some Old Order Amish and conservative-minded Mennonites. Some 12,000 volunteers per year donate time at this warehouse, preparing about 8,000 food boxes each month for distribution in Eastern Europe, Latin America, Africa, and the Middle East.

Amish have not disappeared. Indeed, they have grown in numbers and, in recent years, even increased their rate of growth.

The explanations and implications of such growth vary, but the increases themselves are readily recognizable. For its part, the Beachy Amish church has expanded to include more than 150 congregations in 23 states and one province, along with 39 other churches in 10 counties on four continents. During the 30 years between 1972 and 2002, the Beachy churches' membership climbed 129 percent.[78] Children reared in Beachy Amish homes are the major source of North-American membership increase. But some of this domestic and much of the international growth have come from systematic mission work during the later decades of the twentieth century.

Beachy mission programs through the Mission Interests Committee and Amish Mennonite Aid have resulted in new congregations in places not historically home to Amish people. Often this mission activity includes the migration of a core group of families whose corporate life together serves as the basis for their witness.[79] While many Beachy Amish are keen to engage in verbal evangelism, they also support agencies such as Christian Aid Ministries (CAM), a large international relief and service organization headquartered in Berlin, Ohio, and founded in 1981 by David N. Troyer, now a Beachy Amish layman. CAM receives solid Beachy backing and provides congregations with a tangible link to other parts of the world.[80]

In contrast, the Old Order Amish are cool to organized and bureaucratized mission programs, skeptical of the ability to communicate faithful living through words. While individual Old Order households—especially those in the New Order affiliation—sometimes contribute money or even time at a CAM warehouse or other domestic service site, they harbor reservations about large institutions disconnected from the demands of daily discipleship.[81] Despite their resistance to missionary strategizing, the Old Orders have grown even more rapidly in recent years. While the Amish do not keep systematic membership records on a national basis, the change in the number of church districts reflects their membership trends. Since Old Orders worship in homes, shops, or barns, whenever a given church district's membership grows too large to comfortably continue such meeting, the church divides into two districts. Those patterns of division and multiplication make it clear that the Old Order circle is growing; in the quarter century between 1974 and 2003, the number of Old Order Amish church districts rose 217 percent.[82]

While older communities expand, Amish families also establish new settlements almost annually.[83] Church districts now stretch from Dover, Delaware, to Springdale, Washington, and from Smyrna, Maine, to Sarasota, Florida. Twenty-eight states and the province of Ontario are home to an ever-growing number of Old Order churches. While Amish populations remain concentrated in Ohio, Pennsylvania, and Indiana, those states account for a smaller share of the Amish population than in the past. In 1974, they were home to three-quarters of all Old Orders, but, by 2003, their share had dropped to 66 percent, with Wisconsin, Michigan, and New York attracting many new settlements. Those states, plus Missouri and Kentucky, now account for more than a fifth of the Amish membership and have eclipsed older areas of residence such as Illinois and Iowa.[84] Those forming new communities seek available, affordable rural acreage, though not necessarily farms, since even in today's new communities, farming is often a minority occupation.

Although it is quite possible for those raised in non-Amish homes to join the Old Order church, very few do so. Instead, large families are the key source of Old Order increase. Yet the presence of children is no guarantee of growth, since those reared in Amish homes must choose church membership and baptism as adults. Central to the Old Order Amish story of recent decades has been the rising percentage of Amish offspring who join their parents' church. Comprehensive studies in northern Indiana, northeast Ohio, and eastern Pennsylvania point to identical trends. In the Elkhart-LaGrange, Indiana, settlement, for example, of those born in the 1930s, 21 percent did not join the Old Order church, but of those born in the 1950s, the dropout rate dipped to 10 percent. In many places, retention rates now are 90 percent or more.[85]

Scholars and the Amish themselves suggest possible reasons for the church's increasing attraction in recent years. The rise of Amish parochial schools as a resource for socializing children and presenting a learning environment in harmony with the church and the home is one important piece. Private schools enroll an increasing percentage of Amish students, even in settlements where public-school attendance is still possible.[86]

Other observers point to the growing gap between Old Order culture and wider society, arguing that increased contact with the world through factory employment or tourism confirms for the Amish their sense of separation. Still others suggest that the growing variety of occupational pursuits in Amish circles now makes it economically easier to remain Amish. The choice to stay, in many communities, is no longer reliant on one's ability to find a farm or succeed in agriculture.[87]

Another factor may be the presence of modest and low-profile institutions that bolster and help to define Amish community. These include the books and magazines of Pathway Publishers, printed in Aylmer, Ontario. The monthly periodical *Family Life*, along with *Young Companion* for teens and children, support Amish values though stories, poems, and editorials. Pathway also issues historical fiction, devotional, and prayer books, as well as Amish school texts. Several Amish communi-

The Old Order Amish remain a growing group in the twenty-first century, not only because of their large families, but also because an increasing percentage of Amish children choose to follow their parents' faith.

ties have established historical libraries to support the transmission of heritage and faith, while other settlements have organized trust funds, offering low-interest loans to church members for mortgages or small business start-ups. Finally, a loose network of "People's Helpers" coordinates the efforts of Amish who in some places act as lay counselors, assisting those with a variety of personal or family problems.[88] It is important to note that, despite their small scale, none of these institutions is uniformly accepted in Old Order circles, especially among more conservative-leaning members, skeptical of activity and organization other than that of the local church. Nevertheless, in many places, these formalized connections have helped nurture a broader sense of peoplehood alongside demographic and geographic expansion.

If some Amish speculate on the social causes of their church's health and strength, they typically are also quick to credit the mystery of divine goodness. There simply is no logical explanation, one Old Order sage remarked, "that can explain the basic fundamentals of their faith that was inherited from ancestors of many generations ago, which was granted to them through the grace of our Lord Jesus Christ." Instead, the Amishman thought, his people had "cultivated as their every day mission" the task of Christian discipleship, and "feel that their mission is to lead an humble life that needs no publicity."[89]

And yet notice comes, even if it is sometimes misguided or misinformed. In a world seeking security in more powerful weapons, happiness in scarce resources, and faith in the individual's ability to hasten human progress, Amish life continues to compel many moderns to stop and think about choices and decisions—watching, weighing, and wondering—as the Amish story continues.

Old Order Amish Church Districts, 1974 and 2003

Location	1974 Church districts	2003 Church districts
Canada		
Ontario	16	26
Honduras	1	—
Paraguay	1	—
United States		
Colorado	—	1
Delaware	5	8
Florida	1	1
Idaho	—	1
Illinois	12	36
Indiana	91	246
Iowa	15	40
Kansas	4	8
Kentucky	3	41
Maine	—	1
Maryland	3	7
Michigan	9	66
Minnesota	3	16
Mississippi	—	1
Missouri	19	49
Montana	—	5
Nebraska	—	1
New York	5	51
North Carolina	—	1
Ohio	136	375
Oklahoma	1	5
Pennsylvania	104	312
Tennessee	4	11

Location	1974 Church districts	2003 Church districts
Texas	—	1
Virginia	1	3
Washington	—	1
West Virginia	—	2
Wisconsin	11	93
Total	**444**	**1,410**

Old Order Amish baptized membership in 2000, approximately 77,000.

Old Order Amish total population (including unbaptized children) in 2000, approximately 175,000.

Statistics in this table are for all horse-driving Old Order subgroups (including New Order Amish and New Order Fellowship).

Church districts in older, established settlements often include 60-75 adult members and 90-100 children. In newer, smaller settlements, districts often include fewer people.

Source: David Luthy, "Old Order Amish Settlements in 1974," *Family Life,* (December 1974), 13-16; and "Amish Settlements Across America: 2003," *Family Life* (October 2003),17-23. Luthy's periodic tabulations are the most accurate statistics. See also his compilations for the years 1984 and 1991 in the December 1984 and April 1992 issues of *Family Life.*

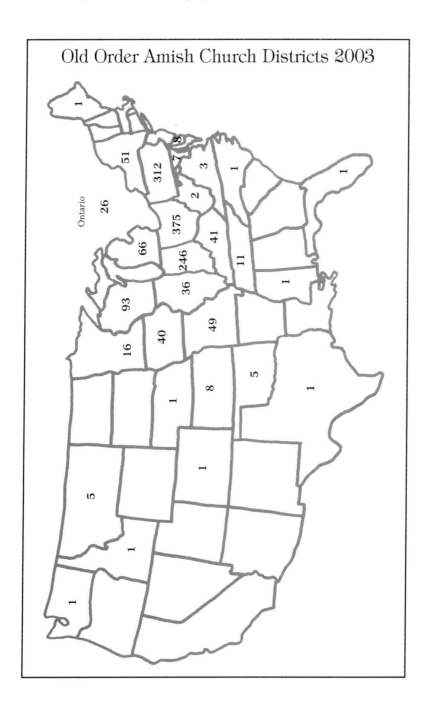

Old Order Amish Church Districts 2003

Beachy Amish Congregations and Members, 1972 and 2002

Location	1972 Congregations	Members	2002 Congregations	Members
Belgium	—	—	1	16
Belize	2	33	6	139
Canada				
Ontario	4	324	10	361
Costa Rica	—	—	10	268
El Salvador	1	19	9	177
Ireland	—	—	1	16
Kenya	—	—	5	319
Nicaragua	—	—	2	52
Paraguay	1	18	2	45
Romania	—	—	1	29
Ukraine	—	—	2	74
United States				
Alabama	—	—	2	67
Arkansas	1	10	2	92
Florida	1	41	2	168
Georgia	1	177	2	274
Illinois	1	74	4	308
Indiana	10	662	14	938
Iowa	2	179	2	187
Kansas	1	176	4	369
Kentucky	—	—	8	550
Maine	—	—	1	12
Maryland	1	31	1	55

Location	1972		2002	
	Congregations	Members	Congregations	Members
Michigan	1	26	1	63
Minnesota	1	39	1	82
Missouri	—	—	2	82
New York	—	—	3	146
Ohio	12	664	19	1,482
Oklahoma	1	42	1	38
Pennsylvania	13	1,129	16	1,680
South Carolina	2	76	3	205
Tennessee	—	—	4	247
Texas	—	—	2	102
Virginia	5	304	9	568
West Virginia	—	—	1	8
Total	**61**	**4,024**	**153**	**9,219**

Source: *Mennonite Yearbook 1972* (Scottdale, Pa.: Mennonite Publishing House, 1972); and *Mennonite Church Information 2002* (Harrisonburg, Va.: Christian Light Publications, 2002).

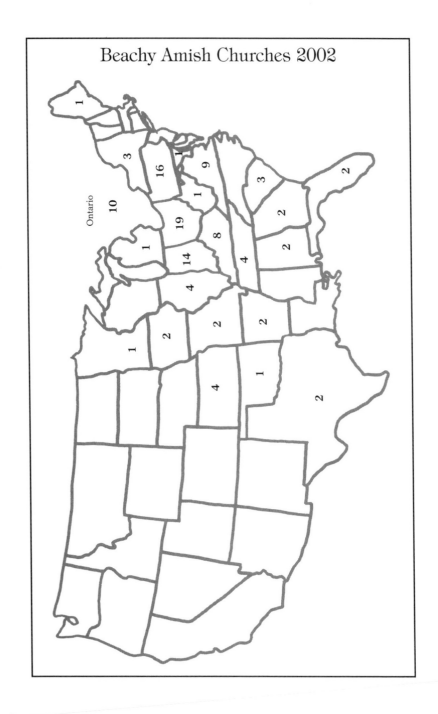

Beachy Amish Churches 2002

Endnotes

Abbreviations used in these endnotes:
AMCUSA-G   Archives of the Mennonite Chuch USA—Goshen, Goshen, Ind.
HHL   Heritage Historical Library, Aylmer, Ont.

Chapter 1 (pages 3-26) Notes

1. Jonathan K. Hartzler, "Fifty Years in the Amish Mennonite Churches of Pennsylvania," *Herald of Truth,* June 1902, 163-164.

2. Hartzler quoted Lamentations 3:22-23.

3. Anabaptism was a geographically diverse movement with many roots and expressions. The summary description in this chapter highlights those places, themes, and events most closely tied to the Amish story. For a balanced introduction to Anabaptism, see Snyder (1995). A brief, classic interpretation from a Mennonite confessional perspective is the 1943 American Society of Church History presidential address of Bender (1944). An encyclopedic compendium of Anabaptists and related sixteenth-century groups and movements is Williams (1992). Selected Anabaptist primary sources appear in English translation as Klaassen (1981) and Dyck (1995).

4. For an overview of Luther's thought, see George (1988). This book also compares Zwingli, Calvin, and Menno, as well as provides an introduction to late medieval Christian thought.

5. The writings of this group, and especially of member Konrad Grebel, are available in English as Harder (1985). A biographical narrative of these events is Ruth (1975). See also Blanke (1961) for the story of an early Anabaptist congregation at Zollikon, near Zurich.

6. See Snyder (1995:101-28) on the dynamics of Anabaptism's spread.

7. Schowalter (1957). Clasen (1972:437) documents Anabaptists executed between 1525 and 1614 in Switzerland, the Rhine Valley, Swabia, Hapsburg territories, southeastern Germany, Franconia, and Thuringia-Fulda.

8. Violence against the Anabaptists in the Low Countries lasted about 50 years. In Switzerland and south Germany, executions continued for approximately 90 years after 1525.

9. Yoder (1973:8).

10. The writings of Menno are available in English as Menno (1956).

11. Snyder (1995:211-24, 317-26, 339-50).

12. Some of the many biblical passages that point to the practice of social shunning are Matthew 18:17; Romans 16:17; 1 Corinthians 5:9-11; 2 Thessalonians 3:6, 14-15; 2 Timothy 2:3-5; Titus 3:10.

13. Shunning was also tied theologically to the particular understanding of Christology among Dutch Anabaptists. See Oyer (1984:222-24).

14. Bender (1927:57-66) and Gross (1991).

15. The most accurate translation is Horst (1988). Another version is more widely available in Leith (1982:292-308). See also Horst (1982), and for an Amish perspective, Stoll (2000). Important though it was, the Confession was not adopted by all Dutch and north German Anabaptist groups.

16. Roth (1993a:145-46).

17. This was Rudolph Egli; see Roth (1993a:106).

18. Roth (1993a:95, and n.29).

19. Hein (1959:110).

20. Background on the Swiss Brethren migration to Alsace is given in Séguy (1984:207-209).

21. Yoder (1973:9).

Chapter 2 (pages 27-50) Notes

1. Gratz (1953:37).

2. Furner (2001) details these strategies.

3. Quotes from Roth (1993a:8).

4. MacMaster (1985:30).

5. Primary source material on the controversy that eventually resulted in schism is contained in a set of contemporary letters written by the participants and translated as Roth (1993a). The letters also appear in German in an issue of the Swiss Mennonite Historical Society periodical as *"Briefsammlung"* (1987:26-61). Narrative accounts of the Ammann-Reist division include Roth (1993a:1-18), Yoder (1987a:43-59), and Gascho (1937:235-66), though Gascho presents Ammann in a particularly unfavorable light. For an overview of interpretations, see Meyers (1996).

6. Roth (1993a:22).

7. Roth (1993a:31). The younger ones here may as likely refer to junior ministers in terms of seniority, as to a literal age difference of older and younger men.

8. Roth (1993a:118).

9. Roth (1993a:24, 118).

10. Roth (1993a:24).

11. Roth (1993a:26).

12. Roth (1993a:26).

13. A common contemporary Swiss naming practice involved shortening surnames by dropping the last syllable and adding an "i" with a long "e" sound. Thus *Ammann* might have been said as *Ami* (Ah-mee). In this form the transition to *Amisch* or *Amish* is more plausible. See Luthy (1978a).

14. Roth (1993a:27-28).

15. Roth (1993a:43).

16. The issue of salvation for the True-Hearted may have become more acute as Swiss Brethren/Mennonites picked up themes and impulses from Continental Pietism. For suggestions in this regard, see Schelbert (1985:118-27) and Hostetler (1996). For reasons too lengthy to detail here, I find this argument less than persuasive in light of recent reinterpretations of Continental Pietism and our growing understanding of the Alsatian Anabaptist context.

17. On Ammann's followers in the Bernese Oberland, see Gratz (1953:45-48).

18. Furner (2001:467) makes an interesting economic point in this regard.

19. Roth (1993:94).

20. Roth (1993a:113-14). Apparently Uli Ammann was a somewhat tolerant and pastoral leader as evidenced in a letter he wrote to the church at Markirch, probably around 1720, in Roth (1993a:123-27).

21. Roth (1993a:69-70).

Chapter 3 (pages 51-71) Notes

1. Baecher (1998) and (2000). The quote from the priest is from (2000:151).

2. Gerlach (1990:3).

3. Schmölz-Häberlein and Häberlein (2001: 479) note, for example, that after 1722 Anabaptists in the Margravate of Baden-Durlach had to pay an annual protection fee similar to that demanded of resident Jews, but the tax also became a basis for recognized toleration.

4. Séguy (1973) and Guth (1995:5-8).

5. Guth (1995:53-54); Schmölz-Häberlein and Häberlein (2001:475).

6. Springer (forthcoming); Correll (1955:70); Stoll (1974).

7. Guth (1995:59); Schmölz-Häberlein and Häberlein (2001).

8. See examples in Gratz (1952:5-7). A 100-Taler reward went to anyone turning in an Anabaptist minister, 50 Taler for a deacon, 25 for a layman, and 12½ for a female member.

9. MacMaster (1985:53).

10. Guth (1995:57, 264-66). Von Gunten was not the father of Barbara's child (he was related to one of Hans Hochstättler's in-laws and was a man of some means), but his offer of marriage would have allowed her to move away and begin a new life without social stigma, which is likely why her father was so eager to have the wedding carried out.

11. For example, Visser (1996:101-102); the Amish disciplines of 1752, 1759, and 1779 discuss marriage and the ban in ways that also suggest this sort of situation. See Springer (forthcoming) for texts of these confessions.

12. Wenger (1981); Beiler (1969). For the experience of Lutheran-turned-Amish Martin Bornträger, see Luthy (1991:19).

13. Schmölz-Häberlein and Häberlein (2001: 486-90).

14. Gratz (1952:9).

15. This narrative is found in Gratz (1952:13-18), Smith and Krahn (1981:87-94), and Smith (1929:70-72).

16. See the memory recorded in Bachmann (1934) and Smith (1929:71-72).

17. Visser (1996); Smith and Krahn (1981:92-94, 134); Gratz (1952:5-21).

18. Frost (1990).

19. Luthy (1988b:20); Hostetler (1980:65, n.34; 56, n.12).

20. MacMaster (1985:59).

21. MacMaster (1985:69-70).

22. See Fogleman (1996:28-35) on the migration destinations of German-speakers at the time.

23. For the story of the Galician and Volhynian Amish and Mennonites, see Stahly (1994), Schrag (1974), and Stucky (1981).

24. For more on the Hutterites, see Hostetler (1974).

25. On these meetings and their resulting documents, see Springer (forthcoming); quotes that follow are from Springer.

26. Nafziger's 1788 and 1790 letters appear in Guth (1995:281-90); this quote from p. 286.

27. Correll (1928:66-79, 198-204); Guth (1987:130); Guth (1995:285-86).

28. Correll (1928:200-204); Guth (1995:279).

29. Guth (1995:289).

30. Guth (1995:286).

Chapter 4 (pages 72-95) Notes

1. Fogleman (1996:67-99).

2. An important source is a series of articles by Joseph F. Beiler entitled "Our Fatherland in America," which appeared regularly in *The Diary* beginning in May 1972. See Beiler

(1976/1977), (1974a), (1977a), and (1983); Stoltzfus (1954); and Fisher (1984). Recent secondary reviews of early settlements include MacMaster (1985:86-88, 125-27) and Kauffman (1991:19-24). Also of interest are the maps and text of *Early Amish* (1991).

3. Beachy (1954); Kauffman (1991).

4. Luthy (1981a).

5. On the debate over rights to a certain meetinghouse in the wake of the Ammann-Reist division, see Roth (1993a:81).

6. On the unique Chester County community see the thoughts of Mook (1955). Apparently the young adults in this settlement often married non-Amish; perhaps one reason the church here eventually dissolved.

7. Brunk (1982).

8. Beiler (1974b:119-20).

9. Beiler (1978). See also MacMaster (1985:151, n.28).

10. MacMaster (1985:70-72, 86-88, 125-27).

11. Wenger (1937:399).

12. Beiler (1975a) provides biographical data but suggests too strongly that Hertzler was the first Amish leader in America. On suggestions of earlier leaders, see Kauffman (1991:20).

13. Kauffman (1991:32).

14. MacMaster (1985:127), Beiler (1976/1977: 46), Stoltzfus (1954:240), and Murray (1981: 16).

15. MacMaster (1985:97-98).

16. Stoltzfus (1954:259-62).

17. Beachy (1954:265).

18. Fogleman (1998:44). Of all arrivals to the British "13 colonies" between 1700 and 1775, 47 percent were slaves, 9 percent were sentenced convicts, 18 percent were indentured servants or redemptioners, and 26 percent were free labor.

19. MacMaster (1985:101, and n.47).

20. MacMaster (1985:100). The redemptioner system differed in an important way from traditional indentured servitude. Indentured servants arrived in North America with contracts stipulating fixed terms of work; only the contract price was negotiable. Redemptioners, in contrast, arrived with a fixed price for passage, and then negotiated the terms and work conditions. In short, shipping transporters bore more of the financial risk of indentured servants, while redemptioners themselves bore more of their own risk; see Fogleman (1998:51-56).

21. MacMaster (1985:74). For nineteenth-century examples, see Hostetler (1989:35) and Gingerich (1961), and the comments of Amish immigrant Louis Jüngerich in Levine, et al. (1997:5).

22. For peace churches in this period, see MacMaster (1979:61-164).

23. Kauffman (1979:15).

24. Butler (1990:164-93).

25. Beiler (1977b) and Hostetler (1989:199-200). It is unknown exactly when Drachsel was silenced and left the Amish church. He was preaching in a non-Amish congregation by at least 1782 and seven years later attended an organizing conference of the United Brethren in Baltimore. In 1804 he moved from Dauphin (now Lebanon) County to Westmoreland County, where he died.

26. Hostetler (1983); Kaffman (1991:31). For information on the German Baptist Brethren tradition, begin with Durnbaugh (1997).

27. The best source, combining primary texts and interpretation, is MacMaster (1979).

28. Durnbaugh (1978) provides case study examples.

29. Quoted with context in Ruth (1976:129); the quotation is from the diary of Pennsylvania German Lutheran minister Henry Melchior Muhlenberg.

30. MacMaster (1979:245-46).

31. MacMaster (1985:254).

32. MacMaster (1979:474-77).

33. MacMaster (1979:464-66) and Mast (1952).

34. Kauffman (1991:30-31).

35. Kauffman (1979:16).

36. Beiler (1975b).

37. Beiler (1975b).

38. Gingerich and Kreider (1986:xiii).

39 Kauffman (1979:13).

Chapter 5 (pages 96-117) Notes

1. Gerlach (1990:5-6); Luthy (1986:288). Other Amish members of that invasion force were not so fortunate—see Estes (1993b:50-51 and notes).

2. Gerlach (1990:5-6).

3. On the impact of the French Revolution and the Napoleonic era on French Amish, see Séguy (1984:212-23).

4. Quoted in Correll (1955:72).

5. Correll (1956).

6. Smith and Krahn (1981:213).

7. Neff (1957).

8. The quotations in this and two following paragraphs are drawn from translations in Estes (1993b:42-51).

9. Grieser and Beck (1960:34).

10. Guth (1995:290, 15).

11. Guth (1995:17-18).

12. Guth (1995:80).

13. Séguy (1973). Excerpts from letters and reports chronicling the Amish-leased Böhmer estates near Zweibrücken during the years 1838-1853 are reproduced in Guth (1995:291-311). On the cattle breeding of the Grabers, see Springer (forthcoming).

14. Varry (1984). See also Yoder (1954). The almanac was issued until 1845.

15. Guth (1995:108-48).

16. Sommer and Hostetler (1957); Guth (1995: 74). The two Ixheim groups reunited in 1909.

17. In 1832, some of the Hessian Amish who immigrated to Butler County, Ohio, brought pianos among their belongings, one of which is now in the Butler County Historical Society, Hamilton, Ohio. See Schlabach (1988:64).

18. See the comments of Swiss Mennonite Niklaus Wütrich in 1807 who criticized both shunning and footwashing, in Roth (1993a:129-40). For a window onto Amish worship during this time, see the sermon by Klopfenstein (1984).

19. Devoted (1984) is the Amish edition; a fresh translation is Gross (1997). See also Luthy (1981b) and Luthy (1984c).

20. Catechism (1905).

21. Schabalie (1975).

22. Zijpp (1956) and (1957).

23. Schrag (1974:62-66) and Stahly (1989). See Stahly (1994:108) for an 1830 observation of a Prussian Mennonite that the Volhynian Amish Mennonites were "very restrictive in external life, on dress, beards, and hooks [instead of buttons on coats]."

24. Gingerich (1982:185).

25. Gerlach (1990:4).

26. Historical (1975:106).

27. Guth (1995:40, 81, 111).

28. Quoted in Smith (1983:78).

29. Estes (1993b:51-56).

30. Smith (1983:57).

31. Hostetler (1989:35).

32. Estes (1984:30).

33. For a list of some of the Amish immigrants during the years 1804-1810, see Luthy (1988b:21).

34. See, for example, Gerlach (1990:2-3). Also Luthy (1973:16). An 1821 letter reproduced in Schmidt-Lange (2002) details reasons for migration from Hesse to North America.

35. Levine, et al., (1997:10). Schmidt-Lange (2002:9) provides another example of such a church letter, dated 18 March 1819, for Chris-

tian Schwartzentruber and signed by elder Samuel Brennemann.

Chapter 6 (pages 118-156) Notes

1. Stoltzfus (1954).

2. Luthy (1972a).

3. Schlabach (1978:1-2), (1981:6-8); Kaufman and Beachy (1991:10-17); Luthy (1986:339-42).

4. Kauffman (1991:100-105).

5. Page and Johns (1983:9-10).

6. Lehman (1978:57).

7. Estes (1993b:33).

8. Estes (1984:21); Luthy (1986:166).

9. At least one Pennsylvania Amish household, that of Christian and Barbara (Yoder) Troyer, had lived in Ontario as early as 1789, but had not remained permanently. Christian Troyer had come to Welland County, Ontario, from Bedford County, Pennsylvania; Troyer then returned to Pennsylvania to encourage other family members to join him and then resettled in Norfolk County. By the time they left Canada for Holmes County, Ohio, in 1815, they were living in York County, Ontario. The lack of a larger church community, the defection of family members to other denominations, and possibly harassment from the Canadian government during the War of 1812 all induced the Amish Troyers to move to Ohio. Christian's son David Troyer and his wife Catherine Hooley remained Amish and also moved to Ohio. Other children joined various denominations and remained in Canada. Roth and Grant (1986:13-17).

10. Guth (1995:312-13); Gingerich (2002:27-41); Roth (1998:9-14).

11. Weber (1931:84).

12. Hostetler (1989:35).

13. There is some debate as to which Christian Zook this was. Steven R. Estes believes it was Christian Zook/Zug (1758-1829) who married Magdalena Mast. Christian Zook who served as an Amish minister in Chester County, Pennsylvania, died 8 October 1826.

14. Mast and Mast (1982:46-47).

15. Levine, et al. (1996:2-3, 6) and (1997:5). Jüngerich became a highly successful and wealthy merchant, eventually leaving the Amish church to join the (Swedenborgian) Church of the New Jerusalem and moving to Philadelphia.

16. Springer (1998).

17. Wenger (1961:328). On the Elkhart-LaGrange settlement beginnings, see Amish and Mennonites (1992:4-18) and Borntreger (1988).

18. Miller (1971).

19. Luthy (1995).

20. Smith (1983:61) and Estes (1990:45-46). Baechler was born in Europe.

21. Yoder (1991:118).

22. Weber (1931:83-87) is a translation of their son's account.

23. Luthy (1986:118-19).

24. Gingerich (1955b:12).

25. Habegger (2002:7-14, 45ff).

26. Luthy (1986:241).

27. Umble (1947:1).

28. Grieser and Beck (1960:26); Stoltzfus (1969:79-80).

29. The eight congregations were Partridge Creek, Busch Gemein, Dillon Creek, Mackinaw River, Rock Creek, Hessian Amish, Bureau Creek, and Ohio Station.

30. Bender (1934:93-95).

31. For more information on the 1809 and 1837 meetings, see Bender (1934). On an 1849 meeting in Ohio, see Gingerich (1965). For a listing of all such known gatherings between 1809 and 1862, see Yoder and Estes (1999:400-403).

32. Yoder (1991:31-32) and (1999); Miller (1959).

33. Yoder (1991:121-34). For the later views of Lancaster County deacon John Stoltzfus, see Yoder (1979a:41-42, 44-47, 170-77). A few Amish—mostly in Mifflin County, Pennsylvania—practiced stream baptism until about 1910. Today stream baptism is not practiced in Old Order Amish churches.

34. George Jutzi letter, Hist. Mss. 1-10, Long, AMCUSA-G. Jutzi's critique of the Methodists was of their use of a so-called "anxious bench" where religious seekers figuratively wrestled for their soul's salvation. Jutzi compared the practice with emotionally intense Roman Catholic devotional rituals that involved sitting before particular images. The anti-Catholic Methodist with whom Jutzi discussed the matter was not pleased with the parallel Jutzi drew!

35. The standard history of the Apostolic Christian Church is Klopfenstein (1984).

36. Yousey (1987:46-59).

37. Gingerich (2002:41); Roth (1998) offers helpful context.

38. Bushman (1992).

39. Umble (1948:103).

40. Nolt (1999).

41. Estes (1982:11-12). Schmidt-Lange (2002) suggests some of the cultural tensions between nineteenth-century Amish arrivals from Hesse and long-established Somerset County, Pennsylvania Amish churches.

42. Examples of Swiss conservatism even into the twentieth century are mentioned in Scott (1981:76-78), (1986:116), and (1988:63, 89, 101). On these settlements, see Ringenberg (1976) and Habegger (2002).

43. The Chester County, Pennsylvania, Amish had had a meetinghouse during the relatively brief life of their settlement, but that building seems not to have set a precedent for later Amish church buildings. Likewise, the temporary log structure used near Louisville, Stark County, Ohio, in the 1830s and the "log chapels" in some Ontario Amish cemeteries as early as 1859 did not represent the same sort of change-minded approach to church life that the meetinghouses built in 1851 did.

44. Boylan (1988).

45. Umble (1941b:20-21).

46. After 1840, some Ontario Mennonites and Pennsylvania Amish conducted Sunday schools on an occasional basis, but none of these experiments lasted.

47. Umble (1963:1-8), (1941b:16-28).

48. Umble (1933:82).

49. Estes (1984:40-41).

50. Kauffman (1991:118-19).

51. Bender (1934:94).

52. Luthy (1984b).

53. Among those concerned were northern Indiana's John E. "Hansi" Borntreger (1988:12); Lancaster, Pennsylvania's David Beiler, in Umble (1948); Iowa's Jacob Schwarzendruber, in Bender (1946). Political involvement was common in Butler County, Ohio; see Page and Johns (1983); and in the large central Illinois settlement and in Mifflin County, Pennsylvania, discussed below.

54. Ellis and Evans (1883:928, 932-33). In 1849, the Pennsylvania Supreme Court ordered recalcitrant Upper Leacock Township to open a public school after its residents had repeatedly refused. Ebersol was elected a school director in 1858.

55. Kauffman (1991:144-47).

56. Hostetler (1964:280-84). For more on Zook, see Luthy (1989b).

57. Estes (1982:47-50).

58. Nolt (1995) and Nolt (1996). Because of its potential interstate nature, the Farnis' case was actually heard by the U.S. Supreme Court as *Farni v. Tesson* (1862).

59. Estes (1984:85-88).

60. Reschly (2000:96-104).

61. Estes (1982:50-51). The most prominent Amish-connected member of the military was

U.S. Brigadier General Samuel Kurtz Zook, grandson of Chester County, Pennsylvania, Amish church members. Samuel's parents, however, were not Amish and had not raised him in the Amish faith. At some point, the patriotic Zook seems to have changed his middle name from *Kurtz* (a common Amish surname) to *Kosciusko* (after Thaddeus Kosciusko, the Polish and U.S. revolutionary hero). See Gambone (1996).

62. Luthy (1989a) includes the story of two generations of an Allen County, Indiana, Graber family who received draft exemptions.

63. Yoder (1991:95).

64. Bender (1946).

65. Yoder (1991:95).

66. Lehman (1978:58).

67. Luthy (1986:241-42).

68. Yoder (1971:26).

69. Gingerich (1939:62-64).

70. Bender (1946:223-25).

71. Umble (1948:105).

Chapter 7 (pages 157-192) Notes

1. On the schisms in Ontario and Iowa, see Roth (1993b) and Reschly (2000:158-72).

2. For discussion of the *Ordnung* by a twentieth-century Old Order Amish minister, see Beiler (1982).

3. Occasionally local gatherings of ministers would publish a brief, written *Ordnung*, but these documents usually summed up only important or controversial points.

4. Gingerich (1986).

5. This chapter identifies these two northern Indiana church districts by their home counties—Elkhart and LaGrange— even though contemporaries often called the church in LaGrange County the "Elkhart church" because its members lived near the Little Elkhart River (in LaGrange County), and called the Elkhart County church the "Clinton church" because its members' homes were in Clinton Township (in Elkhart County). See Yoder (1991:117-121).

6. Borntreger (1988:10).

7. Borntreger (1988:11).

8. Yoder (1991:130-34). According to contemporaries, Yoder taught that the sin of the first humans was not disobedience to God's command, but only lying about what they had done. An account of the controversy in Ohio from the perspective of a conservative is Troyer (1998:130-38).

9. Umble (1948:105).

10. Yoder (1987c:37).

11. For a list of these meetings, see Yoder and Estes (1999:401-405).

12. Yoder (1991:142).

13. Yoder (1987c:63-65).

14. Yoder (1987c:66).

15. The minutes ("Proceedings") of all 17 *Diener-Versammlungen* are available in German in many Amish and Mennonite historical libraries. Yoder and Estes (1999) provide an English translation of the minutes, as well as related documents.

16. Yoder and Estes (1999:5).

17. Yoder and Estes (1999:47, 49, 53-54, 56).

18. For example, see Yoder and Estes (1999:36, 38).

19. Yoder and Estes (1999:39).

20. Yoder and Estes (1999:49). On these problems, see Yoder (1985:2-9).

21. In a 12 February 1863 letter, Mifflin County, Pennsylvanian Shem Zook informed deacon John Stoltzfus that bishops Jonas D. Troyer and John Schmucker had ordained a bishop for the Hessian Amish church. Zook reported that this had happened because "the[Hessians'] playthings [i.e., musical instruments] have been put away." See Yoder (1987c:101-102).

22. Yoder and Estes (1999:16-17, 36-38, 53).

23. Yoder and Estes (1999:13-14, 38, 47, 49, 52).

24. Yoder and Estes (1999:51, and possibly 36).

25. Umble (1948:107).

26. Yoder (1991:159-61).

27. Yoder and Estes (1999:47).

28. English translations of the conservatives' statements are Bender (1934:95-98) and Yoder and Estes (1999:258-60).

29. Yoder and Estes (1999:258-59).

30. Yoder and Estes (1999:259).

31. Yoder and Estes (1999:64). David A. Troyer, one of the signatories, later reflected this disappointment in Troyer (1998:136, 138).

32. See Yoder (1996) for a contemporary Lancaster document outlining the issues (meetinghouses, stream baptism, and Sunday school) from the change-minded standpoint.

33. The Old Orders themselves claimed the designation *Alt Amisch* (Old Amish). The etymology of "Old Order Amish" is elusive; see discussion in Yoder (1991:261). For a definition of "Old Order" emerging from a comparison of Old Order Amish, Old Order Mennonite, Old German Baptist, and Old Order River Brethren beginnings, see Hostetler (1992).

34. Yoder and Estes (1999:71-72, 74-75).

35. Yoder and Estes (1999:82, 90).

36. Yoder and Estes (1999:84).
37. Yoder and Estes (1999:91-92).
38. Yoder and Estes (1999:202).
39. Yoder and Estes (1999:202).
40. A brief account sympathetic to Egly is Nussbaum (1991:2-11). See also Yoder (1991: 184-87).
41. Helpful discussion of Egly's theology is found in Weaver (1997:126-29, 178-87, 212-15, 302-303). Egly (1965) is a translation of an article he penned, and which has the feel and tone of a sermon, and may suggest the content of his preaching. Egly moved to Indiana in 1850; his initial spiritual awakening in the early 1840s occurred while he was still living in Butler County, Ohio.
42. Claudon and Claudon (1947).
43. Egly's thoughts on baptism were outlined in an 1866 letter available in Yoder and Estes (1999:262-64).
44. Nussbaum (1991:2).
45. Historian Joe Springer and genealogist Donald Roth have made the point that much of Egly's support came from churches and communities linked in a close network of immigrant family ties.
46. Jacob Rupp from Fulton County, Ohio, spoke as one sympathetic to Egly's concerns, though he only may have met Egly for the first time at the 1865 gathering. For Rupp's and others' concerns and the meeting's responses, see Yoder and Estes (1999:64, 72-73, 119-20).
47. "Henry Egly's autobiography," Hist. Mss. 1-542, Box 1, folder 3 (English translation), AMCUSA-G.
48. An interpretation of the separation is Estes (1982:66-68).
49. Estes (1982:83-86), Yoder (1991:187-94), and Smith (1983:88-91).
50. Estes (1982:52).
51. Estes (1982:53).
52. Weaver (1926:72) offered the sympathetic view that although Stuckey "was sometimes blamed for splitting churches," in fact "he was only trying to care for those who had left the old church and were without a leader."
53. Estes (1982:48-49, 81) and Clark (1929).
54. Estes (1982:80-81); Yoder and Estes (1999:118-19; and related document 260-62). On universalism and the nineteenth-century American religious scene, see Bressler (2001).
55. Yoder and Estes (1999:155-56). The German poem appears in Estes (1982:291-95); an English translation of the poem is in Estes (1982:296-300) and Yoder and Estes (1999:282-

288). A photocopy of what may be Joder's handwritten original is in the Edwin O. Ropp Papers, Illinois Mennonite Archives, Metamora, Ill. Interestingly, *Der Fröhliche Botschafter* was the name of the German-language universalist periodical that was published 1829-1838. It carried articles in German and some poems in the Pennsylvania Dutch dialect. Published in western Lancaster County, Pennsylvania, it circulated in German-speaking communities well beyond that region; see Yoder (1944).
56. Stuckey had even been the subject of an investigation by committees from the *Diener-Versammlungen*. See Yoder and Estes (1999:136-37).
57. Yoder and Estes (1999:175-76); Estes (1982:70-86).
58. Estes (1982:94-95).
59. Yoder and Estes (1999:136).
60. Yoder and Estes (1999:231).
61. Biographical information on Yoder is found in chapter 4 of Lehman (1978). A brief biography of King is found in Stoltzfus (1969:77).
62. Yoder (1991:196-201).
63. An example of Amish reunion and reconnection facilitated by the ministers' meetings deserves mention. In 1874 the Mennonites living in Russian Volhynia immigrated to Kansas and what would become South Dakota. Some of these Mennonites had been of Amish background, for the most part descendants of Alsatian and Montbéliard Amish who had moved to Volhynia and joined Mennonites there. After settling in North America, however, some of the Volhynian immigrant ministers heard about the Amish *Diener-Versammlungen* and attended as Amish ministers. In 1875, 1876, and 1878 preacher Johannes Schrag of Tuner, Dakota Territory, participated in the gatherings, as did Jacob Stucky of Lakeview, Kansas, in 1875; see Stahly (1994:110-13). Although the *Diener-Versammlungen* temporarily united an extended church family, divided geographically for three-quarters of a century, the Volhynian Amish-turned-Mennonites did not continue their fraternal links with other North American Amish after the ministers' meetings ended. They affiliated instead with the General Conference Mennonites on the Great Plains.

Chapter 8 (see pages 193-230) Notes

1. C. B. Newhause, et al., "From Tennessee," *Herald of Truth*, October 1871, 152.
2. The *Herald of Truth* includes scores of examples of Amish Mennonite and Mennonite

cooperation or joint activity. Illustrative examples from Indiana alone include John Ringenberg, "Letter from Locke, Ind." *HT,* July 1864, 43; John M. Christophel, "Letter from Indiana," *HT,* January 1865, 7; Daniel Brenneman, "A Visit," *HT,* January 1867, 11-12; G. Z. Boller, "From Noble Co., Ind.," *HT,* February 1867, 25. Letters and articles also appeared in the German-language companion paper *Herold der Warheit,* such as Ringenberg (above) in *HW,* July 1864, 43.

3. Roth (1993b); and Reschly (2000:158-72).

4. Yoder (1991:267).

5. Lind (1990:45-46).

6. Quotes here and in the paragraphs that follow from the Mahala Yoder Collection, Hist. Mss. 1-12, Small Collection, Long Box, 1871-76 Diary, AMCUSA-G.

7. Yoder (1991:228-30).

8. Mast and Mast (1982:63-70).

9. The text of the 1889 16-article Oak Grove discipline may be found in Lehman (1978:110-11).

10. On the reaction both of first-generation leaders like Stoltzfus and King and second-generation Amish Mennonites surprised by the rapid pace of change, see examples in Yoder (1991:252-60).

11. Hiller (1968/1969); Gingerich (1971); Miller (1970). For an appraisal by C. Henry Smith of Spirit preaching, which he witnessed as a boy, see Smith (1962:132-35).

12. Reschly (2000:132-57); Hostetler (1980).

13. Stutzman's relatives transcribed and printed her revelations as *Revelations* (n.d.).

14. O. A. Graber, "Gleanings from Yesterday," *Die Botschaft,* 8 February 1984, 14.

15. Sermons from the two are found in Troyer (1879) and (1880); and Kauffman (1953).

16. See, for example, Presbyterian Spirit preacher Constantine Blackmon Sanders (1831-1887) and others in Yoder (1968/1969). See also Schlabach (1988:220).

17. Gingerich (1959).

18. The paper's masthead from April 1, 1893 to December 15, 1895.

19. Amish Mennonite leaders here had met as early as 1882 but did not organize their conference until 1890. For the story of the Western District Conference formation, see Hartzler and Kauffman (1905:306-307), and Weber (1931:187-96).

20. Historical (1975:379).

21. Lehman (1978:134-35) and Yoder (1991:231).

22. On Oak Grove Amish Mennonite (Smith-

ville, Ohio) support for Elkhart Institute, see Lehman (1978:135-42).

23. Smith (1962).

24. For a biography of Smucker, see Yoder and Smucker (1990).

25. Lehman (1990:6-30).

26. See Yoder (1991:220-22) for examples of the last few Amish Mennonite attempts at shunning. Hartzler and Kauffman (1905:306-308) imply that the abandonment of the practice of shunning was a more formal decision on the part of Amish Mennonites.

27. Yoder and Estes (1999:78). The ministers were responding to the hopes for unity expressed by Ohio Mennonite bishop John M. Brenneman, whose proposal "Unity among the Brethren" in the March 1866 *Herald of Truth* is reprinted in Yoder and Estes (1999:264-68).

28. Yoder (1991:247).

29. Joseph Holdeman, "A Visit to Clinton and Haw Patch," *Herald of Truth,* February 1871, 25-26.

30. J. D. Troyer, et al., "Correspondence," *Herald of Truth,* 1 March 1886, 73-74.

31. Gingerich (2002:85, 88).

32. The traditional rendering of the history of this group is Wenger (1966). More recent presentations include Schlabach (1988), Juhnke (1989), and Toews (1996), although these books also deal with other groups in addition to the "old" Mennonites. In 2002 most of the "old" Mennonites and the General Conference Mennonites merged to form two new denominations: Mennonite Church Canada and Mennonite Church USA.

33. For a chronology, see Bair (1952).

34. Yoder (1991:17).

35. Yoder (1987a:83).

36. Erb (1974:468-69).

37. Umble (1964).

38. The Western Ontario Mennonite Conference did join two other Mennonite bodies in 1988 to form the Mennonite Conference of Eastern Canada, but by that time the question of Amish identity was hardly an issue.

39. Yoder (1991:17).

40. The standard history of the group is Miller (1985), but see also Scott (1996:122-36) for more recent developments.

41. In 1971 when the "old" Mennonites reorganized themselves as the Mennonite Church General Assembly, the Conservative Conference loosely affiliated with that body; however, those connections ended in the early 1990s. In 2000, about 18 Conservative Conference congregations concerned about the decline in plain

dress and other signs of nonconformity in Conservative Conference circles left that group and formed Mennonite Biblical Alliance.

42. A standard history of the General Conference is Pannabecker (1975). More recent presentations include Schlabach (1988), Juhnke (1989), and Toews (1996), although these books also deal with other groups in addition to GC Mennonites. In 2002 the GC Mennonites and most of the "old" Mennonites merged to form two new denominations: Mennonite Church Canada and Mennonite Church USA.

43. Pannabecker (1968:18-22) and Pannabecker (1975:69).

44. Pannabecker (1968:18-22).

45. Gingerich (1942:14) reprints the newspaper account.

46. Pannabecker (1968:22-24) and Pannabecker (1975:71-72).

47. Pannabecker (1968:24-25) and Pannabecker (1975:72-73).

48. There were several other congregations of Amish background that joined the GC Mennonites. The GC church at Ransom, Kansas, may have had Amish background. See Haury (1981:54-56), although it does not exactly match Erb (1974:207-209). In 1889, in Lancaster County, Pennsylvania, six families left the Millwood Amish Mennonite Church and under the leadership of minister Samuel Lantz formed a congregation affiliated with the GC Eastern District. See Yoder (1996:25).

49. Summaries of Stuckey Amish history include Weber (1931:435-536) and Smith (1983:88-110).

50. Yoder (1991:193).

51. General Conference Mennonite Church leader Christian Krehbiel visited Stuckey, hoping to persuade Stuckey to join the GC Mennonites. See Krehbiel (1961:65-66).

52. Estes (1982:118-20).

53. Estes (1982:93-94).

54. Weaver (1926:94-95) and Weber (1931: 485-96).

55. Juhnke (1979:67-68) and Weber (1931: 377-92, 519-25).

56. Weber (1931:402-11).

57. Weaver (1926:179-83) and Bush (2000). At the time, the college technically was sponsored only by the General Conference's Eastern and Middle Districts.

58. The Central Conference joined the GC Mennonite Church as a "district conference" in 1946; 11 years later the Central Conference merged with the Middle District of the GC Mennonite Church (the Central Conference and Middle District overlapped geographically) to form the Central District Conference of the General Conference. See Estes (1993a).

59. See Nussbaum (1991) and Smith (1983: 111-31).

60. Schlabach (1988:116). The first Egly Amish conference was held in 1882 in Illinois; the gatherings became annual affairs starting in 1895.

61. Weber (1931:377-401).

62. For a history of the Missionary Church Association, see Lugibihl (1950).

63. Kauffman and Driedger (1991:174).

64. In 2003, EMC convention delegates not only changed their denominational name, but also adopted a seven-point Corporate Core Values statement that included a general reference to "Anabaptist distinctives."

65. Séguy (1982:25).

66. Hostetler (1980:65). Gerlach (1990:3) lists Amish church membership statistics for the mid-to-later nineteenth century, and estimates only 1,659 to 1,859 total members by 1888.

67. Estes (1990:42-46) and Springer (forthcoming) document this third wave of Amish immigration. Estes cites a European Amish immigrant to America as late as 1924. In many cases, these third wave immigrants joined progressive Amish Mennonite congregations in the Midwest, or if they settled in the Pacific West, they did not maintain any Amish or Mennonite ties. Virtually none became Old Order.

68. Yousey (1987:74-75); Luthy (1986:290).

69. Gerlach (1990:2).

70. Neff (1959) and Yoder and Estes (1999: 271-76). A few weeks later the French Amish adopted most of the Offenthal statement.

71. Gingerich (1982:182).

72. Séguy (1984:206-17).

73. Correll (1955).

74. Fretz (1957).

75. Yoder (1955).

76. Guth (1995:94).

77. Sommer and Hostetler (1957).

78. Gerlach (1990:8).

79. Hostetler (1955:215, 218-19).

Chapter 9 (pages 231-256) Notes

1. See United States (1941:2:1005-1006). The reports include statistics for 1906, 1916, 1926, and 1936. Numbers for the Old Order Amish may be a bit low due to uncompleted questionnaires. The 1890 U.S. Federal Census gathered membership and congregational data

on religious bodies, including the Amish; however, the numbers are incomplete and in some cases confuse known Old Order churches with decidedly progressive Amish Mennonite ones.

2. Smith (1983:132-33).

3. Luthy (1972/1973). The articles cover other time periods, as well.

4. See Luthy (1986) for stories of numerous settlements begun and dissolved in this time. See Stoll (1997) for the Daviess County settlement.

5. Luthy (1978c); Yoder (1966); Yoder (1990).

6. HHL has several of these autograph books.

7. Letters from Isaac Ebersol to Sarah Lapp Zook, and from Andrew Ebersol to Sarah Lapp Zook, in the Sarah Lapp Zook Papers, private collection of a relative, Lancaster, Pa. (hereafter SLZ Papers).

8. Isaac Zook to Sarah Lapp, 8 January 1897, SLZ Papers.

9. Sallie J. Fisher to Sarah Lapp, 23 December 1888, SLZ Papers. Christmas trees were a widely shared Pennsylvania German ethnic tradition, see Shoemaker (1999:45-74), and would have been uncommon among Amish in the Midwest.

10. Bettsy Speicher to Sarah Lapp, 30 October 1891; Speicher to Lapp, 2 March 1896, SLZ Papers.

11. Rebecca S. Smucker to Sarah Lapp, 25 March 1896, SLZ Papers.

12. Reschly (2000:43-63, 177-81); Deeben (1992:21-29). Using data somewhat different from Reschly, Cosgel (1993) also argues for a distinct approach to farming among the Kalona, Iowa, Amish

13. Scott (1981:60, 72). Apparently Amish carriages in Pennsylvania were covered only during the latter part of the nineteenth century. See Scott (1981:51, 55-56).

14. The biblical text here in Amish teaching is 1 Corinthians 11:1-16. Scott (1986:98-103) gives more explanation. All of Scott (1986) is an excellent explanation of plain dress. Gingerich (1970) is also a standard work on dress.

15. Gibbons (1882:59).

16. See, for example, Luthy (1995) and Stoltzfus (1995).

17. Swartzentruber (1950); Reschly (2000:164-72, 205-209).

18. Samuel D. Guengerich, "Value of Education," Hist. Mss. 1-2, box 8, AMCUSA-G.

19. Samuel D. Guengerich diaries, 10 March 1864, Hist. Mss. 1-2, box 1, AMCUSA-G.

20. Hostetler (1989:180-82); Luthy (1972/1973).

21. Luthy (1981c). Judging from the hymns and hymn numbers recorded in the *Diener-Versammlungen* minutes, the gatherings of 1873, 1875, and 1876 sang from the "Baer book" rather than the *Ausbund*. The Baer book would have been a fairly recent publication at the time, but may have received a warm reception at the ministers' meetings since it had been compiled by *Diener-Versammlung* proponent Shem Zook. See Yoder and Estes (1999:400-401).

22. Amish Aid Society began in 1885 according to Fisher (1978:335, 379). Amos J. Stoltzfus (1984:191-92) cites apparently the same source, but gives an 1875 date. Stoltzfus is preferred since HHL has a printed policy from the plan dated 1879. Landis (1955) gives an overview of the plan as it spread to other places, but also gives too late a beginning date. Gingerich (1955a) offers a description of similar programs begun by Midwestern Amish in the twentieth century.

23. Luthy (1981a). Later, about half the community (mostly those living south of the Pennsylvania-Maryland border) left the Old Order church to affiliate with the Conservative Amish Mennonite Conference. The Old Order Amish in Somerset County, Pennsylvania, continue to use meetinghouses for their biweekly services.

24. Swartzendruber (1977:12-13).

25. Luthy (1986:271-76).

26. Kauffman (1991:118-19). A study of clothing among these Amish is Weiser (1998).

27. Troyer (1998:52, 57-64). For a discussion of how two early twentieth-century Amishmen thought about theology and ethics, see Biesecker-Mast (1999).

28. Another method of handling such situations followed this procedure: a baptized member of an Old Order church would join an Amish Mennonite congregation. The Old Order group would excommunicate and shun the individual, but, after a period of time, "lift" the ban when the person had demonstrated serious intent to be faithful to the Amish Mennonite church.

29. The story is recounted in Yoder (1991: 266-73); Mast and Mast (1982:83-87); and Yoder (1987a:103-106).

30. Mast and Mast (1982:37-39).

31. Mast and Mast (1982:57).

32. See Yoder (1991:273-74); other parts of the story provided by Joni Helmuth's nephew Orva Helmuth, Arthur, Illinois, in a telephone interview, 14 May 1992. Helmuth (1961);

Smith (1983:141, 169). The Arthur Amish Mennonite Church existed from 1897 to 1914 and was a member of the Western District Amish Mennonite Conference. Orva Helmuth made one correction to the document cited in Yoder (1991:274, n.38). Joni Helmuth's middle initial was *F* and not *J*. Among many Midwestern Amish families, children received as their middle initial the first letter of their father's first name. Since Joni's father was Joseph, many assumed that his middle initial was J; however, the Helmuth family had not followed this naming tradition. Joni Helmuth later left the Amish Mennonite Church, as well, and joined the Churches of Christ.

33. Ritter (1997).

34. Luthy (1986:85-91, 134-39, 177-83, 213-18, 221-28, 305-32) for some of these stories.

35. "Notes from the Hoosier State," *The Budget,* October 22, 1896, p. [4]. Thanks to Karl N. Stutzman for this citation.

36. Williams (1978).

37. The material in this paragraph and the one that follows, including quotations from *The Budget,* comes from Luthy (1982:23-26).

Chapter 10 (pages 257-290) Notes

1. Welty (1908). The analysis that follows is dependant upon Weaver-Zercher (2001:14-17).

2. The author's husband, Benjamin Franklin Welty, was an Ohio attorney of Mennonite heritage, who was also a convinced political Progressive and two-term Congressman.

3. Martin (1905) and Weaver-Zercher (2001: 34-39). On early tourism and popular images of the Amish in the early twentieth century, see Luthy (1994:113-18) and Weaver-Zercher (2001:47-60).

4. Quoted in Yoder (1990:332).

5. On Delaware, see Clark (1988:21-74). Between 1900 and 1915, new Old Order churches also organized in Alabama, Arizona, California, Colorado, Georgia, Montana, Texas, Virginia, and Wisconsin, but did not survive long; see settlements listed in Luthy (1986).

6. On Lancaster, Pa., Amish reaction to the automobile, see Kraybill (2001:214-17). For an Old Order Amish discussion of the car, see Wagler (n.d.).

7. Yoder (1987a:106-10).

8. On the role of technology decisions (as opposed to excommunication practice) in the division, see Kraybill (2001: 189-92, 199-200). Amish farm life from 1900 through the 1920s

in this community is described in Glick (1994:4-139).

9. Umble (1996:63-133) details the telephone story in this community, including the response of Old Order Mennonites.

10. Gingerich (1939:311-14).

11. History (1999). In the 1920s two other similarly ultra-conservative settlements formed near Medford, Wisconsin and Atlantic, Pennsylvania.

12. Luthy (1998); Kraybill (1994); Kraybill and Hostetter (2001:150). Information from Stephen E. Scott: during 1917-1922 the Swartzentruber Amish divided, leading to the formation of the Daniel Wengerd group. In 1934, the Wengerd group reunited with the majority Holmes County Old Orders; however, they remained somewhat more conservative than that group. Many former Wengerd group members left the mainline Old Order again in 1955-1957 with the conservative Andy Weaver group. The Swartzentrubers do derive belt power from engines mounted on carts in order to power some equipment, but do not use belt power from self-propelled tractors.

13. Janzen (1990:167-97). The larger Canadian story was more complex than the Ontario Amish situation summarized here, since Ottawa dealt with immigrant groups on the basis of historic provisions arranged at their respective times of immigration. Thus, Mennonites, Doukhobors, and other COs in western Canada who had arrived from Europe in the later 1800s were treated under a set of provisions different from those applied to Ontario Mennonites and Amish who had come to Ontario in the 1700s and early 1800s. Janzen details the entire Canadian picture.

14. Quoted in Keim and Stoltzfus (1988:32).

15. Abrams (1933).

16. Homan (1994) presents a comprehensive account of Mennonite and Amish World War I experience. See also Juhnke (1989:208-42).

17. Letter from Peachey's granddaughter Donella Peachey Clemens, 26 May 1992.

18. Keim and Stoltzfus (1988:46-52).

19. Juhnke (1989:236).

20. Quoted in Keim and Stoltzfus (1988:40).

21. Stoltzfus (1981:7-24).

22. Even years later, many of the stories of men who had lived as COs in army camps were full of emotion. Some men did not want the notoriety of being named but shared anonymous stories. See the collections Stoltzfus (1981) and Beechy and Beechy (199-).

23. Examples include Homan (1994:77-78), Mast and Mast (1982:132-33), and Estes (1984:216-19).

24. Teichroew (1979:107). On local suspicion of Amish loyalty in LaGrange County, Indiana, see Pratt (1997:95-112).

25. Luthy (1972b).

26. Reason cited in File No. 186400-18, Department of Justice, Washington, D.C., as quoted in Luthy (1972b).

27. See, for example, Belfry (1923).

28. For an articulate explanation of Old Order objections to state-sponsored secondary education, see Stoll (1975).

29. Pratt (1997:167-80, 189-98) details this controversy. While authorities made more than two dozen arrests, the total number of individuals arrested is difficult to determine because some may have been arrested more than once. The controversy lasted from 1921 to 1925. See also Bontreger (1982:20-21).

30. Keim (1975:14-15); Luthy (1986:513-14); Meyers (2003:93). Already in 1914, Geauga County, Ohio school officials had fined Amish parents whose children had stopped attending school before age 16. For an annotated chronology of Amish school court cases, see Keim (1975:93-98). An expanded and annotated list is Place (2003).

31. Just then conservative Canadian Mennonites were also moving to Mexico to avoid new Manitoba higher education statutes. See Sawatzky (1971).

32. Luthy (1986:514-21).

33. Weaver-Zercher (2001:60-81) discusses the national notoriety the events generated.

34. The school was originally slated to cost $112,000, but the final cost increased to $125,000. Of that sum, $52,250 was Federal Public Works Administration money. Reporters marveled that people would reject government dollars for constructing a new school when many communities were hoping for increased funding from Washington.

35. "Education: Amish Folk Shun Their New PWA School," *Literary Digest*, 4 December 1937, 32-34. Kraybill (2001:162-68) narrates the story.

36. This petition and the list of signers are reproduced in Lapp (1991:141-67).

37. Text is Hostetler (1989:136-37).

38. Keim (1975:94). A number of East Lampeter Township Amish families had not sent their children to school in 1937 and did not again in the fall of 1938. The boycott drew national attention, e.g., "Amish Lose Fight for Old Schools," *New York Times*, 28 June 1938, 22; "Amish Threaten School Succession," *New York Times*, 21 July 1938, 23; "New Amish School Strike Looms in Pennsylvania, *New York Times*, 5

September 1938, 15; "Amish Pupils Back in 1-Room School," *New York Times*, 29 November 1938, 25; "Amish Hit High School," *New York Times*, 21 September 1938, 26; "Plain People Win Right to their Own Schools as well as Way of Life," *Newsweek*, 12 December 1938, 32. By 1937, there was a small but largely unknown precedent of Amish parochial schools in Delaware, North Carolina, and Mississippi. On the Delaware school, named Apple Grove School, which operated 1925-1926, see Clark (1988:111-28, 195). On the North Carolina school that operated 1925-1926, see Luthy (1986:299-300). On the origins of Lancaster County's Amish school movement, see Esh (1977).

39. Amish Moving (1965).

40. Yoder (1987a:112-16).

41. Yoder (1987a:116-20) and Beachy (1955). For a perspective very sympathetic to Beachy, see Mast (1950).

42. Beachy (1955).

43. Lapp (2003:37-44) is a detailed account.

44. For more chronology, see Yoder (1987a:126-27) and (1987a:128-38) for further discussion of group consolidation and growth.

45. See settlements listed in Luthy (1986).

46. The 1940 draft census administered by Mennonite Central Committee and sent to all Amish bishops asked the bishops to report the current employment of conscription-age men in each district. The incomplete returns show a few men listed under factory work. This documentary evidence of industrial employment by 1940 matches local anecdotal memory. See Peace Section Census, 1940, Questionnaires: Old Order Amish, Indiana, IX-7-1, Box 1, Folder 7, AMCUSA-G.

47. An Amish minister writing anonymously, "Amish Life" (1971:20).

48. "Amish Life" (1971). Many memories of the Depression era are recorded in Yoder and Yoder (1998) and Glick (1994:158-77).

49. "An Amishman Speaks," Lancaster (Pa.) *Intelligencer Journal*, 23 February 1931, 1.

50. Jellison (2002:109-12, 116). The published USDA survey is Kollmorgen (1942). More detailed analysis appears in Reschly and Jellison (1993).

51. Historical (1975:483).

52. "Amish Life" (August 1971:19).

53. "Amish Gratitude," *Time*, 29 November 1937, 37. The article again mentioned the Smoketown school controversy.

54. John M. McCullough, "Amish Curb Crops—But Not for AAA Pay, *Philadelphia Inquirer*, 2 April 1933.

55. It is worth noting, however, that despite the widespread Amish criticism of New Deal-style politics and programs, a tiny number of hard-pressed Amishmen did end up working in federal Works Progress Administration jobs, as documented in the 1940 draft census cited in note 46, above.

56. Luthy (1984a).

57. A detailed history of peace churches in the U.S. between the world wars is Keim and Stoltzfus (1988:56-102); on the Canadian scene, see Janzen (1990:198-208).

58. The Mennonite statement was Peace (1937); the Amish document was "Statement" (1939). See also the statement written by David L. Schwartz (19—), an Adams County, Indiana, Swiss Amishman and printed as a pamphlet for drafted Amishmen to present to their draft boards when called.

59. Peace (1937).

60. On CO provisions and alternative service in Canada, see Regehr (1996:35-59) and Janzen (1990:198-244).

61. On the CPS program, see Wagler and Raber (1986); Keim (1990); Gingerich (1949); Hershberger (1951); and Keim and Stoltzfus (1988:103-26).

62. Unruh (1952:286). See the Amish CPS directory, which lists some 600 men in Wagler and Raber (1986:97-127). The book also includes first-person accounts of Amish who served as forest firefighters, on dairy farms, in psychiatric hospitals, in publc health projects, in Puerto Rico, for the Fish and Wildlife Service, and as human "guinea pigs" for medical research.

63. Huntington (1956:547-48).

64. For an Amish critique of the Mennonite-administered CPS camp to which he was assigned, see Wagler (1991). Wagler found the administrators liberal and out of touch with Old Order values.

65. Bontreger (1982:23-25, 30-33); Wagler and Raber (1986:75).

66. Luthy (1978b).

67. "Rationing" file collection, HHL.

68. Dick Snyder, "Amish Undisturbed by War Shortages, Have Always Done without Autos and Such," *New York Times*, 12 April 1942, II-10.

69. Unruh (1952:227-29). See also "Sea-Going Cowboys" file collection, HHL.

Chapter 11 (pages 291-340) Notes

1. Luthy (1994b:119).

2. Patterson (1996). On TV ownership, see Historical (1975:796).

3. "Urge Amish Use Tractors to Boost Yield of Wheat," newspaper clipping dated Saturday, 27 April 1946, 5. Probably from a Lancaster, Pennsylvania, newspaper. Pasted inside a copy of Steinfeldt (1937) housed in the archives of the Lancaster Mennonite Historical Society. On 1940s changes in agriculture as experienced by U.S. Mennonites, see Bush (1999:136-40); the wider context is detailed in Shover (1976).

4. "Amish Life" (1971:20). The Kokomo, Indiana, and Kalona, Iowa, settlements were among the few that adopted tractor farming at this time. Oral interviews suggest that in some cases the impetus for mechanization was lack of field hands during World War II when men were drafted out of the community and into alternative service assignments. Kraybill (2001:222-30) discusses the debate over field tractor use in the Lancaster settlement.

5. Luthy (1986:366-69).

6. The story of the 1948 conscription law, the Korean War demand for alternative service for COs, and the development of the I-W program is recounted in Keim and Stoltzfus (1988:127-46) and Bush (1999:171-73).

7. Bush (1999:196-97, 239) discusses some of the negative aspects of the I-W program, though from a Mennonite perspective. Amish reservations and frustrations would have been somewhat different. Some of the negative implications of the program for the Amish are discussed in Keim (2003:56-61).

8. A fourth man received a suspended sentence and probation after he agreed to take a I-W assignment.

9. Huntington (1956:579).

10. Associated Press story carried in the Lancaster, Pa. *Intelligencer Journal*, 28 June 1957.

11. Other examples available in the file "Amish," Clippings Collection, AMCUSA-G. Many of the clippings are from the *South Bend* (Ind.) *Tribune*, but other newspapers are represented, as well. On Miller, see "Amish Farmer Jailed," *New York Times*, 19 March 1960, 9. Stories of Amish convicted of refusing induction into the I-W program also are found in the pages of *The Reporter for Conscience Sake*, the official publication of the National Service Board for Religious Objectors, Washington, D.C. A related story from the national press noted the Amish peace position: in 1955 the *New York Times* ran a story calling attention to the Amish as "pacifists." ("Amish Visit U.N. as Peace Symbol," *New York Times*, 25 May 1955, 35.) The article reported a group of Lancaster, Pa., Amish visiting New York for another rea-

son arranged for a tour of the United Nations while there. Led by 76-year old Daniel Bawell, Bareville, Pa., the Amish said they wanted to visit the U.N. because it works for peace.

12. *South Bend* (Ind.) *Tribune*, 28 October 1953, 1. This case drew particular attention because the LaGrange County draft board halted all induction and demanded state and federal officials take action against the Amish. No action was taken against the church, however, and Selective Service persuaded the draft board to resume regular activity.

13. Information from various *Wooster* (Ohio) *Daily Record* articles, July 1957, in "Amish," Clippings Collection, AMCUSA-G.

14. David Wagler writing in *The Budget*, quoted in Yoder (1990:279).

15. Quoted in Yoder (1961:3).

16. The letter appeared in "The Editor's Corner," *The Budget*, 15 April 1965, 6; however, the editor clearly was not the author.

17. Yoder (1987a:229-30, 293-95) and Keim (2003:59).

18. Stoll (1966:1).

19. Anderson (1966:3).

20. Keim (2003:59).

21. On Steering Committee formation and function, see Olshan (2003) and Olshan (1994). The Committee's first officers were Andrew S. Kinsinger, Lancaster County, Pa., chair; David Schwartz, Allen County, Ind., secretary; and Noah Wengerd, Adams County, Ind., treasurer. Kinsinger served as chair until 1989 when Christian Blank, also of Lancaster, succeeded him. See Kinsinger (1997) for his Amish perspective on the Steering Committee.

22. Primary sources detailing the meeting and agreements are Steering (1973).

23. Meyers (2003) surveys these conflicts. See also lists of cases in Keim (1975:93-98) and Place (2003).

24. Primary sources appear in Lapp (1991: 191-518). The vocational school compromise was in place 10 April 1956. For narrative, see Kraybill (2001:171-72). Ontario information from David Luthy, Aylmer, Ontario.

25. The Hazelton story summarized here is detailed in Erickson (1975b); see also "The Old Order," *Newsweek*, 6 December 1965, 38.

26. Lindholm (2003) details his involvement.

27. Erickson (1975a) and Keim (1975:97-98).

28. Erickson (1975a:73).

29. Keim (1975:98, 114-23).

30. Keim (1975:98) and Ball (1975:120).

31. Supreme (1972). The decision's text also appears in Keim (1975:149-81). For newspaper accounts of the Yoder case, see Lapp (1991:547-56). Discussions of the case include Hostetler (1975), Pfeffer (1975), and Epps (2003).

32. Ed Klimuska, "A Harrisburg Attorney Won the Supreme Court Case for the Amish," *Lancaster* (Pa.) *New Era*, 26 May 1989, A-10. Ball reflected on the implications in Ball (1988) and (2003).

33. Nearly all Beachy Amish children, for example, attend private Beachy Amish schools, and many do not complete high school; see Yoder (1987a:209-10, 270-71). On Old Order Amish school students, teachers, and performance, see Hostetler and Huntington (1992) and Huntington (1994).

34. Luthy (1994a:246) and Fisher and Stahl (1986:18).

35. The Amish mission movement summarized here is detailed in Nolt (2001).

36. On the related Mennonite context of those years, see Toews (1996:54-55, 207-208, 226-28, 285-97).

37. Yoder (1987a:79-80); Huntington (1956: 693-700). In fact, as early as 1952 after preaching in the Lancaster, Pa., settlement, bishops there told Miller he should not return.

38. The congregation, still in existence, took the name Zion Amish Mennonite.

39. Nolt (2001:33-36).

40. Nolt (2001:35).

41. Kraybill (1994:55-56). See also Ohio (1973:14-17); some of this information is reprinted in later editions of this settlement directory, but the size and layout make it easiest to read in the 1973 edition.

42. The New Order Amish story is best summarized in Kline and Beachy (1998); see also Yoder (1987:79-82).

43. Parallels in Matthew 24:13, Mark 13:22, Luke 21:19; see also Revelation 2:5. On the other side, a vocal advocate of assurance of salvation teaching was Mifflin County, Pennsylvanian John R. Renno. He was excommunicated by his Amish church for insisting too strongly on the matter of assurance. His sharp defense is Renno ([1976]).

44. Kline and Beachy (1998:8).

45. Beiler (n.d.), Scott (1991), and Lapp (2003:271-79). In February and April 1966 about 100 families withdrew from the Lancaster Old Order church and formed two so-called "New Order" church districts. The Lancaster Old Orders did not excommunicate or shun those who left at that time, because they considered the incident a church schism and not an act of individual disobedience or independence on the part of those who left.

46. Such as those in Raber's *Almanac* and Luthy (1974), (1985), and (1992); and (1994a).

47. Kline and Beachy (1998:16).

48. See, for example, Beachy (n.d.), Burkholder (n.d.), Kline (n.d.a) and (n.d.b), Miller (n.d.), and Truth (1983). A good discussion of Old Order Amish theology is Oyer (1994).

49. Kline and Beachy (1998:14-17); Kraybill and Hostetter (2001:148-49).

50. Graham (1976).

51. Conflict with the Internal Revenue Service is detailed in Ferrara (2003).

52. "Unto Caesar," *Time*, 3 November 1958, 21; Robert Metz, "The Amish and Taxes," *New York Times*, 22 May 1961, 45.

53. "U.S. Sells 3 Mares for Amish Tax Debt," *New York Times*, 2 May 1961, 34; and Robert Metz, "The Amish and Taxes," *New York Times*, 22 May 1961, 45. Mark Andio of Youngstown, Ohio, bought Byler's animals. Byler owed $308.96. The horses sold for $460. Auction coasts were $113.15. The remaining $37.89 was refunded to Byler.

54. Clarence W. Hall, "The Revolt of the Plain People," *Reader's Digest*, November 1962, 74-78.

55. "Amish are Granted Exclusion," *New York Times*, 31 July 1965, 8. An earlier attempt was Pennsylvania's Rep. Richard S. Schweiker, reported as "Bill Would Exempt the Amish," *New York Times*, 7 November 1963, 29.

56. Ferrara (2003).

57. For complete treatment of the issues involved, see Olshan (2003), Zook (2003), Huntington (2003), and Bontrager (2003).

58. Regehr (1995) argues that in 1953, Canada had a more fully developed welfare state than the U.S. Nevertheless, it is clear that the Amish did not perceive this to be the case.

59. Thomson (1993) includes more detail. See also Janzen (1990:245-71) for context.

60. Meyers (1994a:170-71); the 1940 draft census administered by Mennonite Central Committee and sent to all Amish bishops asked the bishops to report the current employment of conscription-age men in each district. The incomplete returns show a few men listed under factory work. This documentary evidence of industrial employment by 1940 matches local anecdotal memory. See Peace Section Census, 1940, Questionnaires: Old Order Amish, Ind., IX-7-1, Box 1, Folder 7, AMCUSA-G.

61. Greksa and Korbin (2002:377); unpublished data from the 2002 Elkhart-LaGrange church directory, calculated by Thomas J. Mey-

ers; and Kraybill (2001:81) compared similar data in the 1989 edition of the same book. For similar data, see Troyer and Willoughby (1984:52-80, esp. 61).

62. Stoltzfus (1973) examined some of these innovative approaches. By 2002, the organic produce market seemed to be fairly successful in some quarters but has by no means been adopted universally. In parts of Ohio and Indiana, Amish farmers selling grade B milk worked to establish area cheese factories that have played important economic roles.

63. Meyers (1994b); Greksa and Korbin (2002) actually found a reverse relationship between these factors.

64. Kraybill and Nolt (1995) explore many aspects of small-business ownership among the Amish. See also Kraybill and Kanagy (1996).

65. Meyers (1994a), and unpublished data from the 2001 Nappanee church directory.

66. Weaver-Zercher (2001:60-81).

67. Luthy (1994b:119-22).

68. First known as the Chamber Tourism Committee, it is today known as the Pennsylvania Dutch Convention and Visitor's Bureau; see Stoltzfus (2000).

69. Dorothy E. Steinmeier, "Overlooked Indiana," *Travel: The Magazine That Roams the Globe*, June 1967, 28-33; Bill Thomas, "Ohio's Amish Country," *Travel: The Magazine that Roams the Globe*, April 1968, 52-53, 62-63. See also Luthy (1994b:122-29). The first Amish-theme attraction in Indiana was Amishville, near Berne, which opened in 1968; the much larger Amish Acres complex near Nappanee opened to the public two years later. Both were located on formerly Amish-owned farms.

70. de Angeli (1944).

71. Keene (1955).

72. Weaver-Zercher (2001:104-14).

73. Kraybill (2001:280-84). Weaver-Zercher (2001:152-80).

74. For example, Nadya Labi, "Amiss among the Amish," *Time*, July 6, 1998, 81.

75. Weaver-Zercher (2001:181-96).

76. Kraybill (2001:287-94).

77. For one Amish perspective, see Fisher (1978:361-70).

78. *Mennonite Yearbook* (1972:90-91) and *Mennonite Church Information* (2002:16-26).

79. See, for example, Paul [Pablo] Yoder (1998).

80. CAM distributes clothing, medicine, and other material aid, along with Christian literature, in about two dozen countries. Donations of cash and material gifts-in-kind are around

$130 million a year. A majority of CAM board members are Beachy Amish, but members of the Conservative Mennonite Conference and Weaverland Mennonite Conference are also on the board. Founder David Troyer is of New Order Amish background, but joined the Beachy Amish. For an example of Beachy Amish mission and service efforts in one congregation, see details in Lapp (2003).

81. It is common for New Order Amish to volunteer labor at the CAM warehouse in Berlin, Ohio; some Indiana Old Orders volunteers at the CAM warehouse in Shipshewana. Old Order Amish in Lancaster, Pennsylvania, sometimes volunteer at the Mennonite Central Committee (MCC) warehouse in Akron, Pennsylvania, or the regional CAM center nearby. Old Orders in various communities volunteer to help with MCC meat-canning or CAM clothing-packing; in either case, commodities for shipment overseas.

82. For statistics, see Luthy (1974), (1985), (1992), (1994a), and (2003); and Kraybill and Hostetter (2001).

83. Luthy (1994a) discusses migration patterns and motives. On migration, see also Meyers (1991) and Greksa and Korbin (2002). Not all new settlements thrive or endure; see Luthy (2000).

84. For statistics, see Luthy (1974), (1985), (1992), (1994a), and (2003); and Kraybill and Hostetter (2001). While virtually complete, Kraybill and Hostetter omitted the Maine and Idaho Amish church districts in existence in 2000.

85. Meyers (1991) and (1994b), though Meyers shows that retention/defection is not uniform, and certain factors influence the decision to join or leave. Greksa and Korbin (2002) for Geauga and adjacent counties, Ohio, demonstrate the same retention trends and nearly identical percentages, though they found somewhat different variables affecting choice. Greksa and Korbin also review the literature on similar studies in other places, especially Lancaster, Pa. See also Kraybill (2001:117, 187). Kraybill (1994) shows differences in retention rates among different Amish affiliations (subgroups).

86. Hostetler and Huntington (1992). Enrollment rates from unpublished data from Indiana Old Order study conducted by Thomas J. Meyers and Steven M. Nolt.

87. Meyers (1991:319).

88. For *Family Life* excerpts, see Igou (1999). Pathway publications catalogues are available by writing Pathway Publishers, 52445 Glencol-in Ln, RR 4, Aylmer, ON N5H 2R3. Amish Libraries include the Heritage Historical Library, Aylmer, Ontario; Ohio Amish Library, Millersburg, Ohio; and the Pequea Bruderschaft Library, Gordonville, Pa. The first two revolving mortgage funds were the Family Assistance Fund of the Arthur, Illinois, Amish community, followed in 1990 by the Amish Mutual Mortgage Fund of the Nappanee, Ind., settlement. The literature on Amish mental health from a professional clinical perspective is sizable. The People's Helper's movement is a loose network of Amish interested in counseling at a lay level and unconnected in a formal way to professional centers (though some sympathetic ties exist in certain communities). Those interested in People's Helpers meet annually, usually in an Amish community in Michigan.

89. Fisher (1978:320).

Bibliography

Archival sources, newspaper, and news magazine articles appear as full listings only in the Endnotes.

Abbreviations used in this bibliography:
  AP   Ambassador of Peace, Amish-published periodical for their men performing alternative service in lieu of the military draft, 1966-1970. It was succeeded by the monthly Amish youth periodical *Young Companion*, 1971-present.
  FL   Family Life, monthly magazine issued by Old Order Amish Pathway Publishers, Aylmer, Ont.
  ME   Mennonite Encyclopedia. Scottdale, Pa.: Herald Press, 4 vols., 1955-1959; vol. 5, 1990.
  MFH   Mennonite Family History, a genealogical magazine published at Elverson, Pa.
  MHB   Mennonite Historical Bulletin, publication of the Mennonite Church USA Historical Committee.
  ML   Mennonite Life, historical journal published by Bethel College, North Newton, Kans.
  MQR   Mennonite Quarterly Review, major journal of Anabaptist-Mennonite Studies, published at Goshen, Ind., by the Mennonite Historical Society, Goshen College, and Associated Mennonite Biblical Seminary.
  PMH   Pennsylvania Mennonite Heritage, quarterly journal of the Lancaster Mennonite Historical Society, Lancaster, Pa.
  TD   The Diary, monthly magazine serving Old Order Amish and published at Gordonville, Pa.

Abrams, Ray H.
1933   *Preachers Present Arms*. Philadelphia: Round Table Press.
Amish and Mennonites in Eastern Elkhart and LaGrange Counties, Ind., 1841-1991
1992   Goshen, Ind.: The Amish Heritage Committee.
"An Amish Church Discipline of 1781"
1930   *MQR* 4 (April): 140-48.
"Amish Life in the Great Depression, 1930-1940"
1971   *FL* 4 (July): 18-21; (August): 18-21.
The Amish Moving to Maryland
1965   Gordonville, Pa.: A. S. Kinsinger.
Anderson, Calvin E.
1966   "[Editorial] Introduction," *AP* 1 (February): 3-4.
Ausbund, Das ist: Etliche schöne christliche Lieder
1997   Lancaster, Pa.: Verlag von den Amischen Gemeinden in Lancaster County, Pa. First partial edition was in 1564.
Bachman, Peter
1934   *1784-1934, Mennoniten in Kleinpolen: Gedenkbuch . . . .* Lemberg: Verlag der Lemberger Mennonitengemeinde in Lemberg.
Baecher, Robert
1998   trans. by Kevin J. Ruth, "1712: Investigation of an Important Date," *PMH* (April): 2-12.
2000   "'The Patriarche' of Sainte-Marie-aux-Mines," *MQR* 74 (January): 145-58.
Bair, Ray
1952   "The Merger of the Mennonite and the Amish Mennonite Conference[s] from 1911 to 1928," *MHB* 13 (October): 2-4.
Ball, William Bentley
1975   "Building a Landmark Case: *Wisconsin v. Yoder*," in *Compulsory Education and the Amish: The Right Not to be Modern*, ed. by Albert N. Keim, 114-23. Boston: Beacon Press.
1988   "An External Perspective: The Constitutional Freedom to be Anabaptist," *Brethren Life and Thought* 33 (Summer): 200-204.
2003   "First Amendment Issues," in *The Amish and the State*, ed. by Donald B. Kraybill, 253-65. Baltimore: The Johns Hopkins University Press.
Beachy, Alvin J.
1954   "The Amish Settlement in Somerset County, Pennsylvania," *MQR* 28 (October): 263-92.
1955   "The Rise and Development of the Beachy Amish Mennonite Churches," *MQR* 29 (April): 118-40.

Beachy, Lester
n.d.   *The Cross: Bitter or Sweet?* Baltic, Ohio: Amish Brotherhood Publications.
Beechy, William and Malinda Beechy, comps.
[199-]   *Experiences of C.O.'s in C.P.S. Camps, in I-W Service in Hospitals, and during World War I.* LaGrange, Ind.: W. and M. Beechy.
Beiler, Abner F.
n.d.   "A Brief History of the New Order Amish Church, 1966-1976," unpublished paper, Lancaster Mennonite Historical Library, Lancaster, Pennsylvania.
Beiler, Joseph F.
1969   "Two Hundred Years in America: The Stoltzfus Family," *TD* 1 (January): 6, 8.
1974a   "The Amish in the Pequea Valley Before 1800," *TD* 6 (July): 162-64.
1974b   "Landgrants," *TD* 6 (May): 120, 119.
1975a   "Bishop Jacob Hertzler," *TD* 7 (July): 168, 165-67.
1975b   "Revolutionary War Records," *TD* 7 (March): 71.
1976/1977 "Eighteenth Century Amish in Lancaster County," *Mennonite Research Journal* 17 (October): 37, 46; 18 (January): 1, 10; (April): 16.
1977a   "Amish History in Lancaster County," *Mennonite Research Journal* 17 (April): 16.
1977b   "The Drachsel Family," *TD* 9 (March): 70.
1978   [land grant map including Christian Rupp parcel], *TD* 10 (January): 13, 32.
1982   "Ordnung," *MQR* 56 (October): 382-84.
1983   "A Review of the Founding of the Lancaster County Church Settlement," *TD* 15 (December): 17-22.
Belfry, Paul E.
1923   *The Community and Its High School.* New York: D. C. Heath.
Bender, Harold S.
1927   ed., "The Discipline Adopted by the Strasburg [sic] Conference of 1568," *MQR* 1 (January): 57-66.
1934   ed., "Some Early American Amish Mennonite Disciplines," *MQR* 8 (April): 90-98.
1944   *The Anabaptist Vision.* Scottdale, Pa.: Herald Press.
1946   ed., "An Amish Bishop's Conference Epistle of 1865," *MQR* 20 (July): 222-29.
Biesecker-Mast, Gerald J.
1999   "Anxiety and Assurance in the Amish Atonement Rhetorics of Daniel E. Mast and David J. Stutzman," *MQR* 73 (July): 525-38.
Blank, Benuel S.
2001   *The Amazing Story of the Ausbund.* Narvon, Pa.: B. S. Blank.

Blanke, Fritz
1961   Joseph Nordenhauge, trans. *Brothers in Christ.* Scottdale, Pa.: Herald Press.
Bontrager, Herman D.
2003   "Encounters with the State, 1990-2002," in *The Amish and the State*, ed. by Donald B. Kraybill, 235-50. Baltimore: The Johns Hopkins University Press.
Bontreger, Eli J.
1982   *My Life Story.* [Goshen, Ind. : Manasseh E. Bontreger].
Borntreger, John E. (Hansi)
1988   Elizabeth Gingerich, trans., *A History of the First Settlers of the Amish Mennonites and the Establishment of Their First Congregation in the State of Indiana . . . .* Topeka, Ind.: Dan Hochstetler. First issued in German by Bontreger in 1907.
Boylan, Anne M.
1988   *Sunday School: The Formation of an American Institution, 1790-1880.* New Haven: Yale University Press.
Braght, Thieleman J. van
1998   *The Bloody Theater; or Martyrs Mirror of the Defenseless Christians.* Joseph F. Sohm, trans. Scottdale, Pa.: Herald Press.
Bressler, Ann Lee
2001   *The Universalist Movement in America, 1770-1880.* New York: Oxford University Press.
"Briefsammlung"
1987   *Informations-Blaetter/Feuilles d'Information: Schweizerischer Verein fuer Taeufergeschichte/Societé Suisse d'Histoire Mennonite* 10: 26-61. A German edition of the letters detailing the Amish schism of 1693-97.
Brunk, Ivan W.
1982   "Mennonites in the Carolinas," *PMH* 5 (January): 14-21.
Burkholder, David G.
n.d.   *The Inroads of Pietism.* Baltic, Ohio: Amish Brotherhood Publications.
Bush, Perry
1999   *Two Kingdoms, Two Loyalties: Mennonite Pacifism in Modern America.* Baltimore: The Johns Hopkins University Press.
2000   *Dancing with the Kobzar: Bluffton College and Mennonite Higher Education, 1899-1999.* Telford, Pa.: Pandora Press U.S.
Bushman, Richard L.
1992   *The Refinement of America: Persons, Houses, Cities.* New York: Alfred A. Knopf.
Butler, Jon
1990   *Awash in a Sea of Faith: Christianizing the American People.* Cambridge, Mass.: Harvard University Press.
Catechism, or Plain Instruction From the Sacred Scriptures
1905   Elkhart, Ind.: Mennonite Publishing Company. An English translation of the well-

loved 1797 "Waldeck Catechism" of the Waldeck, Hesse, Amish. The Waldeck Catechism was itself originally the 1783 Elbing, Prussia, Mennonite catechism.

Clark, Allen B.
1988 *This Is Good Country: A History of the Amish of Delaware, 1915-1988*. Gordonville, Pa.: Gordonville Book Shop.

Clark, Olynthius
1929 "Joseph Joder, Schoolmaster-Farmer and Poet, 1797-1887," *Transactions of the Illinois State Historical Society* (1929): 135-65.

Clasen, Claus-Peter
1972 *Anabaptism: A Social History, 1525-1618, [in] Switzerland, Austria, Moravia, South and Central Germany*. Ithaca, N.Y.: Cornell University Press.

Clauden, David N. and Kathryn Egly Claudon
1947 *Life of Bishop Henry Egly, 1824-1890*. n.p.

Correll, Ernst
1928 "The Value of Family History for Mennonite History, Illustrated from Nafziger Family History Material of the Eighteenth Century," *MQR* 2 (January): 66-79; (July): 198-204.
1955 "Alsace," S.v. in *ME*, 1:66-75.
1956 "French Revolution," S.v. in *ME*, 2:392.

Cosgel, Metin M.
1993 "Religious Culture and Economic Performance: Agricultural Productivity of the Amish, 1850-80," *Journal of Economic History* 53 (June): 319-31.

de Angeli, Marguerite
1944 *Yonie Wondernose*. New York: Doubleday.

Deeben, John P.
1992 "Amish Agriculture and Popular Opinion in the Nineteenth and Twentieth Centuries," *PMH* 15 (April): 21-29.

A Devoted Christian's Prayer Book
1984 Aylmer, Ont. and LaGrange Ind.: Pathway Publishing Corp. An English language translation of *Die Ernsthafte Christenpflicht*.

Durnbaugh, Donald F.
1978 "Religion and Revolution: Options in 1776," *PMH* 1 (July): 2-9.
1983 ed. *The Brethren Encyclopedia*. Philadelphia, Pa.: The Brethren Encyclopedia, Inc.
1997 *Fruit of the Vine: A History of the Brethren, 1708-1995*. Elgin, Ill.: Brethren Press.

Dyck, Cornelius J.
1995 trans. and ed. *Spiritual Life in Anabaptism*. Scottdale, Pa.: Herald Press.

Early Amish Land Grants in Berks County, Pennsylvania
1991 Gordonville, Pa.: Pequea Bruderschaft Library.

Egly, Henry
1965 "The Kingdom of Peace of Jesus Christ," *The Evangelical Mennonite*, August, 8-10.

Ellis, Franklin and Samuel Evans
1883 *History of Lancaster County, Pennsylvania, with Biographical Sketches of Many of its Pioneers and Prominent Men*. Philadelphia: Everts and Peck.

Epps, Garret
2003 "The Amish and the American Oyster," in *The Amish and the State*, ed. by Donald B. Kraybill, 267-75. Baltimore: The Johns Hopkins University Press.

Erb, Paul
1974 *South Central Frontiers: A History of the South Central Mennonite Conference*. Scottdale, Pa.: Herald Press.

Erickson, Donald A.
1975a "The Persecution of LeRoy Garber," in *Compulsory Education and the Amish: The Right Not to be Modern*, ed. by Albert N. Keim, 84-92. Boston: Beacon Press.
1975b "Showdown at an Amish Schoolhouse," in *Compulsory Education and the Amish: The Right Not to be Modern*, ed. by Albert N. Keim, 43-83. Boston: Beacon Press.

Esh, Levi A.
1977 "The Amish Parochial School Movement," *MQR* 51 (January): 69-75.

Estes, Steven R.
1982 *A Goodly Heritage: A History of the North Danvers Mennonite Church*. Danvers, Ill.: North Danvers Mennonite Church.
1984 *Living Stones: A History of the Metamora Mennonite Church*. Metamora, Ill.: Metamora Mennonite Church.
1990 *From Mountains to Meadows: A Century of Witness of the Meadows Mennonite Church*. Chenoa, Ill.: Historical Committee of Meadows Mennonite Church.
1993a "The Central Conference and Middle District Merger of 1957," *ML* 48 (March): 11-15.
1993b *Love God and Your Neighbor: The Life and Ministry of Christian Engel*. Metamora, Ill.: Illinois Mennonite Historical and Genealogical Society.

Ferrara, Peter J.
2003 "Social Security and Taxes," in *The Amish and the State*, ed. by Donald B. Kraybill, 125-43. Baltimore: The Johns Hopkins University Press.

Fisher, Amos L.
1984 "History of the First Amish Communities in America," *TD* 16 (September): 35-39.

Fisher, Gideon
1978   *Farm Life and Its Changes.* Gordonville, Pa.: Pequea Publishers.
Fisher, Jonathan B.
1911   *A Trip to Europe and Facts Gleaned on the Way.* New Holland, Pa.: Jonathan B. Fisher.
1937   *Around the World by Water and Facts Gleaned on the Way.* [Bareville, Pa.]: Jonathan B. Fisher.
Fisher, Sara E. and Rachel K. Stahl
1986   *The Amish School.* Intercourse, Pa.: Good Books.
Fogleman, Aaron S.
1996   *Hopeful Journeys: German Immigration, Settlement, and Political Culture in Colonial America, 1717-1775.* Philadelphia: University of Pennsylvania Press.
1998   "From Slaves, Convicts, and Servants to Free Passengers: The Transformation of Immigration in the Era of the American Revolution," *Journal of American History* 85 (June): 43-76.
Fretz, Clarence Y.
1957   "Luxembourg," S.v. in *ME*, 3:422-23.
Fretz, J. Winfield
1978   "Witnessing a Community's Death." Unpublished paper, Heritage Historical Library, Aylmer, Ont.
n.d.   "The Amish in Paraguay." Unpublished paper, Heritage Historical Library, Aylmer, Ont.
Friedmann, Robert
1949   *Mennonite Piety Through the Centuries: Its Genius and Its Literature.* Goshen, Ind.: The Mennonite Historical Society.
Frost, J. William
1990   *A Perfect Freedom: Religious Liberty in Pennsylvania.* Cambridge: Cambridge University Press.
Furner, Mark
2000   "On the Trail of Jakob Ammann," *MQR* 74 (April): 326-28.
2001   "Lay Casuistry and the Survival of Later Anabaptists in Bern," *MQR* 75 (October): 429-70.
Gambone, A. M.
1996   *The Life of General Samuel K. Zook: Another Forgotten Union Hero.* Baltimore: Butternut and Blue.
Gascho, Milton
1937   "The Amish Division of 1693-1697 in Switzerland and Alsace," *MQR* 11 (October): 235-66.
Geiser, Samuel
1959   "Reist, Hans," S.v. in *ME*, 4:281-82.
George, Timothy
1988   *Theology of the Reformers.* Nashville, Tenn.: Broadman Press.

Gerlach, Horst
1990   "Amish Congregations in Germany and Adjacent Territories in the Eighteenth and Nineteenth Centuries," *PMH* 13 (April): 2-8.
Gibbons, Phebe Earle
1882   *"Pennsylvania Dutch," and Other Essays.* Philadelphia: J. P. Lippincott.
Gingerich, Hugh F. and Rachel W. Kreider
1986   *Amish and Amish Mennonite Genealogies.* Gordonville, Pa.: Pequea Publishers.
Gingerich, James Nelson
1986   "Ordinance or Ordering: Ordnung and Amish Ministers Meetings, 1862-1878," *MQR* 60 (April): 180-99.
Gingerich, Josef
1982   Elizabeth Horsch Bender, trans. "The Amish Mennonites in Bavaria," *MQR* 56 (April): 179-88.
Gingerich, Melvin
1939   *The Mennonites in Iowa.* Iowa City: State Historical Society of Iowa.
1942   "Amish Ministers' Meeting, 1874," *MHB* 4 (December): 1-4.
1949   *Service For Peace: A History of Mennonite Civilian Public Service.* Akron, Pa.: Mennonite Central Committee.
1955a   "Amish Aid Plan," S.v. in *ME*, 1: 89.
1955b   intro. *Joseph Goldsmith (1796-1876) and His Descendants.* Kalona, Ia.: John W. Gingerich.
1959   "Sleeping Preacher Churches," S.v. in *ME*, 4: 543-44.
1961   "Mennonite Indentured Servants," *ML* 16 (July): 107-109.
1965   "A List of Amish Ministers in 1849," *MHB* 26 (July): 7.
1970   *Mennonite Attire through Four Centuries.* Breinigsville, Pa.: The Pennsylvania German Society.
1971   "Sleeping Preachers," *MHB* 32 (January): 4-6.
Gingerich, Orland
2002   *The Amish of Canada.* Kitchener, Ont.: Pandora Press. First ed., 1972.
Glick, Aaron S.
1994   *The Fortunate Years: An Amish Life.* Intercourse, Pa.: Good Books.
Graham, Otis, Jr.
1976   *Toward a Planned Society: From Roosevelt to Nixon.* New York: Oxford University Press.
Gratz, Delbert L.
1951   "The Home of Jacob Amman [sic] in Switzerland," *MQR* 25 (April): 137-39.
1952   "Bernese Anabaptism in the Eighteenth Century, I," *MQR* 26 (January): 5-21.
1953   *Bernese Anabaptists and Their Ameri-*

can Descendants. Goshen, Ind.: The Mennonite Historical Society.

Greksa, Lawrence P. and Jill E. Korbin
2002 "Key Decisions in the Lives of the Old Order Amish: Joining the Church and Migrating to Another Settlement," *MQR* 76 (October 2002): 373-98.

Grieser, Orland R. and Ervin Beck, Jr.
1960 *Out of the Wilderness: History of the Central Mennonite Church, 1835-1960.* Grand Rapids: The Dean Hicks Co.

Gross, Leonard
1991 "The First Mennonite Merger: The Concept of Cologne," in *Mennonite Yearbook, 1991-1992.* Scottdale, Pa.: Mennonite Publishing House.
1997 trans. and ed. *Prayer Book for Earnest Christians.* Scottdale, Pa.: Herald Press.

Guth, Hermann
1987 "Preacher Johannes Nafzinger of Essingen, Germany," *MFH* 6 (October): 129-31.
1995 *Amish Mennonites in Germany: Their Congregations, The Estates Where They Lived, Their Families.* Morgantown, Pa.: Masthof Press.

Habegger, David L.
2002 *The Swiss of Adams and Wells Counties, Indiana, 1838-1862.* Fort Wayne: D. L. Habegger.

Harder, Leland, ed.
1985 *The Sources of Swiss Anabaptism: The Grebel Letters and Related Documents.* Scottdale, Pa.: Herald Press.

Hartzler, H. Harold
1991 *Amishman Travels Around the World: The Life of Jonathan B. Fisher.* Elverson, Pa.: Mennonite Family History.

Hartzler, Jonas S. and Daniel Kauffman
1905 *Mennonite Church History.* Scottdale, Pa.: Mennonite Book and Tract Society.

Hartzler-Miller, Gregory
1997 "'Der Weiss' Jonas Stutzmann: Amish Pioneer and Mystic," *MHB* 58 (October): 4-12.

Haury, David A.
1981 *Prairie People: A History of the Western District Conference.* Newton, Kans.: Faith and Life Press.

Hege, Lydie and Christoph Wiebe
1996 eds., *Les Amish: Origine et Particularismes, 1693-1993.* Ingersheim: Association Française d'Histoire Anabaptiste-Mennonite.

Hein, Gerhard
1959 "Palatinate," S.v. in *ME* 4:106-12.

Helmuth, Orva
1961 "History of the Arthur Amish Mennonite Church," *MHB* 22 (October): 3-4.

Hershberger, Guy F.
1951 *The Mennonite Church in the Second World War.* Scottdale, Pa.: Herald Press.

Hertzler, Enos
1985 *Time Out for Paraguay.* Gordonville, Pa.: Gordonville Print Shop.

Hiller, Harry H.
1968/1969 "The Sleeping Preachers: An Historical Study of the Role of Charisma in Amish Society," *Pennsylvania Folklife* 18 (Winter): 19-31.

Historical Statistics of the United States: Colonial Times to 1970
1975 Washington, D.C.: United States Department of Commerce, Bureau of the Census.

History and Happenings of the Buchanan County Amish, 1914-1997
1999 Sugarcreek, Ohio: Carlisle Printing.

Homan, Gerlof D.
1994 *American Mennonites and the Great War, 1914-1918.* Scottdale, Pa.: Herald Press.

Horst, Irvin B.
1982 "Dordrecht Confession of Faith: 350 Years," *PMH* 5 (July): 2-8.
1988 trans. and ed. *Mennonite Confession of Faith, ...* Lancaster, Pa.: Lancaster Mennonite Historical Society.

Hostetler, Beulah Stauffer
1992 "The Formation of the Old Orders," *MQR* 66 (January): 5-25.
1996 "The Amish and Pietism: Similarities and Differences," in *Les Amish: Origine et Particularismes, 1693-1993,* ed. by Lydie Hege and Christoph Wiebe, 253-61. Ingersheim: Association Française d'Histoire Anabaptiste-Mennonite.

Hostetler, Harvey
1912 ed., *The Descendants of Jacob Hochstetler, the Immigrant of 1736.* Elgin, Ill.: Brethren Publishing House.

Hostetler, John A.
1955 "Old World Extinction and New World Survival of the Amish: A Study of Group Maintenance and Dissolution," *Rural Sociology* 20 (September-December): 212-19.
1964 "Memoirs of Shem Zook," *MQR* 38 (July): 280-99.
1974 *Hutterite Society.* Baltimore: The Johns Hopkins University Press.
1975 "The Cultural Context of the Wisconsin Case," in *Compulsory Education and the Amish: The Right Not to be Modern,* ed. by Albert N. Keim, 99-113. Boston: Beacon Press.
1983 "Amish," S.v. in *The Brethren Encyclopedia,* ed. by Donald F. Durnbaugh. Philadelphia: Brethren Encyclopedia, Inc.
1989 ed., *Amish Roots: A Treasury of History, Wisdom, and Lore.* Baltimore: The Johns Hopkins University Press.
1993 *Amish Society,* fourth ed. Baltimore: The Johns Hopkins University Press.

Hostetler, John A. and Gertrude Enders Huntington
1992   *Amish Children: Education in the Family, School, and Community*, second ed. New York: Harcourt, Brace, Jovanovich College Publishers.

Hostetler, Pius
1980   *Life, Preaching and Labors of John D. Kauffman*. Gordonville, Pa.: Gordonville Print Shop.

Huntington, Gertrude Enders
"Dove at the Window: A Study of an Old Order Amish Community in Ohio." PhD dissertation, Yale University.
1994   "Persistence and Change in Amish Education," in *The Amish Struggle with Modernity* ed. by Donald B. Kraybill and Marc A. Olshan, 77-95. University Press of New England.

Hüppi, John
2000   "Identifying Jakob Ammann," *MQR* 74 (April): 329-39.

Igou, Brad
1999   comp. *The Amish in Their Own Words: Amish Writings from 25 years of* Family Life Magazine. Scottdale, Pa.: Herald Press.

Janzen, William
1990   *Limits on Liberty: The Experience of Mennonite, Hutterite, and Doukhobor Communities in Canada*. Toronto: University of Toronto Press.

Jellison, Katherine
2002   "The Chosen Women: The Amish and the New Deal," in *Strangers at Home: Amish and Mennonite Women in History*, eds. Kimberly D. Schmidt, Diane Zimmerman Umble, and Steven D. Reschly, 102-18. Baltimore: The Johns Hopkins University Press.

Juhnke, James C.
1979   *A People of Mission: A History of General Conference Mennonite Overseas Missions*. Newton, Kans.: Faith and Life Press.
1989   *Vision, Doctrine, War: Mennonite Identity and Organization in America, 1890-1930*. Scottdale, Pa.: Herald Press.

Kauffman, J. Howard and Leo Driedger
1991   *The Mennonite Mosaic: Identity and Modernization*. Scottdale, Pa.: Herald Press.

Kauffman, John D.
1953   *Kauffman's Sermons*. Saint Joe, Ark.: Martin Printers.

Kauffman, S. Duane
1979   "Miscellaneous Amish Mennonite Documents," 2 *PMH* (July): 12-16.
1991   *Mifflin County Amish and Mennonite Story, 1791-1991*. Belleville, Pa.: Mifflin County Mennonite Historical Society.

Kaufman, Stanley A. with Leroy Beachy
1991   *Amish in Eastern Ohio*. Walnut Creek, Ohio: German Cultural Museum.

Keene, Carolyn
1955   *The Witch Tree Symbol*. New York: Simon and Schuster, Inc.

Keim, Albert N.
1975   ed., *Compulsory Education and the Amish: The Right Not to be Modern*. Boston: Beacon Press.
1990   *The CPS Story: An Illustrated History of Civilian Public Service*. Intercourse, Pa.: Good Books.
2003   "Military Service and Conscription," in *The Amish and the State*, ed. by Donald B. Kraybill, 43-65. Baltimore: The Johns Hopkins University Press.

Keim, Albert N. and Grant M. Stoltzfus
1988   *The Politics of Conscience: The Historic Peace Churches and America at War, 1917-1955*. Scottdale, Pa.: Herald Press.

Kinsinger, Andrew S.
1997   *A Little History of Our Parochial Schools and Steering Committee from 1956-1994*. Gordonville, Pa.: Gordonville Print Shop.

Klaassen, Walter
1981   ed., *Anabaptism in Outline: Selected Primary Sources*. Scottdale, Pa.: Herald Press.

Kline, Edward A.
n.d.a   *A Sure Path for Mankind*. Baltic, Ohio: Amish Brotherhood Publications.
n.d.b   *A Theology of the Will of Man and Some Practical Applications for the Christian Life*. Baltic, Ohio: Amish Brotherhood Publications.

Kline, Edward A. and Monroe L. Beachy
1998   "History and Dynamics of the New Order Amish of Holmes County, Ohio," *Old Order Notes* 18 (Fall-Winter): 7-19.

Klopfenstein, Joseph
1984   Elizabeth Horsch Bender, trans. "An Amish Sermon," *MQR* 58 (July): 296-317.

Klopfenstein, Perry A.
1984   *Marching to Zion: A History of the Apostolic Christian Church of America, 1847-1982*. Fort Scott, Kans.: Sekan Printing Co.

Kollmorgen, Walter M.
1942   *Culture of a Contemporary Rural Community: The Old Order Amish of Lancaster County, Pennsylvania*. [Washington, D.C.]: U.S. Dept. of Agriculture.

Krabill, Russell
1991   "The Coming of the Amish Mennonites to Elkhart County, Indiana," *MHB* 52 (January): 1-5.

Kraybill, Donald B.
1994   "Plotting Social Change Across Four Affiliations," in *The Amish Struggle with Modernity*, ed. by Donald B. Kraybill and Marc A. Olshan, 53-74. Hanover, N.H.: University Press of New England.

2001   *The Riddle of Amish Culture*, rev. ed. Baltimore: The Johns Hopkins University Press.
2003   ed. *The Amish and the State*, rev. ed. Baltimore: The Johns Hopkins University Press.

Kraybill, Donald B. and C. Nelson Hostetter
2001   *Anabaptist World USA*. Scottdale, Pa.: Herald Press.

Kraybill, Donald B. and Carl F. Bowman
2001   *On the Backroad to Heaven: Old Order Hutterites, Mennonites, Amish, and Brethren*. Baltimore: The Johns Hopkins University Press.

Kraybill, Donald B. and Conrad L. Kanagy
1996   The Rise of Entrepreneurship in two Old Order Amish Communities," *MQR* 70 (July): 263-79.

Kraybill, Donald B. and Steven M. Nolt
1995   *Amish Enterprise: From Plows to Profits*, rev. ed. Baltimore: The Johns Hopkins University Press. A revised edition of this book is slated for release in 2004.

Kraybill, Donald B. and Marc A. Olshan
1994   eds., *The Amish Struggle with Modernity*. Hanover, N.H.: University Press of New England.

Krehbiel, Christian
1961   *Prairie Pioneer: The Christian Krehbiel Story*. Newton, Kans.: Faith and Life Press.

Landis, Ira D.
1955   "Amish Aid Society," S.v. in *ME*, 1:89-90.

Lapp, Aaron, Jr.
2003   *Weavertown Church History: Memoirs of an Amish Mennonite Church*. Sugarcreek, Ohio: Carlisle Printing.

Lapp, Christ S.
1991   *Pennsylvania School History, 1690-1990*. Gordonville, Pa.: Christ S. Lapp.

Lears, T. J. Jackson
1981   *No Place for Grace: Antimodernism and the Transformation of American Culture, 1880-1920*. New York: Pantheon Books.

Lehman, James O.
1978   *Creative Congregationalism: A History of the Oak Grove Mennonite Church in Wayne County, Ohio*. Smithville, Ohio: Oak Grove Mennonite Church.
1990   *Uncommon Threads: A Centennial History of Bethel Mennonite Church*. West Liberty, Ohio: Bethel Mennonite Church.

Leith, John H.
1982   ed., *Creeds of the Churches: A Reader in Christian Doctrine from the Bible to the Present*, third ed. Louisville, Ky.: John Knox Press.

Levine, Neil Ann Stuckey, Ursula Roy, and David J. Rempel Smucker
1996   "Trans-Atlantic Advice: An 1822 Letter by Louis C. Jüngerich (1803-1882)," *PMH* 19 (July): 2-16.
1997   "The View of Louis C. Jüngerich (1803-1882) in 1826: It is Best to Come to This Country Well Prepared," *PMH* 20 (July): 2-15.

Lind, Hope Kauffman
1990   *Apart and Together: Mennonites in Oregon and Neighboring States, 1876-1976*. Scottdale, Pa.: Herald Press.

Lindholm, William C.
2003   "The National Committee for Amish Religious Freedom," in *The Amish and the State*, ed. by Donald B. Kraybill, 109-23. Baltimore: The Johns Hopkins University Press.

Lugibihl, Walter H.
1950   *Missionary Church Association*. Berne, Ind.: Economy Printing Concern.

Luthy, David
1972a "An Amishman's City," *FL* 5 (February): 23-25.
1972b "The Arrest of an Amish Bishop—1918," *FL* 5 (March): 23-27.
1972/1973 "New Names Among the Amish," *FL* 5 (August/September): 31-35; (October): 20-23; (November): 21-23; 6 (February): 13-15; (June): 13-15.
1973   "The Amish in Europe," *FL* 6 (March): 10-14; (April): 16-20.
1974   "Old Order Amish Settlements in 1974," *FL* 7 (December): 13-16
1978a "Concerning the Name Amish," *MHB* 39 (April): 5.
1978b "Forced to Sell Their Farms," *FL* 11 (January): 19, 20.
1978c "A History of *The Budget*," *FL* 11 (June): 19-22; (July): 15-18.
1980   "'White' Jonas Stutzman," *FL* 13 (February): 19-21.
1981a "Amish Meetinghouses," *FL* 14 (August/September): 17-22.
1981b "A History of *Die Ernsthafte Christenpflicht*," *FL* 14 (February): 19-23.
1981c "Replacing the *Ausbund*," *FL* 14 (November): 21-23.
1982   "An Amish View of the Panic of 1893 and the Election of 1896," *FL* 15 (May): 23-26.
1984a "A History of Raber's Bookstore," *MQR* 58 (April): 168-78.
1984b "An Important Pennsylvania Broadside of 1812," *PMH* 7 (July): 1-4.
1984c "Significant Books for Amish and Mennonites: A Brief Summary," *PMH* 7 (January): 6
1985   *Amish Settlements Across America*. Aylmer, Ont.: Pathway Publishers.

1986   *The Amish in America: Settlements That Failed, 1840-1960*. Aylmer, Ont. and LaGrange, Ind.: Pathway Publishers.

1988a   "Amish Beginnings: Three Centuries of Migration," *MFH* 7 (July): 110-16.

1988b   "Two Waves of Amish Migration to America," *FL* 21 (March): 20-24.

1989a   "The Graber Family Comes to America," *FL* 22 (April): 21-24.

1989b   "Two Amish Writers: The Zook Brothers, David and Shem," *FL* 22 (November): 19-22; (December): 19-21.

1991   "Martin Bornträger and His Descendants," *FL* 24 (March): 19-21.

1992   "Amish Settlements Across America: 1991," *FL* 25 (April): 19-24.

1994a   "Amish Migration Patterns, 1972-1992," in *The Amish Struggle with Modernity*, ed. by Donald B. Kraybill and Marc A. Olshan, 243-59. Hanover, N.H.: University Press of New England.

1994b   "The Origin and Growth of Amish Tourism," in *The Amish Struggle with Modernity*, ed. by Donald B. Kraybill and Marc A. Olshan, 113-29. Hanover, N.H.: University Press of New England.

1995   *Amish Folk Artist Barbara Ebersol: Her Life, Fraktur, and Death Record Book*. Lancaster, Pa.: Lancaster Mennonite Historical Society.

1998   "The Origns and Growth of the Swartzentruber Amish," *FL* 31 (August/September): 19-22.

2000   *Why Some Amish Communities Fail: Extinct Settlements, 1961-1999*. Aylmer, Ont: Pathway Publishers.

2003   "Amish Settlements Across America: 2003," *FL* (October): 17-23.

MacMaster, Richard K.

1979   et al., *Conscience in Crisis: Mennonites and Other Peace Churches in America, 1739-1789, Interpretation and Documents*. Scottdale, Pa.: Herald Press.

1985   *Land, Piety, Peoplehood: The Establishment of Mennonite Communities in America, 1683-1790*. Scottdale, Pa.: Herald Press.

Martin, Helen Reimensnyder

1905   *Sabina: A Story of the Amish*. New York: The Century Publishing Company.

Mast, C. Z.

1952   "Imprisonment of Amish in Revolutionary War," *MHB* 13 (January): 6-7.

Mast, C. Z. and Robert E. Simpson

1942   *Annals of the Conestoga Valley in Lancaster, Berks, and Chester Counties, Pennsylvania . . . .* Elverson, Pa. and Churchtown, Pa.: C. Z. Mast and Robert E. Simpson.

Mast, J. Lemar and Lois Ann Mast

1982   *As Long as Wood Grows and Water Flows: A History of the Conestoga Mennonite Church*. Morgantown, Pa.: Conestoga Mennonite Historical Committee.

Mast, John B.

1950   ed., *Facts Concerning the Beachy A. M. Division of 1927*. Myersdale, Pa.: Menno J. Yoder.

Menno Simons

1956   John C. Wenger, ed. *The Complete Writings of Menno Simons, c.1496-1561*. Scottdale, Pa.: Herald Press.

Mennonite Church Information

1999-   Harrisonburg, Va.: Christian Light Publications.

Mennonite Yearbook

1905-1997 Scottdale, Pa.: Mennonite Publishing House.

"Mennonites on the Move"

1968   *Mennonite Research Journal* 9 (October): 44.

Meyer, Rich H.

1999   "Why Don't We Tell the Beginning of the Story? Native Americans Were Here First," *MHB* 60 (July): 1-8.

Meyers, Thomas J.

1990   "Amish," S.v. in *ME*, 5:20-22.

1991   "Population Growth and Its Consequences in the Elkhart-LaGrange Old Order Amish Settlement," *MQR* 65 (July): 308-21.

1994a   "Lunch Pails and Factories," in *The Amish Struggle with Modernity* ed. by Donald B. Kraybill and Marc A. Olshan, 165-81. Hanover, N.H.: University Press of New England.

1994b   "The Old Order Amish: To Remain in the Faith or to Leave," *MQR* 68 (July): 378-395.

1996   "The Amish Division: A Review of the Literature," in *Les Amish: Origine et Particularismes, 1693-1993*, ed. by Lydie Hege and Christoph Wiebe, 72-93. Ingersheim: Association Française d'Histoire Anabaptiste-Mennonite.

2003   "Education and Schooling," in *The Amish and the State* ed. by Donald B. Kraybill, 87-107. Baltimore: The Johns Hopkins University Press.

Miller, Harvey J.

1959   "Proceedings of Amish Ministers Conferences," 1826-1831," *MQR* 33 (April): 132-42.

Miller, Ivan J.

1985   *History of the Conservative Mennonite Conference, 1910-1985*. Grantsville, Md.: Ivan J. and Della Miller.

Miller, John S.

1971   "A Statistical Survey of the Amish Settlers in Clinton Township, Elkhart Coun-

ty, Indiana, 1841-1850." Unpublished manu-
script at the Mennonite Historical Library,
Goshen, Ind.
Miller, Levi D.
1970   "Another Sleeping Preacher," *MHB*
31 (April): 5-6.
Miller, Levi P.
n.d.   *Teaching Emphases That Hinder Discipleship*. Baltic, Ohio: Amish Brotherhood
Publications.
Mook, Maurice A.
1955   "An Early Amish Colony in Chester
County, Pennsylvania," *MHB* 16 (July): 1-3.
Murray, John F.
1981   "Blank/Plank Ancestry of the Amish
Mennonite Tradition," *PMH* 4 (July): 13-19.
Neff, Christian
1957   "Ibersheim Resolutions," S.v. in *ME*,
3:2.
1959   "Offenthal Conference," S.v. in *ME*,
4:21-22.
Neff, Christian and Nanne van der Zijpp
1957   "Napoleon I," S.v. in *ME*, 3:812.
Nolt, Steven M.
1995   "The Rise and Fall of an Amish Distillery: Economic Networks and Entrepre-
neurial Risk on the Illinois Frontier," *Illinois
Mennonite Heritage* 22 (September): 45, 53-
63; and (December): 65, 75-79.
1996   "Christian Farni and Abraham Lincoln: Legal Advice and the Election of 1860,"
Illinois Mennonite Heritage 23 (March): 1, 13-
14.
1999   "Plain People and the Refinement of
America," *MHB* 60 (October): 1-11.
2001   "The Amish 'Mission Movement' and
the Reformulation of Amish Identity in the
Twentieth Century," *MQR* 75 (January): 7-36.
Nussbaum, Stan
1991   *You Must Be Born Again: A History of
the Evangelical Mennonite Church*. Fort
Wayne, Ind.: Evangelical Mennonite
Church.
*Ohio Amish Directory: Holmes County
and Vicinity*
1973   Ervin Gingerich, comp. Baltimore:
Division of Medical Genetics, The Johns
Hopkins University School of Medicine.
Olshan, Marc A.
1994   "Homespun Bureaucracy: A Case
Study in Organizational Evolution," in *The
Amish Struggle with Modernity* ed. by Donald
B. Kraybill and Marc A. Olshan, 199-213.
Hanover, N.H.: University Press of New
England.
2003   "The National Amish Steering Com-
mittee," in *The Amish and the State*, ed., by
Donald B. Kraybill, 67-85. Baltimore: The
Johns Hopkins University Press.

Oyer, John S.
1984   "The Strasbourg Conferences of the
Anabaptists," *MQR* 58 (July): 218-29.
1994   "Is There an Amish Theology?" in *Les
Amish: Origine et Particularismes, 1693-1993*, ed.
by Lydie Hege and Christoph Wiebe, 278-302.
Ingersheim: Association Française d'Histoire
Anabaptiste-Mennonite.
Oyer, John S. and Robert S. Kreider
2003   *Mirror of the Martyrs*, sec. ed. Intercourse, Pa.: Good Books.
Oyer, V. Gordon
1994   ed. *Proceedings of the Conference: Tradition and Transition, An Amish Mennonite Heritage of Obedience. 1693-1993*. Metamora, Ill.:
Illinois Mennonite Historical and Genealogical
Society.
Page, Doris L. and Marie Johns
1983   *The Amish Mennonite Settlement in Butler County, Ohio*. Trenton, Ohio: Trenton Historical Society.
Pannabecker, Samuel Floyd
1968   *Faith in Ferment: A History of the Central District Conference*. Newton, Kans.: Faith
and Life Press.
1975   *Open Doors: The History of the General
Conference Mennonite Church*. Newton, Kans.:
Faith and Life Press.
Patterson, James T.
1996   *Grand Expectations: The United States,
1945-1974*. New York: Oxford University Press.
*Peace, War, and Military Service: A State-
ment of the Position of the Mennonite
Church*
1937   Resolutions adopted by the Mennonite
General Conference at Turner, Oregon. August.
Peachey, Titus and Linda Gehman Peachey
1991   *Seeking Peace*. Intercourse, Pa.: Good
Books.
Pfeffer, Leo
1975   "The Many Meanings of the *Yoder
Case*," in *Compulsory Education and the Amish:
The Right Not to be Modern*, ed. by Albert N.
Keim, 136-48. Boston: Beacon Press.
Place, Elizabeth
2003   "Appendix: Significant Legal Cases," in
The Amish and the State, ed. by Donald B. Kray-
bill, 277-88. Baltimore: The Johns Hopkins
University Press.
Pratt, Dorothy A. O.
1997   "A Study in Cultural Persistence: The
Amish in LaGrange County, Indiana, 1841-
1945," Ph.D. dissertation, University of Notre
Dame.
Raber, Ben J.
1930- comp., *Der Neue Amerikanische
Kalendar*. Baltic, Ohio: Raber's Bookstore.
Since 1970 the Almanac has also been issued
under the title *The New American Almanac*.

Regehr, T. D.
1995 "Relations Between the Old Order Amish and the State in Canada," *MQR* 69 (April): 151-77.
1996 *Mennonites in Canada, 1939-1970: A People Transformed*. Toronto, Ont.: University of Toronto Press.
Renno, John R.
[1976] *A Brief History of the Amish Church in Belleville*. Danville, Pa.: John R. Renno.
Reschly, Steven D.
2000 *The Amish on the Iowa Prairie, 1840 to 1910*. Baltimore: The Johns Hopkins University Press.
Reschly, Steven D. and Katherine Jellison
1993 "Production Patterns, Consumption Strategies, and Gender Relations in Amish and Non-Amish Farm Households in Lancaster County, Pennsylvania, 1935-1936," *Agricultural History* 67 (Spring): 134-62.
The Revelation of Barbara Stutzman, Deceased, to All Mankind
n.d. n.p. copy at the Mennonite Historical Library, Goshen, Ind.
Ringenberg, William C.
1976 "Development and Division in the Mennonite Community in Allen County, Indiana," *MQR* 50 (April): 114-31.
Ritter, Gretchen
1997 *Goldbugs and Greenbacks: The Antimonopoly Tradition and the Politics of Finance in America, 1865-1896*. New York: Cambridge University Press.
Roth, John D.
1993a trans. and ed. with Joe Springer, *Letters of the Amish Division: A Sourcebook*. Goshen, Ind.: Mennonite Historical Society. Note: pagination in this book differs slightly from a 2003 reprinting; citations in *A History of the Amish* are from the original 1993 printing.
Roth, Lorraine
1993b "The Amish Mennonite Division in Ontario, 1886-1891," *Ontario Mennonite History* 11 (March): 1-7.
1998 *The Amish and Their Neighbours: The German Block, Wilmot Township, 1822-1860*. Waterloo, Ontario: Mennonite Historical Society of Ontario.
Roth, Lorraine and Marlene J. Grant
1986 "Canadian Amish Mennonite Roots in Pennsylvania," *PMH* 9 (April): 13-17.
Ruth, John L.
1975 *Conrad Grebel, Son of Zurich*. Scottdale, Pa.: Herald Press.
1976 *'Twas Seeding Time: A Mennonite View of the American Revolution*. Scottdale, Pa.: Herald Press.

Sawatzky, Harry Leonard
1971 *They Sought a Country: Mennonite Colonization in Mexico with an Appendix on Mennonite Colonization in British Honduras*. Berkeley: University of California Press.
Schabalie, John Philip [Schabaelje, Jan Philipsz.]
1975 *The Wandering Soul, or Conversations of the Wandering Soul with Adam, Noah, and Simon Cleophas*. Baltic, Ohio: Raber's Book Store. First edition was 1635 in Dutch.
Schelbert, Leo
1985 "Pietism Rejected: A Reinterpretation of Amish Origins," in Frank Trommler and Joseph G. McVeigh, eds. *America and the Germans: An Assessment of a Three-Hundred-Year History, Vol. 1: Immigration, Language, Ethnicity*. Philadelphia: University of Pennsylvania Press.
Schlabach, Ervin
1978 *A Century and a Half with the Mennonites at Walnut Creek*. Walnut Creek, Ohio: Walnut Creek Mennonite Church.
1981 *The Amish and Mennonites at Walnut Creek*. Millersburg, Ohio: Ervin Schlabach.
Schlabach, Theron F.
1988 *Peace, Faith, Nation: Mennonites and Amish in Nineteenth-Century America*. Scottdale, Pa.: Herald Press.
Schmidt, Kimberly D. Schmidt, Diane Zimmerman Umble, and Steven D. Reschly
2002 eds. *Strangers at Home: Amish and Mennonite Women in History*. Baltimore: The Johns Hopkins University Press.
Schmidt-Lange, Anne Augspurger
2002 "Roast Bear? No, Thank You!—An 1821 Letter from Kurhessen, Germany, to Daniel and Christian Schwartzentruber in Somerset County, Pennsylvania." *PMH* (October): 9-20.
Schmölz-Häberlein, Michaela and Mark Häberlein
2001 "Eighteenth-Century Anabaptists in the Margravate of Baden and Neighboring Territories," *MQR* 75 (October): 471-92.
Schowalter, Paul
1957 "Martyrs," S.v. in *ME* 3:521-25.
Schrag, Martin H.
1974 *The European History (1525-1874) of the Swiss Mennonites from Volhynia*. North Newton, Kans.: Swiss Mennonite Cultural and Historical Association.
[Schwartz, David L.]
19— "Articles of Faith of the Old Order Amish Mennonite Church, Berne, Indiana." [Berne, Ind.: David L. Schwartz].
Scott, Stephen E.
1981 *Plain Buggies: Amish, Mennonite, and Brethren Horse-Drawn Transportation*. Intercourse, Pa.: Good Books.

1986   *Why Do They Dress That Way?* Intercourse, Pa.: Good Books.
1988   *The Amish Wedding and Other Special Occasions of the Old Order Communities.* Intercourse, Pa.: Good Books.
1991   ["Information About the Groups Originating from the New Order Division Among the Lancaster County Amish,"] unpublished paper, personal papers of Stephen E. Scott.
1996   *An Introduction to Old Order and Conservative Mennonite Groups.* Intercourse, Pa.: Good Books.
Scott, Stephen E. and Kenneth Pellman
1990   *Living Without Electricity.* Intercourse, Pa.: Good Books.
Séguy, Jean
1973   Michael Shank, trans. "Religion and Agricultural Success: The Vocational Life of the French Anabaptists from the Seventeenth to the Nineteenth Centuries," *MQR* 47 (July): 179-224.
1980   Mervin Smucker, trans. "The Bernese Anabaptists in Sainte-Marie-aux-Mines," *PMH* 3 (July): 2-9.
1982   "The French Mennonites: Tradition and Change," *International Journal of Sociology and Social Policy* 2 (No.1): 25-43.
1984   "The French Anabaptists: Four and One-Half Centuries of History," *MQR* 58 (July): 206-17.
Shoemaker, Alfred L.
1999   *Christmas in Pennsylvania: A Folk-Cultural Study.* Mechanicsburg, Pa.: Stackpole Books.
Shover, John L.
1976   *First Majority, Last Minority: The Transformation of Rural Life in America.* DeKalb, Ill.: Northern Illinois University Press.
Smith, C. Henry
1929   *The Mennonite Immigration to Pennsylvania in the Eighteenth Century.* Norristown, Pa.: Pennsylvania German Society.
1962   *Mennonite Country Boy: The Early Years of C. Henry Smith.* Newton, Kans.: Faith and Life Press.
Smith, C. Henry and Cornelius Krahn
1981   *Smith's Story of the Mennonites*, fifth ed. Newton, Kans.: Faith and Life Press.
Smith, Willard H.
1983   *Mennonites in Illinois.* Scottdale, Pa.: Herald Press.
Snyder, C. Arnold
1995   *Anabaptist History and Theology: An Introduction.* Kitchener, Ont.: Pandora Press.
Sommer, Pierre and John A. Hostetler
1957   "Ixheim," S.v. in *ME*, 3:58.
Songs of the Ausbund, v. 1: History and

Translations of Ausbund Hymns
1998   Millersburg, Ohio: Ohio Amish Library.
Springer, Joe A.
forthcoming   Montbéliard church book. A translation of this important European Amish Mennonite congregational source will be published soon, along with supporting documents and data on immigration from Montbéliard to North America.
Springer, Nelson P.
1998   "Schoolteacher by Accident, Churchman without Office: Christian Erismann, 1835-1905," *Illinois Mennonite Heritage* 24 (December): 73, 78-93.
Stahly, Jerold A.
1989   "The Montbeliard Amish Move to Poland in 1791," *MFH* 8 (January): 13-17. Stahly followed this article with other *MFH* pieces that traced the stories of individual families who had been a part of the migration and later immigration.
1994   "The Amish in Eastern Europe," in *Proceedings of the Conference: Tradition and Transition, An Amish Mennonite Heritage of Obedience. 1693-1993*, ed. by V. Gordon Oyer, 101-16. Metamora, Ill.: Illinois Mennonite Historical and Genealogical Society.
"Statement in 1939 Concerning the Position of Non-resistance signed by Old Order Amish bishops . . ."
1939   original copy at the Heritage Historical Library, Aylmer, Ont.
Steering Committee
1973   *Minutes of the Old Order Amish Steering Committee, vol. 1, 1966-1972.* Gordonville, Pa.: Gordonville Print Shop.
Steinfeldt, Bernice
1937   *The Amish of Lancaster County: A Brief, but Truthful Account of the Actual Life and Customs of the Most Unique Class of People in the United States.* Lancaster, Pa.: Arthur G. Steinfeldt.
Stoll, Joseph
1966   "Introducing a New Paper," *AP* 1 (January): 1-2.
1972   "The Amish Settlement at Guaimaca, Honduras," *TD* 4 (October): 200, 196-99.
1974   "The Amish Church of Montbéliard, France (Founded 1713)," *TD* 6 (January): 19-23.
1975   "Who Shall Educate Our Children?" in *Compulsory Education and the Amish: The Right Not to be Modern*, ed. by Albert N. Keim, 16-42. Boston: Beacon Press.
1996   *Sunshine and Shadow: Our Seven Years in Honduras.* Aylmer, Ont.: J. Stoll.
1997   *The Amish in Daviess County, Indiana.* Aylmer, Ont.: J. Stoll.

2000 *How the Dordrecht Confession Came Down to Us*. Aylmer, Ont: Pathway Publishers.

Stoltzfus, Amos J.
1984 *Golden Memories*. Gordonville, Pa.: Pequea Publishers.

Stoltzfus, Grant M.
1954 "History of the First Amish Mennonite Communities in America," *MQR* 28 (October): 235-62.
1969 *Mennonites of the Ohio and Eastern Conference from the Colonial Period in Pennsylvania to 1968*. Scottdale, Pa.: Herald Press.

Stoltzfus, Louise
1995 *Two Amish Folk Artists: The Story of Henry Lapp and Barbara Ebersol*. Intercourse, Pa.: Good Books.
2000 *The Story of Tourism in Lancaster County, Pa*. Lancaster, Pa.: Pennsylvania Dutch Convention and Visitor's Bureau.

Stoltzfus, Nicholas
1981 comp. *Nonresistance Put to Test*. Salem, Ind.: the author.

Stoltzfus, Victor E.
1973 "Amish Agriculture: Adaptive Strategies for Economic Survival of Community Life," *Rural Sociology* 38 (Summer): 196-206.

Stucky, Solomon
1981 *The Heritage of the Swiss Volhynian Mennonites*. Waterloo, Ont.: Conrad Press.

Supreme Court of the United States
1972 *State of Wisconsin, Petitioner, v. Jonas Yoder, Adin Yutzy, and Wallace Miller*. On Writ of Certiorari to the Supreme Court of Wisconsin. [May 15], No. 70-110.

Swartzendruber, A. Lloyd
1950 "Samuel D. Guengerich," *MHB* 11 (October): 1, 3.

Swartzendruber, William
1977 et al., *Upper Deer Creek Conservative Mennonite Church Centennial Anniversary*. n.p.: Upper Deer Creek Conservative Mennonite Church.

Teichroew, Allan
1979 ed., "Military Surveillance of Mennonites in World War I," *MQR* 53 (April): 95-127.

Thomson, Dennis L.
1993 "Canadian Government Relations," in *The Amish and the State*, ed. by Donald B. Kraybill, 235-48. Baltimore: The Johns Hopkins University Press. Note: this chapter appears only in the 1993 edition of this book, not in the 2003 revised edition.

Toews, Paul
1996 *Mennonites in American Society, 1930-1970: Modernity and the Persistence of Religious Community*. Scottdale, Pa.: Herald Press.

Troyer, David A.
1998 Paton Yoder, trans. *The Writings of David A. Troyer Published after his Death: An English Translation*. Aylmer, Ont.: Pathway Publishers.

Troyer, Henry and Lee Willoughby
1984 "Changing Occupational Patterns in the Holmes County, Ohio, Amish Community," pp. 52-80 in Werner Enninger, ed. *Internal and External Perspectives on Amish and Mennonite Life*. Essen: Unipress.

Troyer, Noah
1879 *Sermons Delivered by Noah Troyer, the Celebrated Amishman*. Iowa City, Ia.: Daily Republican Job Printers.
1880 *Sermons Delivered by Noah Troyer, a Member of the Amish Mennonite Church, of Johnson Co., Iowa, while in an Unconscious State. Second book, Containing Six Sermons not before Published . . . .* Elkhart, Ind.: Mennonite Publishing Company.
The Truth in Word and Work: A Statement of Faith by Ministers and Brethren of Amish Churches of Holmes Co., Ohio, and Related Areas
1983 Baltic, Ohio: Amish Brotherhood Publications.

Umble, Diane Zimmerman
1996 *Holding the Line: The Telephone in Old Order Mennonite and Amish Life*. Baltimore: The Johns Hopkins University Press.

Umble, John S.
1933 "Amish Mennonites of Union County, Pennsylvania," *MQR* 7 (April): 71-96; (July): 162-90.
1939 ed., "Amish Ordination Charges," *MQR* 13 (October): 233-50.
1941a ed., "Amish Service Manuals," *MQR* 15 (January): 26-32.
1941b *Ohio Mennonite Sunday Schools*. Goshen, Ind.: Mennonite Historical Society.
1947 "Why Congregations Die," *MHB* 8 (October): 1-3.
1948 ed., "Memoirs of an Amish Bishop," *MQR* 22 (April): 94-115.
1954 "An Early Amish Formulary," *MQR* 34 (January): 57-60.
1962 "Amish Membership Certificates," *MQR* 36 (January): 88-89.
1963 *One Hundred Years of Mennonite Sunday Schools in Logan County, Ohio*. West Liberty, Ohio: South Union Mennonite Church.
1964 "The Background and Origin of the Ohio and Eastern Amish Mennonite Conference," *MQR* 38 (January): 50-60.

United States Department of Commerce Bureau of the Census
1941 *Religious Bodies: 1936*. Washington, D.C.: Government Printing Office.

Unruh, John D.
1952   *In the Name of Christ: A History of the Mennonite Central Committee and Its Service, 1920-1951*. Scottdale, Pa.: Herald Press.

Varry, Dominique
1984   "Jacques Klopfenstein and the Almanacs of Belfort and Montbeliard in the Nineteenth Century," *MQR* 58 (July): 241-57.

Visser, Piet
1996   "Some Unnoticed Hooks and Eyes: The Swiss Anabaptists in the Netherlands," in *Les Amish: Origine et Particularismes, 1693-1993*, ed. by Lydie Hege and Christoph Wiebe, 95-116. Ingersheim: Association Française d'Histoire Anabaptiste-Mennonite.

Wagler, David
1991   "Our Forefathers Left the Church," *FL* 24 (March): 40, 32-34.
n.d.   *Are All Things Lawful?* Aylmer, Ont.: Pathway Publishers. An Amishman discusses automobile ownership.

Wagler, David and Roman Raber
1986   *The Story of the Amish in Civilian Public Service*. North Newton, Kans.: Bethel Press. A reprint of the 1945 edition with an expanded directory of Amish who served in CPS.

Warkentin, Abe
1987   *Strangers and Pilgrims*. Steinbach, Man.: *Die Mennonitische Post*/Derksen Printers, Ltd.

Weaver, J. Denny
1997   *Keeping Salvation Ethical: Mennonite and Amish Atonement Theology in the Late Nineteenth Century*. Scottdale, Pa.: Herald Press.

Weaver, William B.
1926   *History of the Central Conference Mennonite Church*. Danvers, Ill.: William B. Weaver.

Weaver-Zercher, David L.
2001   *The Amish in the American Imagination*. Baltimore: The Johns Hopkins University Press.

Weber, Harry F.
1931   *Centennial History of the Mennonites of Illinois, 1829-1929*. Goshen, Ind.: Mennonite Historical Society.

Weiser, Frederick S.
1998   "The Clothing of the 'White Top' Amish of Central Pennsylvania," *PMH* 21 (July): 2-10.

Welty, Cora Gottschalk
1908   *The Masquerading of Margaret*. Boston: C. M. Clark.

Wenger, John C.
1937   *History of the Mennonites of the Franconia Conference*. Telford, Pa.: Franconia Mennonite Historical Society.

1961   *The Mennonites in Indiana and Michigan*. Scottdale, Pa.: Herald Press.
1966   *The Mennonite Church in America, Sometimes Called Old Mennonites*. Scottdale, Pa.: Herald Press.

Wenger, Samuel S.
1981   "Nicholas Stoltzfus in Europe and America," *PMH* 4 (April): 15-17.

Williams, George H.
1992   *The Radical Reformation*, third ed. Kirksville, Mo.: Sixteenth Century Journal Publishers.

Williams, R. Hal
1978   *Years of Decision: American Politics in the 1890s*. New York: Wiley.

Yoder, Don
1944   "*Der Fröhliche Botschafter*: An Early American Universalist Magazine," *The American-German Review* 10 (June): 13-16.
1968/1969   "Trance-Preaching in the United States," *Pennsylvania Folklife* 18 (Winter): 12-18.

Yoder, Elmer S.
1987a   *The Beachy Amish Mennonite Fellowship Churches*. Hartville, Ohio: Diakonia Ministries.
1990   *I Saw It in* The Budget. Hartville, Ohio: Diakonia Ministries.

Yoder, Freeman L. and Lizzie Yoder
1998   comps. *Echoes of the Past: Experiences of the Plain People 1920's through 1940's, during the Depression Years and More*. Middlebury, Ind: F.L. and L. Yoder.

Yoder, Harvey
1966   "*The Budget* of Sugarcreek, Ohio, 1890-1920." *MQR* 40 (January): 27-47.

Yoder, John Howard
1954   "Mennonites in a French Almanac," *ML* 9 (October): 154-56.
1955   "Bitscherland," S.v. in *ME*, 1:349.
1961   *The Christian and Capital Punishment*. Newton, Kans.: Faith and Life Press.
1973   trans. and ed., *The Schleitheim Confession*. Scottdale, Pa.: Herald Press. Written in 1527.

Yoder, Mary Elizabeth
1971   "Amish Settlers and the Civil War," *FL* 4 (March): 26-28.

Yoder, Paton
1985   "The Preaching Deacon Controversy Among the Nineteenth-Century American Amish," *PMH* 8 (January): 2-9.
1987b   "The Structure of the Amish Ministry in the Nineteenth Century," *MQR* 61 (July): 280-97.
1987c   *Tennessee John Stoltzfus: Amish Church-Related Documents and Family Letters*. Lancaster, Pa.: Lancaster Mennonite Historical Society.

1991   *Tradition and Transition: Amish Men-nonites and Old Order Amish, 1800-1900.* Scottdale, Pa.: Herald Press.
1996   trans. and ed. "A Plea by a Change-Minded Pennsylvania Amish Leader to the Traditionalists," *PMH* (April): 25-28.
1999   "A Controversy Among the Amish Regarding the Rebaptism of Mennonites, 1820-1845: A Newly-Discovered Document," *MQR* 73 (January): 87-106.

Yoder, Paton and Steven R. Estes
1999   eds. and trans. *Proceedings of the Amish Ministers' Meetings, 1862-1878.* Goshen, Ind.: Mennonite Historical Society.

Yoder, Paton and Silas J. Smucker
1990   *Jonathan P. Smucker, Amish Mennonite Bishop.* Goshen, Ind.: Silas J. Smucker.

Yoder, Pablo [Paul]
1998   *Angels Over Waslala.* Summersville, Mo.: Harbor Lights Publishers.

Yoder, Paul M.
1964   et al., *Four Hundred Years with the Ausbund.* Scottdale, Pa.: Herald Press.

Yousey, Arlene R.
1987   *Strangers and Pilgrims: A History of Lewis County Mennonites.* Croghan, N.Y.: Arlene R. Yousey.

Zijpp, Nanne van der
1956   "Groningen," S.v. in *ME*, 2:592-95.
1957   "Kampen," S.v. in *ME*, 3:141-42.

Zook, Lee J.
2003   "Slow Moving Vehicles," in *The Amish and the State*, ed. by Donald B. Kray-bill, 145-61. Baltimore: The Johns Hopkins University Press.

Zürcher, Isaac
1992   "Hans Reist House and the 'Vale of Anabaptists,'" *MQR* 66 (July): 426-427.

Index

About the Author

Steven M. Nolt is associate professor of history at Goshen College where he teaches courses in American history and Mennonite history. Since 1999 he has worked with sociologist Thomas J. Meyers to document the history and contemporary life of Indiana's Old Order communities. During the 1990s he joined Donald B. Kraybill in charting the social and economic shifts among Pennsylvania Amish families moving from farming to non-farm occupations.

Nolt graduated from Goshen College and also earned degrees at Associated Mennonite Biblical Seminary (M.A.) and the University of Notre Dame (M.A., Ph.D.). His books include *Foreigners in Their Own Land: Pennsylvania Germans in the Early Republic* (Penn State, 2002) and co-authored volumes *Through Fire and Water: An Overview of Mennonite History* (Herald Press, 1996) and *Amish Enterprise: From Plows to Profits* (Johns Hopkins, 1995).

A native of Lancaster, Pennsylvania, Steve is married to Rachel Miller of Engadine, Michigan. They are the parents of two daughters, Lydia and Esther.